DEATH, DRUGS, AND MUSCLE

Gregg Valentino
and Nathan Jendrick

ECW Press

Copyright © Gregg Valentino and Nathan Jendrick, 2010

Published by ECW Press, 2120 Queen Street East, Suite 200,
Toronto, Ontario, Canada M4E 1E2
416.694.3348 / info@ecwpress.com

LIBRARY AND ARCHIVES CANADA CATALOGUING IN PUBLICATION

Valentino, Gregg
Death, drugs, and muscle / Gregg Valentino, Nathan Jendrick.

ISBN 978-1-55022-921-9

1. Valentino, Gregg. 2. Bodybuilders—United States—Biography.
3. Doping in sports. I. Jendrick, Nathan II. Title.

GV545.52.V35A3 2010   796.41092   C2010-900588-0

Cover and photo section: Rachel Ironstone
Cover image: Gregg Valentino
Typesetting: Mary Bowness
Printing: Webcom   1   2   3   4   5

Printed on 100%
recycled paper

Preserving our environment

Your Publishing Company chose to print the pages of this
book on recycled paper and saved these resources[1]:

energy	water	greenhouse gases	solid waste
60 million BTUs	169,697 L	5384 kg	1747 kg

52
trees were saved
for our forests

Printed by **Webcom Inc.** on 100% post-consumer waste.

[1]Estimates were made using the Environmental Defense Paper Calculator.

This book is set in Minion and Akzidenz

PRINTED AND BOUND IN CANADA

ECW PRESS
ecwpress.com

TABLE OF CONTENTS

Acknowledgments

This book is dedicated to the memory of my mother, Rosemary Valentino, and to the memory of Julissa Rivera. My most heartfelt appreciation goes out to my family: my father, Paul Valentino, and my sister, Jamie Valentino DeRosso; if not for their love, I would never have made it. My love and thanks go out to my children: my son, Paul, and my light and angel, Gina. I would also like to acknowledge many friends, whose support and actions have kept me from being lost in my life — Bob Bonham, Dana Capobianco, and Father Mark Rosetti; they helped me to make it through hell on earth — and my boss and, most importantly, my good friend, Steve Blechman, whom I love and admire. Steve believed in me and gave me a chance when the rest of the world told him he was crazy. His faith in me means more than words can say, and my life would not be the same without him. To Carlon Colker, Garry Michel, Michael Gennusa, Steve Zaccaro, Mitch Farina, Alex Abbay, Mike Lambile, Mike Gentile, Jasmine Bellard, my sweetheart Lucia Moreno, and my friend Nathan Jendrick ... thank you all.
— Gregg Valentino

To all who have helped me with yet another amazing project that I have been blessed to take part in, I offer my deepest gratitude. Foremost, my sincere thanks to Gregg Valentino for allowing me the opportunity to take this ride. To Jack David and the staff at ECW, thank you for believing in this terrific story. To my wife, Megan Jendrick, I could never thank you enough for your patience and love; you are truly wonderful and the biggest blessing in my life. To Tom and Janice Tani, Don Anderson and Christena Warwick, Michael Jendrick, Matt Nader, Jerimy and Maria Edee, Mel and Tiffany Stewart, Mike Heaberlin, and Anjan Mitra: thank you all, the reasons for which would require a book of their own.

– Nathan Jendrick

Prologue

I'm not a superstitious guy. I don't tend to believe things I can't see with my own eyes. But over time, when all the pieces are put together and you look at something without bias, there are moments when you just have to admit that the most unusual things seem not just plausible but also true.

Upstate New York is home to Howe Caverns, described as a "living, limestone cave, carved by an underground river over the course of 6 million years, located 156 feet below the earth's surface." They say now that it's over 10 million years old. Some people will also tell you that it's a powerful and mysterious place — that it's sacred, that it can place a curse on you — and however crazy it sounds I believe it. Keep in mind I don't say this lightly; I'm a headstrong realist. But if the story is true, it took 10 million years for that place to develop into what we know it as today, and after going there myself it took only a couple of months for my entire world to come crashing down.

For much of my life, I did things backward. Often I had my priorities all mixed up, to the detriment of not just myself but my friends and family as well. Years after I married, I found the woman I believed wholeheartedly was my true love, Julissa, and things only became more confused. I couldn't leave my wife because we had a history together, and we had children. But during the time that I should have been nurturing my relationship with my family, I was spending it giving Julissa the life she had never had. I neglected my obligations, and over time everything deteriorated.

Eventually, my marriage couldn't sustain my lack of attention. It fell apart — something that I claim full responsibility for — and my wife and I divorced. That moment was a shock for me, though, and it caused me to revert to a stage of real husbandry. Like I said, I went backward. My now ex-wife was threatening to take the kids away, and the possibility that they could leave my life hit me like a ton of bricks. I knew too that they deserved better from me. Nothing that goes on between parents should ever affect the kids, but my way of living — the money, the sex, the drug deals, the two lives — had always been their burden.

Over the few months after my divorce, I spent less time with Julissa, who felt she should have been my top priority now that I didn't have to hide her, and more time with my ex-wife. Julissa became jealous of this, and now my relationship with her was suffering. And it all comes back to those caverns.

In 2000, I went upstate with my ex-wife and my two children. Even though I was staying with Julissa most of the time, I knew it would be good for my kids to see their parents together and getting along. So Julissa stayed home, keeping an eye on my drug-dealing business as well as my Powerhouse Gym branch, and off on vacation I went. I had been desperately missing spending time with my children.

We visited the Major League Baseball Hall of Fame in Cooperstown, and we stopped by Howe Caverns. They are a fun place that puts its own little spin on everything. All over there are signs telling you not to touch the walls lest you disrupt the "fragile ecosystem" of the caves. They say the moisture and oil from human hands can completely alter what happens in the caves, and those who disrespect them are subject to a curse. It sounds crazy, something made up for the fun of a tourist, yet I truly believe that my disrespect caused a horrible curse that I still carry with me.

By the time we reached the caverns, everything had gone perfectly. The minute we took the elevator down into the caves, though, I needed to use the restroom. I'm not easily embarrassed, so I have no problem telling this story: I had to take a piss like never before in my life. The trip was long, and I was still in training, so throughout it I was sipping water and drinking protein shakes. That was a lot of liquid. And, of course, there are no bathrooms anywhere on the tour.

As we followed a blonde girl who acted as our tour guide, my ex-wife and kids were cracking jokes and making fun of me because they knew the agony I was in. It's no exaggeration when I say that my insides literally hurt because of how badly I needed to go. Eventually, I just couldn't take it anymore. I ran away from the crowd and, between two pillars of rock, started to piss all over the wall. My son ran up behind me, and I could hear his little footsteps before he said, "What are you doing, Dad? Are you crazy?"

My ex-wife came over looking for my son and saw the puddle of piss on the ground. She shook her head at me and scoffed. "You're a fucking idiot, Gregg," she said. "Watch what happens to you now."

I laughed and flipped off the wall as we started walking away. "I'm not afraid of a bullshit curse," I told her.

Most people tell such a story to laugh and brush it off. But days later I would lose the woman I loved and hold her cold, dead body. Weeks later I would be robbed, beaten, and near death, and within a couple of months I would lose everything else I held dear in my life.

I don't need to be told there is no such thing as a curse. I'm living it.

Chapter 1
THE EARLY YEARS

Most people who become an infamous part of history are haunted by a dark past. Whether it was an uneasy childhood or a traumatic event as a teenager, something led them to a life that is so far off the beaten path that it morphed into something evil. Some people use this as an excuse, while others merely point their fingers and say the person was destined to fail. Even worse, some say the person should never have been born. Humanity calls these lapsed people monsters, psychopaths, or even vermin. The law usually calls them felons.

I am a felon, and this is my story. Nothing herein is trumped up, cushioned for effect, or otherwise overstated for shock value. I don't justify what I've done, but neither do I refute it. I'm a man who had it all and watched it get stripped away in one horrifying, numbing incident. I might be convicted in the courts, but many would believe that I was behind a victimless crime. I never hurt anyone, yet so many people hurt me because of my actions.

For years, I was a drug dealer. People hear the term and picture me slinging poison out of baggies stuffed away in the trunk of a beaten-down car. That wasn't me; I never sold poison. My product could even be regarded as medicinal. For many, it is. I sold hormones.

Anabolic steroids were my drug of choice.

In the 1990s, if people were indulging in synthetic forms of what makes up the chemistry of men, they probably got it from me. Maybe not hand to hand, but somewhere along the line I was involved. The operation was big, the profits were large, and the risks were high. Like all things, it eventually came crashing down. And when it did, there was no pretty picture to be painted. Tears had been cried, blood had been shed, lives had been ruined, and the ride came to a screeching halt when I found myself behind bars.

When I was arrested, it was all over the national news. Some newspapers put the name Gregg Valentino in the same sentence as drug kingpins like Pablo Escobar and Manuel Noriega. These guys were traffickers of cocaine and heroin, poisons they knew were taking the life right out of people. I've never wavered in my belief that I was selling a safe product. Every night of my life after I started dealing drugs, I slept well, whether on the 1,200-thread-count Egyptian cotton sheets of my New York home or on the paper-thin and stained rag they give you in jail. The one thing that never bothered me was the thought that I had hurt someone.

I can't tell you where Escobar or Noriega went wrong. Maybe it was at birth, maybe it developed over time; it doesn't matter. Plenty of psychologists have already offered their "professional" opinions. My life doesn't follow suit. I didn't grow up unloved or neglected.

Childhood for me was pleasant. Because of my association with bodybuilding, people assume I lack any intelligence and figure I had some sort of heathen upbringing. My father, Paul, was a successful artist, and my mother, Rosemary, worked in the school district. I was blessed with one sibling, a sister, who is just ten months younger. Our parents were loving, they didn't drink or use drugs, and there was absolutely no drama. The only strange part about my early years is that they were so mundane. We are talking about the 1960s and 1970s, and no

Valentino in our home dabbled in any sort of shady business or drugs. And this was in New York City.

I should mention that a large portion of my story centers on my love affair with my home city. This is God's chosen place. From the seasons to the sports, things here are graceful. From the postcard winters all the way to the Yankees, this has always been my playground. Nowhere else in the world can you get the diversity that New York offers. That comes in both positive and negative ways, as I ultimately found out.

If it weren't for the steroids, I never would have grown the world's largest arms, which Jay Leno would come to measure against his head. They made me both a target — Jon Stewart had fun with my arrest on Comedy Central — and a personality in the bodybuilding community. It was in that community, the brotherhood of iron, that I found comfort. Many children and teenagers participate in organized sports, which I also enjoyed, but to me there was nothing like lifting weights.

It was both a release and the means to end the torment I endured growing up. People see me now, hear about my near-thirty-inch arms, and assume I came out of the womb looking like Popeye. But I was a small kid. So small in fact that, embarrassingly enough, I was afraid to walk home from school because two sisters used to pick on me. I had no confidence, no self-esteem, and certainly no size to intimidate anyone, even girls.

"Quiet and sickly" would be a solid description of me as a child. Again, I had no self-esteem despite my parents' best intentions. It wasn't until the fifth grade when I met a teacher named Ed O'Connor that I started shaping up. That man helped me, guided me, and nurtured me because he saw something no one else did in me: potential. It was over that year I realized my existence had substance. I remember Mr. O'Connor once telling my parents that someday people would be reading about me. Now I laugh because I wonder what he would say after reading about me being busted for running a steroid network, but in any case he was absolutely right.

I was in classes for gifted students, but all I wanted was to be good at sports. I wanted the opportunity to be the best, and if no one was going to give me a shot then I would train myself and become so good that I could just take it myself. This came in the form of shaping my body. I did it to be able to defend myself, but most of all to develop myself inside and out. With my newfound strength, I also started developing a personality. As that happened, I started getting a little rowdy — nothing too serious, but occasionally I would act out or talk up during class when I wasn't supposed to.

A memory I carry with me to this day is having a teacher place his hands on me in such a way that I could feel his hatred toward me and see it emanate from his eyes when he looked at me. As I was becoming what felt like the person I was supposed to be, I was becoming what this man didn't appreciate. One day in class I said something about "mother nature," which this teacher somehow decided to hear as "motherfucker." He split the desks heading directly in my direction, placed his hand around my throat, and lifted me single-handedly out of my chair. He choked me through the door and threw me into the hallway.

My father heard about this incident and knew that I had never said a swear word in my life. This was back in a time when kids didn't use curse words, especially at school. Even though I would take a liking to choice words later on, those words weren't in my vocabulary at the time. My father, having seen me so shaken up and knowing the truth deep down, chose to do something. The next day, while we were sitting in the classroom of this teacher, my father came in with such prominence that every student immediately stared at me because they knew who he was. He dragged the teacher out of the room and straight down to the office, where he gave the principal the opportunity to either discipline him or watch as he got his ass kicked. Subsequently, the teacher apologized, Mr. O'Connor became my main teacher, and somehow out of all that I continued to grow more and more confident.

These random bits all tie together because they carry a constant theme of example. Mr. O'Connor cared, nurtured me, taught me, and believed in me, and my father in my mind was the epitome of a man. By combining these two examples in my life, I was learning the best traits possible. My father didn't use drugs, he didn't beat me or my sister or my mother, he didn't drink alcohol, smoke, or even sip coffee. He was a strong man, both physically and mentally. And if I wanted to be like my father, I needed to be strong like him. Hence, my obsession with training was born. I had never thought about bodybuilding as a sport, but I gave it everything I had. Mr. O'Connor had caused me to believe in myself, and my father's manner helped me to create goals for myself. Even though I didn't know what I was doing, because of the people who believed in me, I knew I would achieve my goals no matter what they were. I began to condense these two figures in my life into an example of who I wanted to be.

In sixth grade, other kids started talking about my "lumps." I had a lot more muscle than everyone else, and people started paying attention to me. I liked that attention, and I started to crave it once girls started noticing me. I saw a magazine called *Muscle Training Illustrated* later on with bodybuilding legend Boyer Coe on the cover, and like any kid I created a hero in my mind. Bodybuilders are made up of superhero-like dimensions as it is, so it wasn't far-fetched to see these guys as being godly powerful. They built their physiques and were getting recognition for it, and ultimately I would develop an addictive personality that wanted the same. At that time in school, I was afraid of getting too muscular because I was told it would take away from my speed in sports like baseball and football, but like most things it all worked itself out.

Fast-forward several years, and I was becoming very proud of my body. I was starting to idolize guys like Arnold

Schwarzenegger and "Incredible Hulk" Lou Ferrigno — both men I would later come to know personally and, in Ferrigno's case, hate — and it was really from that point on that my life started to be dictated by muscle.

By the end of high school, without drugs, I could incline press in the 400 lb range. I learned body part by body part how to train at a YMCA more than twenty miles from my home. I became popular, showing off and happy to receive the attention. At lunchtime in school, I'd often go pump up with some dips and pushups, then stand on a tabletop and rip off my shirt to flex for everyone.

As a senior, I worked in a strip club called the Lake Lounge in Mahopac, New York. The club is still there but is now called Teasers. While that job wasn't so unusual, because the drinking age was only eighteen back then, everyone knew I was in for a different type of life when I brought a stripper to the senior prom. It didn't occur to me at the time what that might have indicated, but those were the types of girls I was hanging out with. I skipped classes, I was always with women, and I was making some money of my own. My parents were just happy I was out of the shell I had been in early on, and to them it was just "That's Gregg." It didn't surprise them that I took a stripper to a dance. It wasn't your traditional dating of a co-worker, but it wasn't awkward for anyone.

I felt on top of the world, and just a few days after the senior prom I had my first run-in with a celebrity. This was the first of many incidents I look back at now and can do nothing but shake my head.

The general public meets a celebrity, gets excited, and collects an autograph or a photo if possible. That never worked for me; for some reason or other, most people with some notoriety I run into seem to have a problem with me, or I have one with them. Several times this conflict revolved around a well-known musician. I would later have some encounters with Mark

Wahlberg that even became the topic of Howard Stern's radio show, but years before that I fought with Twisted Sister, the heavy-metal band. Years before they were a big deal with hits like "I Wanna Rock" and "We're Not Going to Take It," they were just another band from New York City trying to make it. They had been around a couple of years and had a local following, but they weren't tried-and-true "rock stars" yet.

On the weekend of my senior prom, I took the stripper I was dating, who went by "Seven" on stage, to Club Gemini, where Twisted Sister was playing. They weren't much of a traveling act yet, so they were regularly on stage at this place.

My friends and my girl were at the front of the crowd right at the edge of the stage. The lead singer of the band, Dee Snider, carried a rainbow-colored lollipop with him. Every so often he'd take a few licks of it and then put it down between his legs like it was his cock and shove it in the mouth of my girlfriend. She sucked on that thing like the stripper she was. It was a rock show, she was a stripper, and I just didn't care at the time.

Later, during a break the band took, I couldn't find Seven anywhere. Then I noticed her walking out from the back room with the band as they were retaking the stage. I asked her where she had been, and, being a stripper and therefore an excellent performer, she proved to be an expert liar. She spun me a story about being in the back talking to one of the other girls and not hanging with the band.

Her story soon proved to be bullshit. When Twisted Sister started playing again, Snider pulled her up on stage, and another band member, Mark Mendoza, joined him in a dry humping session right there with my girl between them. After a bit of that, she dropped to her knees and in front of everyone — right there on stage — started going after this lollipop like it was, again, his dick. Not surprisingly, when they stepped off the stage, she disappeared with them again.

The next time they came out from the back, they all sat

down in a roped-off section of the club on velvet chairs. The bouncers had stopped me when I tried to get to the back, but now that the band were out on the floor I just stepped over the rope and made my way straight for my girl, who was sitting on Mendoza's lap.

As soon as she saw me, she jumped to her feet and tried to talk to me. I ignored her, marched straight in front of Mendoza, and told him to get up out of his chair. The guy was rock star all the way; he smiled at me, completely relaxed, and let out a very confident "Fuck you, asshole."

I lifted my leg up and kicked him squarely in the chest, sending him and his chair directly backward. I leapt over the legs of the chair to get on top of him, and I started raining punches down on any open spot of his head as he tried to cover up. I got some good shots in, but it didn't take long before Dee Snider, himself a big motherfucker, jumped on my back and started throwing me a beat-down of his own. Shortly thereafter the bouncers jumped in, got in some of their own shots, and dragged me outside. As if that wasn't bad enough, one of them decided to bounce my head off an iron beam on the street. The last I saw of that stripper girlfriend was when she dropped me off at home, bloodied up for no damn good reason other than my own stupidity.

I learned a lot during my time in high school and grew up faster than I probably should have. But nothing that I went through prepared me for what would come later in my life.

Chapter 2
THE LIFE I ALMOST HAD

Decades before I was a convicted felon on drug and gun charges, I was on the other side of the bars. In theory at least. Back when I was content with being a natural, drug-free, amateur bodybuilder, I also aspired to be a police officer. Most people can't see me in a uniform. They see the big, freak-like muscles, they read my "Ramblin' Freak" column and hear my crazy-but-true stories, and they don't think I would ever have made it. They can't even fathom the idea that I wanted to be an officer of the law. But I did, and for a period of time I was a probationary "special" officer — essentially meaning they could get rid of me at any time for any reason — of the Westchester County Police Department, badge 737. Westchester is a very affluent suburb of New York. During my time as an officer, there were nearly 900,000 people living there, and for a county of its size there was surprisingly little to do.

For the first couple of years, any new police officer is at the bottom of the totem poll. New officers get the worst jobs, the worst assignments, and garner little, if any, respect from their fellow officers. Don't get me wrong: "special" police officers may be the lowest of the low, but if something did go down I never had any doubt that the rest of the force would have had my back.

And I would have had their backs. It's a brotherly bond; when you take the oath and make the commitment to become an officer, you do so knowing that you might well have to take a bullet for a member of your new family. You accept it and do your best, praying that it never comes to that. But you're always prepared.

One of my assignments as a probationary "special" was to patrol a stretch of beach in Westchester. It was likely the most tedious, boring job I have ever held. So little happened there that I felt as if my only job was to make sure no one came to steal the sand. And the few things that did occur I often let go.

Many times on the night shift I would park my patrol car in a dark, covered area to stay out of sight. During the summer months when the weather was warm, it wasn't uncommon to watch a couple come to the beach and have sex. Truly, I can't count the number of times I watched a guy lay there while his girl blew him. This isn't legal, and it was my job to stop them, but I didn't see the point. These were people doing what people do, it was dark, no one else was on the beach, and I couldn't have cared less.

Adding to my own poor reflection of my short-lived cop career, I used to have my girlfriend at the time come out and visit me while I was supposed to be ensuring the safety of nothing and no one. Things were so predictable during my time on this beach that I could set my watch to them. I knew that four hours after my shift started an old, overweight, gray-haired man would walk down the sidewalk with his black dog, a mini pinscher named Chewbacca. I knew that exactly an hour later he would walk right back by on his way home. Occasionally, I would get a surprise in the form of car headlights in the distance, but otherwise there was nothing to see and nothing to do. So, to pass the time, my girlfriend would visit. Naturally, this was against the rules, but no one higher ranking than me ever felt I was worth the time to come check on. After all, I was the new guy, and they knew this station was exactly the type of assignment no cop wanted. I figured that, if I was going to get put somewhere where they knew nothing would happen, I'd entertain myself.

Now, a lot of guys have fucked their girlfriends or wives in a car. Not a lot of them have done it in a real patrol car. I have. I found out quickly that it was my favorite way to pass the time. Down on the beach, there was also a small office setup for the cop on shift. Many times we could go in there and have sex right on the desk. I never missed a radio call, and, just like I expected, nothing ever happened on the beach that would have required my undivided attention.

One of my other choice ways of passing the time on shift was going to the gym. I would wear a white shirt under my uniform, and I would park right outside the front door. Inside I would take my shirt and my gun belt off, lock them up, and go train in my department-issued pants and boots. More times than not this went off without a hitch. As they say, though, all good things must come to an end, and I did eventually get caught. Luckily for me, I managed to talk my way out of it.

On one Fourth of July, I went in to train as usual. I called in to the county headquarters from the gym payphone, as I was supposed to do, and said my standard "Special Police Officer 7-3-7 on duty, post 6-4." At this point, I was already late to be at my post, but I trained anyway. By the time I actually did arrive at my post, my lieutenant was there.

"Where the fuck have you been?" he asked me. "You were supposed to be here an hour ago, what the fuck is wrong with you?"

I knew I couldn't tell him the truth and let him know that I was late merely because my workout had run over, so I lied. I told him I was dieting for a bodybuilding show and, because of that, I was eating a lot of green vegetables and other foods that didn't digest so well. I told him this diet had caused me to shit my pants.

My lieutenant looked at me with great big eyes of disbelief. "You've got to be fucking kidding me."

"I swear."

After he berated me, he made me fill out a "greenie," better known as an incident report. "I want you to write that bullshit story up," he said. "I can't go back to headquarters and tell them that's the story. You're going to write it up."

So, just like I had told him, I wrote it up. I wrote that I had actually arrived early, but when I got into the police car I farted and actually shit my pants. Because of that, I had to go home and change so I wouldn't have shit running down my legs all shift. After I wrote it up, I handed it to him and stood there nervously waiting for his response. I followed his eyes as he went over the report, line by line.

"You're really going to stick by this story?" he asked.

I nodded. "That's what really happened."

He yelled at me and ripped the paper down the middle. "I can't go back to headquarters with this! I'm not going to tell my chief that one of my officers shits his fucking pants. The department doesn't issue diapers, Valentino!"

"Sorry, sir."

"Let me tell you something," he said to me. "If you thought this up, you're a smart guy. Because as a probationary officer it would be so easy for me to rip that badge off of you, make you turn in your gun and uniform, and make you drive home in your fucking underwear. If you had said anything else other than this, you'd be done. But I'm going to let you go this one time. This *one* time."

In the end, my potential life as a police officer ended in an accident that resulted in a piece of wire in my eye, paralyzing my retina. I had just gotten into bed one night and felt something poking into my arm. I found a piece of wire sticking up through the mattress and pulled it out. I balled it up and threw it into the waste basket, but the wire came unraveled and shot straight back at me. It was sheer dumb luck where it hit me. I ended up having to get a lens implant and now have a permanently dilated eye. This accident is the reason I usually wear sunglasses — not because I'm trying to act Hollywood — as sunlight bothers my eyes a great deal. When I'm seen without sunglasses on, one of my eyes is a mellow green, while the other is black.

Soon after the wire incident, I was deemed medically unfit to remain an officer and was let go. Today I don't have any hard feelings over it, and I don't try to kid myself and say it wasn't for the best. I believed in what I was supposed to be doing, but I wasn't passionate about it. I can't help but ask myself, though, how much different my life would be if I had finished my term as a "special" probationary officer and eventually become a full-fledged police officer.

Maybe, I tell myself, I would never have touched steroids. Maybe my ex-wife and I would still be together, and my two children would live under the same roof as me. Maybe I would never have met and fallen in love with Julissa, and maybe — and I beat myself up over this every day — she would still be alive.

Chapter 3
MARK WAHLBERG

In 1994, I had my first of what would be a couple of interesting encounters with Mark Wahlberg. Long before he was a movie star, he was a musician trying to make it and had an attitude the size of Long Island.

On Wednesday nights, my great friend Paul, whom I often refer to as my "partner" because he's always there for me through thick and thin, and I would get ready for Freak Night at the Limelight Nightclub in Manhattan. It was when the freaks — the eclectic folks, the hookers, the transvestites, the cross-dressers, and the otherwise very abnormal people — would come out to party. All week long we'd look forward to what we considered the absolute best night of the week to party.

One night we walked in and noticed right away, the second we stepped inside the Limelight, that the crowd was thicker than usual and that the girls were even more gorgeous than we were used to. We quickly found out it was because Wahlberg was sitting upstairs on the second level, looking down over the dance floor. Wahlberg was with a crew that numbered at least twenty-five. All of them were rugged-looking guys who wore skullcaps long before they were considered the fashion. Wahlberg himself was wearing an Elmer Fudd-like hat — a hunting hat with snappy ear flaps — and obviously enjoying being the center of attention. All of the girls in the place were trying to catch his attention and get a piece of the guy who was on the underwear ads in Times Square.

I'm not ashamed to admit that Paul and I made our way over to the newfound celebrity circle to try to catch some of Wahlberg's rejects. But it just wasn't happening. Every woman in the Limelight that night was focused only on him; even his crew was getting rejected.

Paul noticed that every so often one of the guys in a skull-cap would whisper to Wahlberg and point in our direction, and then they'd both laugh. The problem was Paul gets pretty lippy when he gets pissed off, and he didn't like the laughter at all. I tried to grab him and quiet him down because I knew we were outnumbered, and I didn't really feel like trying to fight off the entire entourage.

I got Paul to head back downstairs with me, and all the way down he was mouthing off about how badly he wanted to punch Wahlberg and throw down with him. Paul lived to fight and loved testing himself against anyone who wanted to step up. He used to spar with Alexis Arguello, a former three-time world boxing champion, and could easily have handled himself one on one with anyone in that club. Again, though, I reminded him we were vastly outnumbered. It still didn't seem like he gave a shit.

After another half-hour, Wahlberg and his crew made their way downstairs to be among the masses and ultimately very close to us. Paul and I, even though we weren't on steroids, were pretty muscular and lean and as such were wearing short-sleeve shirts. Over the next few minutes after Wahlberg and his goons came down, we kept hearing people shout "steroids" and "juice-heads" over and over. It was obvious who was doing it even though they were trying to shout fast out the sides of their mouths. The flattering part was that at this point I had never once used any juice.

After about fifteen minutes, I was equal to Paul in being pissed off. Finally, I looked at Wahlberg, straight in the eye, and told him off. "Hey, asshole," I yelled. "You talk big with your boys here, but you're nothing but a punk-ass bitch."

Wahlberg glared back at me and screamed, "Fuck you, you juiced-up freak. You da punk!"

Then Paul came up with a line that we still recite today. He stepped right in front of me and had his turn. "Hey, Marky Mark and the Punky Bunch," he said, smiling. "I'm going to be on *Entertainment Tonight* for kicking your fucking ass!"

With that, Wahlberg put his hands out and said, "Bring it."

I took a running leap straight for Wahlberg and took him right to the floor. Paul took out one of his boys with a single punch, and I locked Wahlberg into the tightest headlock anyone has ever seen, causing him to shout for help like a small child. As I was choking the hell out of him, though, his boys started jumping on me to help him out. I could see up through the masses that Paul was still on his feet and connecting with some great shots, but quickly the numbers caught up to us. Wahlberg was ripped out of my arm by a couple of his boys, and the club bouncers came and grabbed me, a couple on each side. They held me down while Wahlberg started kicking me like a soccer ball.

When the bouncers finally tossed us out, I had a blackened face, and my shirt had been torn off. Paul was bruised a bit and had his knuckles bloodied up good.

"I've got God only knows whose blood on me," he said when we hit the night air.

We left the Limelight that night pretty pissed off. I never got any worthwhile shots in on Wahlberg because he had his crew there, and none of those cocksuckers knew how to fight fairly. Hearing him scream for help was great, but I would have loved to have gotten in a great shot that night.

My redemption, as fortune would have it, came about six

months later at Club USA in Manhattan. This time the club was made up of *my* friends and bouncers with whom I was tight.

As soon as we came within reach, Paul took Wahlberg down, and I started wrestling with his entourage. The bouncers got involved, on our side, and it became a fucking melee in the club. Chairs and tables were flying, bottles were crashing everywhere, and it wasn't until a horde of NYPD cops flooded in that the fight was broken up. Paul and I were able to sneak out before any cuffs were slapped on, and when I didn't see anything in the news the next day I assumed that Wahlberg and his idiots had managed to get away without problem too.

These days I assume Wahlberg has grown up since his punk rapping days, and I haven't seen him since that second fight. Howard Stern did try to get us on the air together for his show, but Wahlberg punked out.

As the *Italian Job* film was hitting theaters, Stern had Stuttering John call me up at 7 a.m. Wahlberg was supposed to be on the show to promote his latest movie, and Stern wanted me to start a little thing with him and challenge him to a boxing match. But Wahlberg, maybe more Hollywood than ever, showed up almost an hour late. Stern was pissed off and didn't have time to go through with it, and I was left with just an hour-long conversation with Stuttering John.

I have no doubt that Wahlberg would have turned me down, afraid that he'd get his ass kicked. I'd still love to go a few rounds with him man to man. I had him at his best, crying for his crew when I had him in that headlock, and I'd be more than happy to do it again. As it goes, though, I can't say I kicked his ass. I did get him down, but ultimately he played kickball with my head.

Chapter 4
ANDREW CRISPO

In the magazines, at contests, and at expos, bodybuilding seems like a real glamour sport. You've got men running around in posing trunks at four percent body fat and tanned to perfection. There are women looking fit and trim and wearing about as many items of clothing as a *Maxim* cover girl. Lights, music, a cheering crowd — everything looks good at show time. But let me tell you, depending on the way you see things, the world of bodybuilding can be sick and as dirty as anything you've ever seen or heard. I want to say that up front because many people don't approve of what goes on in what some call the bodybuilding "underground." Personally, I don't care. I don't care if someone is straight, gay, or transsexual. I don't care what color they are, where they're from, what language they speak, none of that. If people are good to me, I'm good to them. That said, for right or wrong, most people don't think the way I do.

Bodybuilding, like I've said, breeds assholes, and it has nothing to do with steroids. "Roid rage" is a myth. The thing with steroids is that, if someone is an asshole before they take them, they become a bigger asshole after they take them, because suddenly idiots think they're Superman. Eventually, they get their asses kicked and come to know better, but for a while they're completely self-obsessed. It's the ego, the muscle, the testosterone. But, again, not the kind of testosterone that comes out of a vial.

Many people will hate me for what I'm about to say. I'm going to piss off a number of people in the sport — the guys who want the façade of glamour to stick around — but I'm an honest guy, and like I always do I'm going to tell it how it is. I don't spew nonsense about the drugs I've used or the drugs I've sold, so there's no reason to lie about how screwed up bodybuilding really is. On the outside, bodybuilders look put together. Many professionals appear to have a good thing going in the sport, maybe a steady girlfriend, cash, whatever. Most of them are full of shit.

Very few professional bodybuilders can put food on the table from competing. The prize money offered at pro shows is laughable. Think about this: Ronnie Coleman won the biggest contest, the Mr. Olympia, eight times in a row. That made him the premier bodybuilder in the entire world for almost a decade. With investments, he's probably a millionaire, but for many of those years, while winning the most prestigious title in the sport, he still worked full-time as a police officer. If he had been at the top of the baseball world for eight years, though, he'd have hundreds of millions of dollars, houses on both coasts, a private island with a cabana for hookers, two jets, and twenty cars.

What I'm saying is that no one gets into bodybuilding for the money, but every one of these guys has a fucking ego the size of New Jersey. They can't work another job. There's no way you'd catch a guy who has won a pro bodybuilding show working at a Wal-Mart or, God forbid, a job that requires manual labor. I know guys who neglect their kids, won't go play catch with their young sons because they say it expends too much energy, and they need that recovery time to "build muscle."

So what do these "professional athletes" do to keep up the

image? They sell drugs. Just like I did, but on a much smaller scale. They call it "personal training." I can't even count the number of guys I know who compete and say they work as personal trainers when the endorsements don't add up to pay the mortgage.

That isn't to say that bodybuilders don't actually work as trainers. Many of them do. But quite a few take it a step further and build their services, if you will. Big guys attract big guys in the gym, so before you know it someone is asking how to get a bottle of "test" (testosterone). When a guy mentions to a friend that he's taking it, he might get asked for a bottle. He'll get it, even money, no big deal. Then he realizes he can jack up the price from his own cost, and sure enough it becomes deal after deal.

Many professional bodybuilders use their legitimate personal training jobs as fronts on their taxes for selling drugs. They might make ten times as much in a year selling drugs to other bodybuilders as they do training normal, drug-free clients, but the IRS just thinks each to be one hell of a fitness coach.

There is another taboo subject in the world of muscle that keeps the lights on and the furnace hot. It's called "muscle worship." It can be disgusting, it can be vile, but it pays well, and many guys are either doing it right now or have done it in the past. Even Arnold Schwarzenegger was rumored to be into this shit.

Now, muscle worship can mean a lot of things. At one end, it's a buff guy getting paid to pose in his underwear for anywhere from one to a dozen guys or more who jack off to it. Then it goes deeper, no pun intended. For more money, he'll get his own dick hard. A few more bills and he'll get himself off for the pleasure of the audience. Some guys have a price that, if it's paid up-front, means they'll throw the kneepads on and get to work. It doesn't even mean, necessarily, that they're gay. It just means they need the money badly enough.

When people hear me say this, they swear I'm full of shit. I'm not. I swear to God this happens more than anyone imagines, and it's more likely than not that a favorite "pro" of a body-building fan has done it. People want to believe that these big, muscular guys they look at in the magazines are as straight as an arrow, but let me tell you I've watched male professional bodybuilders make out with other guys. My own two eyes and those of many others have watched this stuff happen. That behavior, of course, might be induced by the huge amounts of street drugs many pros do, but that's a story for later.

Now I have to say that not all muscular guys who do muscle worship are bodybuilders. Despite an obesity epidemic, America is ahead of many countries when it comes to fitness. Many guys like to take care of themselves for their own purposes, which have nothing to do with competing on stage. And not all guys who are into muscle worship allow touching, no matter how much money they're offered.

My partner in crime from years ago, Paul, used to do male escort work. He worked with some of the craziest sons of bitches you'll ever hear about, but he also posed for big-money clientele. On more than one occasion, he was even called up by a very famous Latin comedian. Paul was as much of a man as you'll ever meet. And he had business savvy. He knew where the money was, and he didn't mind taking his clothes off for cash, as long as doing so stayed contact-free. And he didn't have a price to break that barrier, either, let me tell you. He once had a sheik from a Middle Eastern country offer him $10,000 to fuck him in the ass. He didn't even hesitate to turn that offer down. As I already said, he worked with high-profile people. Big Wall Street guys, celebrities, you name it.

One of these guys was the infamous Andrew Crispo, the New York art dealer who ran into his own much-publicized trouble later, which became known as the notorious "death mask murder case," when he was accused of killing a fashion student after a wild night full of sex and violence. Crispo also had run-ins with the law later on, including allegations of extortion, threats to kidnap, obstruction of justice, and all sorts of other crimes.

It was around 1994 when Paul called me up and asked me if I wanted to make a couple hundred bucks. At the time, I was broke, had a baby son to feed, was trying to build a gym, and was only able to work part-time as a bouncer. Of course I wanted to make some money, and the offer became even more enticing when he said, "All we have to do is abuse this guy Crispo." At the same time, I was a little nervous. I'd never used my size to make money, unless you count punking some drunken morons out of a club. "Grab a pair of hot skins, a tank top, and some work boots," Paul told me.

Hot skins are basically tight spandex shorts. You have to forgive the fashion sense of the 1980s and early 1990s and just focus on what I'm saying.

Paul told me where to meet up with him, and he said that Crispo was a regular client and that he was usually called in by Crispo's "master." Apparently, this guy was big into S&M stuff and on this occasion wanted a couple of muscle guys.

Paul and I went down to 14th Street and found this building a block off the Westside Highway, which, ironically, is in the meat-packing district. Make your own jokes later. This was a dirty, rundown, seedy commercial area. Not the type of place where you'd expect to see a guy like Crispo, but then again this wasn't the type of thing you'd assume a guy like Crispo would be into.

When we arrived, we took a creaking elevator up to the floor this studio was on. When we stepped off, the first person we saw was this "master." He was naked except for a pair of leather chaps and a police hat, and he was bald except for his handlebar mustache. On the other side of the room was Crispo, naked, tied to a wooden cross setup. His ass was facing us, his package the other direction. The master told me to take off my shirt and leave on just these hot skins and boots.

Don't get me wrong, I thought this was some fucked-up shit, but I needed the money. I did what I was asked to do.

The master handed me a blow dart gun. "Shoot him with these," the guy told me. It was a little dart gun, but it wasn't the type of dart that you throw at a board in a tavern. It shot out little needles when you blew through the back end.

At this point, I figured if I was going to do it I might as well have some fun with it. The guy looked like a total bitch tied to this cross, and if he was paying good money for this it was obviously getting him off. So I took up the dart deal, took in a deep breath, and shot one of those needles right into his ass. Crispo screamed, but it wasn't one of those "Oh, my God, I'm in pain" sort of screams. It was a Christmas-style scream like when you get what you've always wanted. Before then, I would never have known or even guessed that someone actually asked for this type of shit, but who am I to judge? I blew a few of these darts, and with each one I tried to send it harder. It didn't seem to matter; he loved it. A loving, Christmas scream every time. He was like a human dart board, and it was ridiculous.

"You're a fucking disgusting human being," I said before I fired another one off. "You sick little fuck. You're not even a man, you're a pathetic little bitch."

After a few darts to Crispo's ass, the master gave Paul a paddle shaped like a racquetball racquet. Paul wound up and smacked that piece right upside those bare ass cheeks, but nothing changed. The guy was tied up, getting abused, and loving every second of it. We were there because we had muscles, so you can imagine that Paul smacking that thing up against his backside wasn't any sort of love tap. Regardless, despite his ass turning three shades of purple, Crispo let out another healthy scream of joy.

"I should kick you in your fucking balls," Paul yelled.

The whole time we were abusing this guy — if you can even call it that since he was paying for it — his master was yelling at him, telling him to shut up, telling him he was a piece of shit, worthless, all that. A while later Crispo was on trial for some pretty foul charges, so it looked like this guy was just foretelling the future and saying things everyone else would say later.

When Crispo was finally released from his bindings, he bowed to us and groveled at our feet. I had to wonder what kind of fucked-up childhood this guy had had, but my mind changed quickly because now he was getting too close. It's one thing to stand eight feet away and shoot darts at a guy's butt cheeks; it's quite another when he's trying to clean your boots with his tongue and tears.

I don't know what Paul made that night, but before we left I had a check for $300 written in a black felt pen from Andrew Crispo's art company. The moral of the whole story? Bodybuilding is fucked up, but it definitely isn't the only sport that has its share of characters. Even successful, educated individuals have vices they're willing to pay for. All the same, just as with Crispo, it's not up to me to judge. Too many people have done so to me, and I refuse to do the same in return.

See, I don't judge any type of people. After I meet people, if they prove themselves to be assholes, then that's another story. But until that point, I leave people be. If they don't like my muscles, that's just fine. What other people think about me is none of my business.

Me, I like muscles. And I like people. Muscle attracts people. Straight, gay, bi, doesn't matter. Celebrities and average Joe alike. Even world-famous rockers. Steven Tyler, lead singer from Aerosmith, was all over me at a party we both attended in 2003. Looking at his wife and judging by his daughter, the guy has taste in women and the genes to make them and definitely isn't a homosexual. It's just that people can't help but get a feel for themselves because they can't believe what they're seeing with their own two eyes. His hands were all over me, even making a couple trips down to my ass. But, hey, I don't hold it against him, I'm used to it. Besides, he's Steven Tyler; there isn't much he can't do. Bottom line is I can even be in a grocery store, and an old lady I've never seen before will walk up, grab a piece, and say, "Oh, my . . . God."

I want to say something funny when I end up in a situation like that, but I'm never sure that they'd get the joke. In any case, it's better than saying, "Get your fucking hands off me." I know I'm a freak. I accept it, and there are other things that have to be accepted when people look at you the way they look at me.

Ultimately, as cheesy as it might sound, I feel honored when people approach me. Even if they're completely at a loss for words and come off in ways most people would find rude, I don't take it negatively. I greet people, I answer their questions, and often I respect them even more than they respect me. I give them my autograph, I let them touch and gawk and gasp, and usually I smile. People like freaks, and I've been called the king of that bunch.

Chapter 5
STEROIDS 101

I started training in 1972 and had never heard of steroids before. I was a kid, training with passion and reading the muscle magazines and believing everything in them. I thought Arnold was as natural as apples, and I did what I thought everyone did: I ate a lot of food, cut down at contest time, and competed. Back then I was an amateur competing in the AAU.

A friend of mine, Peter Neff, one of the greatest natural bodybuilders of all time, used to tell me he was competing in natural shows. I was clueless. "What's unnatural?" I asked him. I had no idea what he meant by "natural" until he explained to me that other guys were using hormones and called them "steroids." That's how I figured out what they were. I had so much to learn; I wish someone had just handed me a textbook on the subject.

Where I lived, you didn't get magazines the way you do today. From Westchester, New York, I'd have to go all the way into New York City to find muscle magazines. When you got them in the 1970s, you read them from cover to cover and believed every word like they were the Bible. You believed the Weider ads, you believed you needed liver pills. Muscle was a commodity so rarely seen that the guys who had it, when they said this is what they did, you believed it. You thought protein was all these guys ate, you thought they lifted weights and slept a lot. You saw big guys and freaked out and thought they had the secret, and you were blessed because they were sharing it with you.

I learned to lift weights by watching other guys around me lifting them. At first, I didn't know the difference between the biceps and the triceps, until one day I saw a guy who had a huge back half to his arm. I learned by doing, and everything was in its infancy to me.

By the 1980s, after Peter told me about the difference between open and natural shows, I started learning what really went on. I wouldn't actually take part in any of it until I had more than twenty years of training under my belt.

What really bothered me back then was seeing a young guy in the gym who would come up to me and ask me for training tips, and then, when I'd see him a year later, he'd be bigger than me. I kept thinking to myself, what's going on? Time and time again I'd find out that these guys had started taking steroids. Combining the hormone use with the training program I had given out had caused these guys to explode.

In the 1970s and 1980s, it bothered the hell out of me that guys used steroids. I felt cheated and robbed. In a couple of years with steroids, guys were making the gains that it had taken me almost ten years to make. For so long I stayed natural because it was a sense of pride to me that as a natural I was still competing and beating guys who were juicing up. It was like being a natural athlete at the Olympic Games beating competitors who are ducking the rules. I felt good about what I was doing and how I was doing it. That other people wanted to take shortcuts made me even more proud of my progress that had been made with sheer hard work.

Later on I owned my own gym and promoted bodybuilding shows on my own. But times were tough, and there wasn't a lot of money in running gyms and hosting shows even though

everyone knew me as both a good bodybuilder and a show pro-
moter. I was able to bring in the top pros in the sport, like Lee
Haney, who has even eaten dinner at my home. During that
time, everyone was familiar with Gregg Valentino and for all
good reasons. But that doesn't pay the bills.

With my son having been born in 1990 to my wife Veola and
me, people counted on me to keep food on the table, and I was
getting desperate for money. A friend of mine, Fernando, eventually came up to me and said, "Hey, you know everyone. You're
hooked up. I can get a bunch of juice, and you can sell it, and
we can make a bunch of money." He wasn't a bodybuilder, so he
wasn't in the community. He had connections to the drugs but
not to the buyers, and you need to have both to be successful
and make the cash. I didn't know what else to do after a while
and figured what the hell. I told myself, "I'm not going to use it,
but if I can make some money selling it, I have to. I need it. I
need to put food on the table."

We ended up heading out one day and picking up a guy
named Paul, who would eventually become my business partner. We also picked up a slower guy everyone called Beans
before making our way out to Brighton Beach in Brooklyn, to
the Russian area, and we got our hands on a huge quantity of
Russian Dianabol and Russian Sustanon. This was some of the
highest-quality pharmaceutical-grade steroids anywhere in the
world.

I went from taking back bottles and cans to the recycling
center to making a thousand bucks a day. Fernando laughed
when I told him how amazed I was at the money we could
make. He said we'd go back the next week and do it all over
again. You really have to understand where I'd come from to
truly get a grasp on why this was so amazing to me. I didn't
have to worry anymore about putting food on the table or
making sure we had a roof over our heads. This was a means to
an end for me, not something I did out of greed. I felt I had

reached the point of having to do this out of sheer necessity, and it wasn't something I had just decided to do on a whim.

After I closed my gym in 1992, I was destitute. I didn't know what I was going to do. I was used to owning my own business and didn't know where to go. I'd seen guys who had gone from owning their own businesses to absolute rock bottom, and I feared being one of those guys. I didn't want to be just a statistic of yet another failed business.

I had looked at myself as having no skills. I had a high school education, but I wasn't a plumber or an electrician or a skilled carpenter. I just didn't have any particular skills that could put a roof over the heads of my family or food in their stomachs. So, from being the man who made all the decisions on the gym floor and in the offices, I went to working for someone else doing the worst jobs in the gym.

"Gregg, someone pissed on the floor in the locker room. Go clean it up."

I felt low, as low as I could possibly go. I tried to do some other things in the gym, but for whatever reason they had a tendency not to work out, no pun intended.

One thing I was good at, and I knew it, was being a personal trainer. I trained guys to get ready for contests, to burn fat, to get big, whatever they wanted. I tried this at the gym I was doing grunt work at and put some of its clients through my wringer. They all came out in the best shape of their lives. But I never got paid. I got fucked. It was a crashing spiral, and everything that could go wrong for me did. Every financial opportunity busted out.

I went from running the most popular gym around, having Mr. Olympia eating dinner at my house, promoting the biggest of local shows, and being known all around the bodybuilding community to cleaning up shit off the floor. They say money can't buy happiness, but I know when I didn't have it I sure was unhappy. Someone would decide to take a piss anywhere besides the urinal, and I was the guy to go clean it up. But I had a family to provide for, and I had to do whatever was necessary to pay the bills.

People usually think of the guy they see picking up other people's trash as a bum and loser. For a while, I was that guy. Down in the area of New York City known as Little Italy, I would go every year to what's called the Feast of San Gennaro to clean up just so I could recycle the cans and bottles. That was like Christmas to me. Over a million people show up during this event, which runs for a week, and you wouldn't believe the amount of trash that gets left on every street and corner. And like the old saying goes, one man's shit is another's bread and butter. My car would smell putrid and sour, but I'd make a few hundred dollars by taking the aluminum cans and glass bottles to the recycling plants.

When the feast wasn't on, if I saw a beer bottle on the side of the road, I'd still pull over and pick it up. I was half recycling crusader and half desperate man who wanted the nickel for the bottle. When gas was cheap enough, I'd drive around just to look for those very bottles.

Eventually, I started bouncing at a gay nightclub called Stutz after a friend hooked me up with the job, which was like a godsend. I was at the point of scraping the bottom of the bodybuilding barrel and thought seriously about muscle worship, posing for fags like a lot of bodybuilders do. Fortunately for me, I never had to do that. But I'm not ashamed to admit that, if it was my last option for making sure my family stayed warm and fed, I would have done it. In my mind, there is absolutely no shame for a man doing what he has to do — within the law — to provide for those who depend on him. But for me, it was never enough to just get by. The bouncing didn't allow me to give my kids and wife everything I wanted them to have, so I started in with some guys who showed me how to make bigger money, and the rest, as they say, is history. My history. And it got crazy very quickly.

On just the second trip we all made together to pick up some gear, we ended up robbing the guys. We didn't do it on purpose, though, and the whole thing caused a lot of animosity between a large group of people.

Fernando and I had picked up Paul, whom I now considered a friend, as well as Beans. We got down to Brighton Beach and called the drug dealer we were working with. The guy said he couldn't meet us, but the drugs were waiting for us. We went onto the boardwalk, and there was an eatery there. His father owned it, and we were told to go there and tell him we had been sent down. The idea was to give his father the money, and he would give us the package of drugs we were expecting. When we showed up, we handed over the cash, but he passed over far more gear than we had ordered. Fernando elbowed me and told me not to say a word, and we took all of the bags and quickly started walking out.

We were only a block away when we heard a yell behind us. It was the dealer himself, who must have got back just in time to hear his dad tell him he had given us everything. Right away we took off running and knew that if we got caught in that neighborhood we were going to get killed. Only a few blocks down we saw a van coming after us with these Russian mobsters inside. Sprinting, we ended up in my car and bolted down the block. Through the L-tracks, we ended up losing them.

When we finally made it back to my place, we broke open the bags and found that we had picked up about $30,000 worth of D-bol and Sustanon. It was going to be all profit because we hadn't put up any money for most of the stuff. We split it up evenly, and on top of that Fernando gave me his stash, and I took a percentage of what I sold for him.

My first real taste of drug dealing came the week that followed. I made over $10,000 in a matter of days; my gym couldn't even begin to compare to that kind of profit.

Most people think that steroids are basic, low-profile drugs handled only by bodybuilders. But that's not the case at all. The people we worked with were businessmen, not bodybuilders. These Russians were gangsters, true hardcore wiseguys who looked at the steroid game the same way other gangs dealt with cocaine, heroin, and God knows what else. These guys had a sophisticated operation that stemmed from Russia, where the drugs were made; they smuggled them into the country, and they distributed them once they were stateside. This wasn't a small operation to them.

After that day, it would be years before I saw those Russians again, and I never saw Beans again. He had been the go-between, and they knew everything about him; I don't know how he was ever going to explain what happened to them because he was running right alongside us.

Once our bridge was burned with the Russians, we had to find a new way to get product. Fortunately, Paul knew other guys who could get us what we needed. Ultimately, we would settle the mess we had made when we had an unplanned run-in with those Russian dealers in a club — and fortunately everything was very up-front, and the air was cleared — but that wasn't until long after we had set up getting supply from elsewhere.

One thing that really set my dealing apart from that of many others is that I wasn't working with Mexican vet drugs or pulling them into the country like many other guys had to. I was working with a much bigger operation. And honestly, I don't know that I'd have got involved if I'd had to get product through more difficult channels.

Some people go to extremes I wouldn't have even thought of to get their stuff. One guy I knew took vacations to Mexico with his girlfriend and turned them into business trips, so to speak. While he was down there, he would go to local pharmacies and buy tens of thousands of dollars worth of steroids. The first time I asked him how he brought that much shit back over the border was when I realized he was a crafty son of a bitch.

At the border, guards don't have to be very well trained to know that a juiced-up-looking bodybuilder might well have illegal steroids on him when heading back into the United States. Guys get busted for it all the time. But my friend was smarter than the average bodybuilder.

Knowing he'd usually get checked out — he has over twenty-inch arms — he told me that, to keep from getting searched, he would shit for a couple of days into big containers that he took with him. He would then wrap his drugs up inside dirty clothes, place them in his suitcase, and dump the containers of shit all over them. Once he even added two cans of tuna in oil to mix in with the feces. He would then let this mixture sit for a couple of days to get exceptionally foul, then put it in his trunk when he was ready to leave.

When he got to the border, the patrol guards surely asked him to pop the trunk so they could take a look. He always told them "No problem" but added that he had been very sick in Mexico and vomited all over himself and shit his pants more than once. He told them as well that his hotel had no laundry facilities and ranted about how dirty Mexican water is.

Because of how bad things smelled and the story they heard, the guards never questioned it once they opened the suitcase. Usually, he said, they could smell it as soon as the trunk was opened, but even the brave ones who unzipped the suitcase never made it past a quick initial impression. They saw and smelled the shit and closed it right back up.

My methods of obtaining drugs were far cleaner, so to speak. But they were also a hell of a lot more dangerous, and I would quickly come to realize there's no such thing as a "safe drug" when it comes to selling it.

Chapter 6
MEETING JULISSA: A LOVER AND A PARTNER

The most beloved character to have ever been a part of the comedic tragedy I call my life was my love Julissa Rivera. There is no negativity or derogatory meaning behind calling her a character, because that's exactly what she was. She played the loving girlfriend to me, willing to sacrifice for me and willing to clean up after me, the girl willing to fight for me and willing to die for me. How I met her was, fittingly, no less wild.

From the first time I saw Julissa, I knew there was something special about her; she had an appeal that I wanted to get close to. She was like a light.

At a club one night, I was making the rounds, hanging out with my friends, and talking to women all evening. But the whole time, no matter how hot the women right in front of me were, I kept my eyes on this Latina on the dance floor with dark, curly hair, a tight body to die for, and wide, engaging dark eyes. I knew right away she was a working girl — the way she was dancing dirty with this one guy gave it away — but that didn't deter me. Whatever her choice of trade, she was working this guy like a champ. He was clearly acting the part of asshole perfectly, but he was drunk and throwing money around just the way she wanted. For some reason, the way she was hustling this guy just kept my attention, and part of me enjoyed it.

Julissa was a street girl, to be sure, but there's an art to what she was doing that night. Girls like her worked guys like this the same way that Picasso painted pictures; it was an art. Not only was it obvious to me that this Latin street girl had some ghetto in her, but she also had street smarts. Many people might look down on girls like this, but not me. I know what it's like to struggle, I know what it's like to have the odds stacked against you, and it takes strength to survive. That's what this girl was doing, and as she moved her hips and pushed her body against his I could tell she had not only determination but also flavor.

In any case, no matter how drawn to this girl I was, I couldn't bring myself to talk to her because I didn't want to screw up her business. I didn't know if she was trying to find a place to stay that night, I didn't know if she was trying to put food on her table or if she had a child to feed. I wasn't going to screw up her business. Over the course of the night, I started letting her image fade from my peripheral view.

When I eventually left the club, my friend and I made a stop at a diner next door. We took a window seat at a long, white-topped table. On one side was my friend and a girl he had met at the club. I and another friend we had run into at the club were on the other side. While the other two were making out across the table, I was carrying on small talk on my side and enjoying my plate. For no particular reason halfway through my meal, I looked out the window. The second my eyes came into focus I jumped up out of my seat and headed for the door, not stopping to say anything to my friends.

I pushed through the glass double doors that led out of the diner and started running down the dark sidewalk. From my seat, I had seen a guy beating up a girl; once he had knocked her to the ground, I realized it was the same girl I had been eyeing all night long and the same drunken asshole she had been working in the club. As I was heading down the block, he grabbed her by the hair and was dragging her around the corner into a gravel parking lot; she was screaming and crying, pleading with him to let her go.

The second I was within earshot in the busy city night I yelled at him. "Yo, asshole!" I shouted. "Get your fucking hands off of her!"

The prick didn't even look at me when he hollered back, "Mind your fucking business." He was tall and rugged-looking and wore a sports coat over a plain T-shirt. He wore cowboy boots that clicked on the ground with every step he took.

That second, as soon as I digested his words, I snapped. "Listen, motherfucker," I said, close to him now. "Get your hands off of her, or I'll bash your fuckin' head in."

This time he stopped to look at me, and in the process he let go of her hair. She curled up into a ball at his feet, screaming and covering her head.

He spoke as he moved toward me. "I told you, man," he said, "mind your fucking business."

I shook my head. "I'm making it my business, asshole, and I'm not playing with you. Get out of here, or I'm bashing your head in."

He rushed me.

I drew my right fist back and, the instant he was within arm's reach, pushed it into his teeth. He fell to his knees and tried to push off like a lineman into my gut to tackle me, but as his shoulder hit my gut I wrapped my arms under his, drew my knee into his chest, and lifted him up. I twisted his torso and placed my left hand around the front side of his neck and my right hand around the backside. I raised my arms up like I was lifting a sledgehammer, and I brought his head right down onto the hood of a car parked right next to us. I felt his body go limp, and I let him go, turning my focus to the girl on the ground, still crying and covered.

I thought the asshole had been knocked out, but before I

even reached the girl he was screaming obscenities at me. I turned around and looked over my shoulder, and I couldn't close my eyes quickly enough to avoid the handful of gravel he threw at me. It caught me off-guard, and I stumbled just enough that I had to put my hands down on the ground, but I didn't fall. I felt rocks slice into my palms, and I knew blood was coming. I stood back up as he was coming toward me. He reached his arm back as if he was going to strike me, but I threw a short jab with my left hand to catch him off-guard. He leaned back, trying to stop my left with both of his hands, and I reached over the top and caught him on his left eyebrow with my right hand, sending him back to the ground.

I waited there in the lot, breathing heavily, angry, waiting for him to make his next move. Soon enough he decided to crawl backward slowly to distance himself from me and finally returned to his vehicle and drove away.

I turned around and moved toward the girl, who by this point was sitting up and wiping the dirt and dust away from her face and arms, still crying with tears streaming down her cheeks as fast as she could wipe them away. Kneeling next to her, I took in the extent of her damage. Her eyes were black and already swollen, her lower lip was bleeding profusely, and she had cuts on her nose, chin, and cheeks that must have come from being dragged.

The girl looked terrible; that asshole had fucked her up badly. She tried to get to her feet and stumbled, barely able to make it on her second attempt.

"Are you okay?" I asked. I knew the outside was beaten up severely, but I wanted to know how she was feeling inside.

"I'm fine," she said, obviously lying.

"Let me take you to the hospital," I said.

"Oh, please. This isn't the first time I've had my ass beat by a man, and I'm sure it won't be the last." She was trying to hold back her tears, but her words were muffled, her mouth thick with saliva. She spoke with acceptance of the life that a street girl lives. Not pretty, not safe, but true.

My heart was bleeding for her. I felt a connection to this woman, and I couldn't tell why, but I knew inside I was hurting as much as she was on the outside. I ached for her and pleaded with her to let me help her, but obviously she was so used to a life of solitude that she was afraid of me. She didn't want to let me into whatever circle of safety she still felt she had. After I asked again to help her, she snapped at me.

I understood.

For a long minute, I stood there waiting, watching her try to get herself together, and wishing desperately there was something I could do to make all of this okay.

As she brushed herself off, she was still apparently dizzy from having been hit and manhandled. When she tried to take a step, she lost her footing and fell forward. I reached out to grab her, my right hand clasping hers, and I pulled her into me and rested her back against my left arm and chest. I kept a hold of her hand, and she gripped mine tightly.

I looked down to see my hand and hers, and for the first time I saw my palm bleeding. When she pulled her hand just slightly out of mine — our fingers still intermixed — I saw that small drops of blood were slowly pooling together in my palm. We both just stared for a second, not knowing what to say or do, and then I felt something lightly hit the inside of my hand: a drop of her blood. At that moment, something inside of me connected, and I knew, whether she did or not, that I was now attached to this girl, and for better or worse her troubles would be my troubles.

Just as I started taking her image in — cuts and bruises be damned, she still looked gorgeous to me — she pulled away.

"Listen," she said. Her voice cut straight through me to my heart. "Thank you for your help, but I'm fine now." She waited for a long moment. "You can go back to whatever you were doing. But thank you. I just want to be alone now."

At the same time, I felt a moment of rejection but also one of purpose. I had been there when she had needed me, but now she wanted her space. I had no right to take that from her. I simply nodded my head and turned away slowly.

As I walked, I thought to myself how good she looked — her jet black hair glistening in the night — but also how much she needed someone. I could tell she hadn't been doing so well; she was gaunt like most girls on the street. But even looking like she was made of just skin and bones, I was so stricken by her.

I turned around and watched her slowly stumble away. The inside of me still hurt for her, and I was arguing with myself about what to do next. I knew she was lying, I knew she needed someone. But I didn't want to force myself on her because I didn't want her to fear me too. I'm not one who usually believes in fate, but something told me to go back to the diner and wait. I didn't know how long to wait, and part of me said it would be wasted time, but I went back and stood there. I closed my eyes and knew that if I was meant to help this girl further — and in a strange way if she was meant to help me — she would come back.

I call it destiny. Not more than thirty seconds after I opened my eyes back up to the night did I see her coming back toward me. She still had tears in her eyes, and the swelling in her face caused her cheeks and lips to protrude even further, but I looked past that. She was beautiful. When she finally reached me, I could see she was walking only a little better than before. At least now she could keep herself upright.

Her big, dark eyes met mine, and she said, "Hey, listen, I'm still kind of scared that jerk might come back. Can you just sit with me for a while?"

She told me that she was homeless but staying with a friend

for a few days, but she couldn't go back there because her friend was "pulling a date." I knew what that meant; her friend was a hooker and had found a trick for the night.

Even though this girl was scared, I could tell she was trying very hard to get close to me, to trust me. I asked her for her name, and she said to me, "I'm Julissa."

We walked over to my car, and as I opened the door for her she tripped again, this time into my arms. To me it felt like an omen of what was to be. I got her something to eat and something to drink. I'll never forget that night. I bought her a Welch's grape juice, her absolute favorite, and a pack of Newport cigarettes.

For the rest of the night, we just drove around the city and talked. I tried to get to know Julissa without her feeling like I was invading her privacy. While we talked, she would occasionally touch her cheeks and her split lip; I could only imagine the stinging pain she felt. In time, I found out that she was addicted to heroin and that she had been in jail eleven times over her short life. She was only twenty years old, and I was thirty-six, but age wasn't a factor for us. Not that night, not ever.

After we finally got in touch with her friend, Julissa said I could take her back to the apartment she was staying at. By now it was morning, and though I knew my eyes should be burning with desire for sleep I still felt alive and energetic.

When I pulled up to the apartment building, she looked at me and grabbed my hand, and told me, "You're a good man, Gregg. I hope to see you again." And she kissed me lightly on my lips. Then she stepped out of my car and gently closed the door.

The apartment she was staying at looked rundown and seedy. I knew what went on in this type of place, and it pained me to watch her walk into it. It almost felt to me like I was letting her go back to the very life I wanted so badly to take her away from. With the car still running, I jumped out and ran to her, grabbing her small right hand as quickly as I could.

"Let me see you tonight," I said to her.

She took on a small, adorable smile. "Okay," she said. "But I don't have a phone, so I can't call you."

"Don't worry about that," I said. "Just wait for me. I'll be here."

At that moment, she smiled back at me, and, while I knew we had just started something that held great potential to grow, I also knew we had more than that. We had a partnership in so many ways.

Chapter 7
LEARNING TO LIVE TWO LIVES

I knew from the moment I met Julissa that I could fall in love with her. There was something about her — the way she spoke, the way she looked — that just had me from the start. I don't know if it was her vulnerability and that I felt she needed me to protect her or if it was because no matter how frail she was she had the courage to protect herself. Whatever it was, I was hooked, and I was in deep.

But I had a choice to make. I was a married man — married to a fantastic woman at that — but I was head over heels for another woman. I could have been a man and told my wife our marriage was over, but I didn't. Instead I chose to live a second life. It was literally overnight that I went from being a bad guy to worse; now, not only was I selling illegal drugs, but I was also lying to a woman who had committed everything to me, given me my wonderful son, and I was lying to a new woman I was giving my heart to. I had become so good at lying that to me it was all the truth. I didn't lie; there were two parts of me.

There was the daytime Gregg, the devoted husband and father and hard-working, self-respecting New Yorker, and then there was the nighttime Gregg, the one living a life of sex and drugs and underground dirt. But somehow it was comfortable, and I found my niche. But I had to ask myself in a blunt way how I could have gone from loving a beautiful woman who cared about me enough to marry me to loving a ghetto street hooker. I never could answer that question, and to this day I haven't figured it out.

My life with my wife had been deteriorating before Julissa came along, mostly from my doings. We hadn't had sex in what felt like ages, and we weren't even sleeping in the same bed. But I loved her, and she was my wife. Somehow I justified it to myself that it was okay to have a girlfriend on the side to complete what I felt I needed in my marital relationship.

Initially, Julissa didn't know I was married. As I said, I was lying to her as well as my wife. But while I was able to keep things under wraps for a while and prevent either side of my life from visually conflicting with the other, there was no stopping the damage I was doing on a mental level. The more time I spent with Julissa, the less time I spent at home. Both were like hungry mouths that needed to be fed, but the only one I was feeding was my life with Julissa. My wife and son suffered for it.

Spending time with Julissa soon escalated beyond lust. It wasn't like she was a mistress whom I saw only when I wanted to fuck. She was much more than that. I could talk to her about anything, she would share her secrets with me, and I found that her Spanish-speaking ability came in very handy when it came to business. Quickly, Julissa and I became more than lovers. We were a team. A steroid-dealing Bonnie and Clyde, if you will.

Many of my steroid deals were with Latin gang members in Washington Heights. On several occasions, I got screwed on deals because, they said, they misunderstood me. They didn't understand English that well, and somehow that got them off the hook with the powers that be, and I took the loss for it. That was no longer the case with Julissa around; she was Puerto Rican, spoke perfect Spanish, and much to my benefit took absolutely no shit. She was half hitman, half translator. And she was up for anything and just enveloped herself in my lifestyle.

In a business sense, Julissa was much like me because she couldn't stand dishonest people. On the opposite end of the spectrum — sexually — she was a freak just like me. She was so much like me that, no matter where we went or what I was doing, she would enjoy herself and hang out right by my side. Dealing drugs, she was there. Shopping for new clothes and cars, she was there. Hanging out at the strip clubs, she was there. It was like having a best friend who was your lover who was your business partner. I had no reason to spend time away from her.

Except, of course, for my family, whom I was neglecting in a very non-traditional way. By this time, it had grown as well. Along with Veola and my son, Paul, we now had my daughter, Gina. When I did perform my parental duties, I did so in a hollow way. I took my son to baseball practice and karate, I lay in bed with him at night until he fell asleep. I dropped my kids off at day care and picked them up from school, but once the lights went out and they were asleep I left to live my other life they had no idea about. Drug dealers live the night life, and Julissa and I were like vampires. Hindsight, as they say, is always perfect. At the time, I didn't even notice the toll my actions were taking on my wife, and it wasn't long before she figured out what was going on.

I was making typical male assumptions; I was thinking with the wrong head on my body. If my wife complained, I'd feed her bullshit story after bullshit story, and I'd buy her more gifts. Money was no object since I had become a much bigger player in the drug dealing, so I would just buy and buy and buy until she quieted down. But she had women's intuition, she knew something wasn't right with her man, and she wasn't going to put up with it for much longer. But she stopped short of calling me straight out until she was absolutely positive I was fucking around on her.

For my part, I was having so much fun living the night life that I wasn't receptive to my wife's clear hints that I needed to stop what I was doing, be a man, and tend to my business. Fuck that, I figured. I was getting in deeper with Julissa each day, and she was getting in deeper with me. She had my back on drug deals, she helped me make a ton of money, and she never complained. But again, it was because she was getting everything she wanted. She had all of me, and my wife had none. I wouldn't realize until much later that it is absolutely impossible for a man to make more than one woman happy, no matter how smooth he thinks he is. A good woman deserves all of the man she loves — heart, body, and soul — and I wasn't able to give that to either woman in my life. Even Julissa was lacking because I still had to hide things from her.

Finally, I confessed to Julissa that I was married. She wasn't happy with this, of course, but by this point she had fallen so hard for me that she couldn't pull herself away. She was in love with me. I can't help but think how horrible that one decision she made was for her. The thing was, she had nothing other than me. She was a girl from the street who went from man to man just to feed and clothe herself. She had nothing, and I gave her something. She was in love with me, and she wasn't going to be bothered by the fact that I was married to another woman. Even then I felt bad; she was an amazing person, and I had her into very bad things, none of which she deserved.

Heroin was her demon. I took Julissa away from that scene, got her cleaned up, but I only replaced one demon with another. I considered myself a good person who was also into bad things, but I was greedy. I wanted everything and then some, and I had it all, but it was never enough. Julissa should have left me — I was just as bad for her as that heroin — but she didn't see it that way. I still feel that I'm responsible for what happened to her, because I know with great certainty that her final breath came alongside a thought of me.

Chapter 8
UNEXPECTED HOLD-UP

One night I ended up at Scores, the strip club, and met up with my old friend and partner, Paul. At this club, Paul said to me that he wanted to keep up what we had started when it came to selling drugs. He was comfortable with our arrangement, and I wanted to remain involved with Paul because he was a good guy. Even though we were mixed up in some illegal shit, I could tell he was genuine.

Paul took me to meet a jacked bodybuilder named Reggie, who was hooked up with huge quantities of Steris drugs — Deca, testosterone, Dianabol, all kinds of things — and he would front it to us. He would give us tens of thousands of dollars worth of product, which he got straight from a doctor, and let us pay him later.

The doctor Reggie was working with was Dominican. Because Reggie was into bodybuilding the way he was, he told this doctor he knew ways to make big money. And walking into his home, it was obvious that the deal had been working out very well. Reggie had more than a million dollars in cash on his kitchen table, in cabinets, everywhere. He wasn't just moving juice, though. If you took a piss in his house, you could look in the bathtub and find dozens of pounds of marijuana. He was hooked up into any type of drug that would make him some money.

Originally, as the story goes, Reggie was dead broke. He was down and out, had no money, no possessions, nothing of value in his life. Then he started dabbling in this and that, and when his operation started growing he went from sleeping on the floor of Paul's house to a huge house of his own and enormous amounts of cash.

But over time, Reggie started to lose his mind because of the other drugs he was on. He started getting paranoid. One night we were in his house watching a Mike Tyson fight, and Reggie fell dead asleep right on the couch. With seven figures in cash on his table, he had no problem falling asleep or even leaving us alone there. He knew we were honest guys who weren't going to touch a dime, so he often acted like we weren't even there. But after a while, he became a little weird. He would get so high that he even forgot he had fronted juice to us.

The things we were getting from Reggie included bricks of testosterone vials, the sight of which would make any "supplemented" bodybuilder drool. The stuff came in boxes that had five rows with five 10-cc bottles in each row. We'd get dozens of bricks at a time and go sell them. We'd come back and say, "Hey, Reggie, here's your money," and he'd swear up and down he hadn't given us anything and we didn't owe him. Even though he was as high as a kite, we paid him anyway. That's why he trusted us so much, because we were always very honest. But on the flipside, sometimes we'd knock on the door to bring him some cash, and he'd stick a pistol in our faces, not knowing who the hell we were.

Eventually, Paul started getting worried that Reggie could go from forgetting that he ever gave us stuff to forgetting that we actually paid him. Luckily, that never happened, but he was getting in deep with the wrong drugs and really starting to lose it. Nonetheless, for a long time, he was the go-to guy for our product.

During this time, Paul and I were bouncing at a gay bar called Stutz in White Plains, New York. It was the place to be for the rich white guys in the area: publicists for musicians, Hollywood agents, all types. But this club didn't want gay guys as bouncers, so they hired Paul and me, and we ended up making some pretty good money from a legit job too.

This club had a big parking lot with security because people were parking Lamborghinis and Mercedes at this bar, which was only a few blocks from housing projects. I'd watch the door while Paul would run out to Reggie's — still on the clock at the bar — and pick up our drugs. We were making money hand over fist, both legally and not.

After a while, though, we got busted. This was a high-class club, and they had zero tolerance for any kind of drug. One day someone called the club to make an order. This was before cell phones were common, and often we took orders right off the bar phone. The bartenders would answer the phone and just call me in to take the call, and it would be a client wanting some drugs. One call, somehow, ended up on the machine. It picked up an entire drug deal order going down on the phone between me and a guy. The club's owner called us in and played this message and threatened to turn us in to the cops. We didn't get fired, but we were damaged in her eyes. At this point, we had to slow down our business. We knew we had to keep jobs as a front to cover up the money we were making elsewhere.

While we were working at the club, Paul met a guy named Remo — the son of one of America's most notorious gangsters. He was a horrible person; he hated "fags," he hated blacks, he hated Asians. I watched him break the jaw of a transsexual who hung out near the diner where we met. He was bad news, but he had connections for European gear we couldn't get from Reggie.

In time, Reggie got busted and wanted out of the business. He never got caught for selling steroids, he got hammered for dealing pot. By this point, he was almost completely gone. We went over to his place, and he jumped out from behind a couch with a pair of guns pointed at us. After we calmed him down, he finally told us that he was getting out of the business, he was going down, but that the doctor he was working with wanted to keep making money.

Because Reggie was in so good with this physician, he spoke for us. He told the doctor he had to meet us and needed to trust us. In short order, we got in direct contact with this doctor and found out his story. He had clinics in the Dominican Republic, and he told Steris, the company, that this massive amount of hormones was for his chain of clinics. In reality, of course, the stuff never left the United States; it went straight to us.

This doctor told us he'd work with us, but we couldn't deal directly with him. Instead, he gave us the phone number of one of his associates, and we would arrange everything with that guy. We would call him, for example, and say we needed 2,000 bottles of Testosterone Enanthate 250, which would be a 10-cc bottle of testosterone dosed at 250 mg per cc.

The setup was so smooth. We would call, and I would meet him at the location he'd mentioned, he'd get in my car, and we'd go wherever he wanted to pick up the stuff. It was different every time. He'd go in wherever and pick up the drugs, I'd take him back wherever he wanted to go, I'd hand him the cash, and he'd leave the bag in the car.

At various points, though, we would call this doctor and find out the guy we had been dealing with was suddenly no longer "employed" by him. We'd get told the official story that he had left the country, but we would hear things in the background that he had tried to stiff someone along the supply chain and got whacked. Every time a guy left, we'd get a simple explanation. But every time the good word came in that something horrible had happened. One guy was found with a bullet in his ear, another guy had his chest split open, and another guy ended up in the river. No matter what happened, we knew that these outcomes were entirely possible, and we stayed straight to keep that sort of thing from happening to us.

Sometimes we would get a new guy who would overcharge the hell out of us. One guy, Jose, got into the car, and the first words out of his mouth were that he was raising the price five dollars a bottle despite what the doctor had said. The order was for 2,000 bottles, and it ended up costing me an extra $10,000.

Another trip paired me and Julissa, whom I was now dating, with an associate of mine named Timmy. With us were a pair whom Timmy had known, a Russian guy and his girlfriend. The guy was very quiet but had a thick jaw and wide shoulders that carried a lot of muscle. The girl was gorgeous — blond hair, big breasts, small waist — but hardly said a word.

We ended up at Reggie's house, and as soon as we pulled up this Russian guy pulled a gun on me, and his girlfriend pulled a gun on Julissa. I swore so loud I thought the neighbors would hear.

The entire ride I had an uneasy feeling, and I never had liked dealing with new people. I trusted my friends, but my gut was always the best measure of whom to deal with, and when I started in with people I didn't know I wasn't able to check them out first.

The gun was pressed into my neck, and through his thick accent the guy told me to shut up. He was very direct and told me that I had twenty minutes to go into the house and get what he had ordered. I was told in no uncertain terms that if I was even a second over my limit he'd kill Timmy, and his girl would kill Julissa. At that moment, I felt my hands tingle and my face go numb. I had been in bad situations before, this wasn't new, but I knew I'd never forgive myself if something happened to Julissa, and it was like a shot to the gut to have even put her in this situation.

I took a deep breath and opened the car door. I knew there were several ways out of this, none of which involved calling the cops once I was inside. I was a drug dealer; asking the cops for any kind of help never entered my mind. In any case, had they shown up, Julissa and Timmy probably would have been shot anyway, and then all of us who survived would have gone to jail. Anyway, the cops, because of distance, would never have shown up in time. And it was entirely possible that the fucking Russian cocksucker and his girl would both end up dead before I even stepped outside.

What the Russians didn't know was that Julissa had my pistol in her pocket. Usually, I kept it in my glove box, but she had great instincts. Before we all got together, she placed it in her jacket pocket "just in case," she told me. I knew full well that her plan, if I didn't come out in time, would be to shoot this guy's girlfriend and hope to God she could shoot him before she took one in the chest. I had a feeling that, if she did start pulling the trigger, Timmy would get shot too. Not in the cross-fire but by her. She had that Latin temper that was as dangerous as it was attractive. She was extremely loyal to me, and I knew she was as pissed off at Timmy as the other two who held the guns. I thought she was probably calculating how to get rid of all three at once.

I'd been in many scary situations before, but I wasn't really scared this time. I was pissed off. I knew that this Russian fuck didn't actually want to shoot anyone, I could tell it in his voice, but I also knew he was very concerned about being ripped off. While I understood that, the fact that he would pull out a gun before I even had a chance to get his shit was ridiculous.

I stepped through the door and found Reggie strung out over the edge of the couch. His head was notched back over the armrest, and his mouth was hanging half open. "Reggie, get up," I yelled at him. "Where's my shit?"

I started looking around his living room and kitchen, and I was hoping it was already together somewhere. I knew I couldn't tell him what was going on outside because the last thing you tell a drug-dealing tweaker is that someone only a few feet away is ready to murder someone else. I had to stay calm, but I felt my breathing become labored.

"What stuff?" Reggie asked as he rolled his body off the couch.

I bit my lip. I wanted to just go off on him, to put my fist into his face, but I resisted. Any other day this would have been par for the course, normal Reggie-being-Reggie. But today my girlfriend had a gun to her head, and there wasn't a second to spare.

"You know what I ordered, Reggie, and I'm in one major fucking hurry, so get it together!"

As if he had been joking before, he got to his feet and said, "Oh, yeah . . ."

This Russian guy had made a hell of an order. He was looking at more than $20,000 worth of anabolic steroids, which meant hundreds of bottles inside dozens of boxes. First I had to find bags, and then I had to get Reggie to take me to where he kept the stuff. For whatever reason, he would leave countless stacks of cash around his house, weed in the sinks, and only God knows what else in drawers and cupboards, but he hid the steroids extremely well.

Finally, Reggie sauntered down the hall into a small room. He opened up the closet and pulled away a pile of clothes thrown on the floor. Behind the stack was a small door about the size of an old *Rolling Stone* magazine. Through this little gateway, he pulled box after box of drug vials. I pulled a crumpled-up piece of paper out of my pocket and smoothed it out between my hands before I gave it to him. It was the list from the Russian.

While Reggie was going over the list, I grabbed a couple of gym-sized duffel bags off the floor in one of the bedrooms and started piling cases of testosterone inside. I easily filled up the first bag and quickly zipped it up after I set it down. I went back to the same room and grabbed a few more bags and threw them out into the room where Reggie was now sitting on the floor. The one thing he did have plenty of were those bags; we were all bodybuilders, so it never looked suspicious, no matter where we went, that we'd have a full gym bag with us.

Reggie took one and started haphazardly dumping things inside. I looked at my watch and saw I was running out of time. It was almost like I could hear a clock ticking inside my head, and I got a stretching feeling in my chest as if my heart were going to beat right out. I strongly felt this guy didn't want to pull the trigger, but I was concerned that Julissa would escalate the situation.

When there was only room for a few more vials, I heard a loud bang outside, and my arms went limp. I dropped the bag, cases and bottles falling on top of Reggie and spilling onto the floor. He didn't skip a beat and took no notice that my eyes were as wide as cola cans and my mouth hung open. I started to shake and thought of Julissa. I looked down at Reggie, who had gone back to filling the bag, and I bolted out of the room to the nearest window that overlooked the parking area.

I ran until I came within a couple steps of the window, and then I slowed down. I didn't know if I was prepared for what I was going to see. Just before I peeked through the glass, I heard the sound again. I instinctively covered my ears, and my entire body tensed up. When I finally got up the nerve to peek outside, nothing had changed. I saw two scared people and two guns held by a pair of Russians whom at that moment I hated more than anything. I never did find out where the sounds that drew me to that window had come from, and I didn't have time then to reflect.

I ran back into the room where Reggie was still kneeling on the floor in the closet and realized he had barely filled that second bag. For as much product as this guy had ordered, I knew it would take at least four neatly packed bags, five the way

Reggie was handling things. I had only a few minutes left, and I was certain there would be a shootout if I didn't make it. I pulled Reggie out of the way and dropped to my knees. I didn't care what I was grabbing, I just reached into the wall and placed whatever I found into a bag. If I would owe Reggie more money later, it didn't matter.

After I had close to five bags full of drugs, I grabbed them by their straps, three bags in my left hand, two in my right, and I ran down the hallway toward the door. When I reached the door, I set the bags in my right hand down, ripped the door open, picked the bags back up, pushed my shoulder through the screen door, and jumped out onto the porch.

I wanted to yell "Wait!" but knew I couldn't say anything, not wanting to draw attention from the neighbors. I hustled back to the car, and as soon as I could see clearly inside I knew that the image just yards in front of me was only seconds away from becoming a crime scene. I could see three guns drawn and pointed in a triangle. The Russians were screaming in Russian, and Julissa was yelling back in Spanish.

I looked around to see if anyone was watching me. When I was sure no one was around, I stepped hard on the ground to make my footsteps heard, and then I dropped the bags onto the hood of the car. I threw my hands out to let them know everything was cool, I had the drugs, and hoped everything would cool down.

Both of the Russians looked at me, but Julissa kept both hands on her pistol and kept it pointed at the guy. I don't know if she thought the girl wouldn't fire first or if he was just the bigger, easier target. The guy said something I couldn't hear to his girlfriend and lowered his gun. The girl kept hers out but slightly lowered it. I yelled to Julissa to relax and put her weapon down too. She ignored me.

The Russian guy calmly opened the door and stepped out of the car, followed by his girlfriend. After they stood up, Julissa opened the other door, got out, and stepped up beside me. I couldn't see the gun but saw her hand in her pocket. Not surprisingly, she kept her shoulders squared off, ensuring she kept the guy right in front of her.

After peeking inside just one bag, the Russian guy nodded his head as if to tell me he approved. As crazy as it was, after he saw the bag, he became apologetic. He explained that all of the "excitement," as he called it, was just to ensure he wasn't going to be ripped off. Apparently, he was so used to getting jacked that he had decided to take things into his own hands. He paid me every cent he owed and took his drugs, told us he had been serious about killing Timmy and Julissa if I hadn't come back in time, and left.

That was the last time I knowingly worked with someone unfamiliar, and it was one of the last times I saw Reggie. With the cops breathing down his neck, I heard he relocated his operation south of New York.

I never pretended Reggie and I were like brothers or anything, we were mostly conducting a strict business relationship, but it weighed on me for quite a while when I heard news years later that he had never made it out of the business. Steroids are no safer in a legal sense than "recreational" drugs, but the people you deal with are usually very different. With another type of dealer, you have to worry about the clients you keep. A guy high on crack might well be willing to slit your throat for his next hit. With steroids, you never hear of a guy cutting copper pipe or knocking off a convenience store to get his next shot. They aren't that type of drug, and often the people who use them are very affluent and well mannered. Frankly, you have to be very brave or very stupid to deal with hard drugs the way Reggie did. We always told him to stick to steroids, but he never listened.

The news came to me through a former bodybuilder. Reggie was off the drugs himself, I was told. His life was coming together. But he was still dealing harder products and ended up keeping the wrong company. Rumor has it that he was robbed, beaten, and killed slowly. Reggie was Haitian, and I dealt with a lot of Haitian drug dealers. They were some of the most ruthless, crazy, unforgiving criminals I ever came across, and I did my best to stay away from them. Only God knows what really happened to Reggie; I just know he isn't around anymore, and it has been over fifteen years since I heard from him or anything about him. It's a crazy life.

Chapter 9
SAVED BY AN ANGEL

Not only had Julissa proven herself time and time again to be of tremendous value to my business, but she soon turned herself into a private security contractor. She was gritty, and she was comfortable on the streets. Her no-bullshit attitude complemented mine, and she had amazing street sense.

For a while, I was turning over great profits working with a large group of Dominicans to whom I had been introduced through the clinic doctor who brought in all the drugs. I didn't enjoy working with them in the slightest because they were the type of guys who would have no problem slitting my throat for twenty dollars to take their girls on a date to McDonald's, but the cash I was making from the drugs was too good to pass up. They changed their prices constantly, didn't speak English, sold steroids, but didn't lift weights. It was very shady. But I always kept a pistol on me, and when I measured risk against reward it usually turned out in favor of going through with it.

Every so often the doctor would change the group of guys I was working with. I hated it when he did this because some of the guys were cool and some weren't. Just when I'd get into a rhythm with one group and we all got along, it would get changed around, and, as I've mentioned, I'd somehow end up with an asshole.

One night Julissa and I were heading to a meeting at Jimmy Bronx Café off I-87, and I had a large amount of money on me to make a buy. I was supposed to meet my contact and pick up a large quantity of Steris brand anabolic steroids. Then, already on the trip, I was told that things had been changed at the last second, and I was being sent to a totally different part of the Bronx. Any drug dealer will tell you that a change in location is almost a guaranteed fucking. It's uncomfortable because you never know where you're going, and if you had planned for backup in the area you were supposed to make the buy in it's hard to coordinate everyone for the new location.

While I wasn't comfortable with it, I wasn't too alarmed over this sudden change because for once it actually moved the location up in scale. Instead of going to the normal meeting spot, we were headed into a nicer neighborhood in the Bronx described to me as Jose's brothers' house. We were making the switch because Jose felt his neighborhood had become too hot — meaning too many cops around — and his brother lived in a nearly all-white neighborhood that didn't have cops parked on every corner.

Julissa was pissed off right away that the location was being changed. She kept telling me, "Gregg, I don't like this shit," and "Fuck this, don't do it, Gregg." But I had been training hard, I was jacked, I had my pistol in the glove box, loads of cash in my pockets, and visions of making a few hundred grand. My judgment was obviously clouded, and in hindsight I should have listened to her. But when I pulled up to that two-storey brownstone, all I saw were green dollar signs.

"This ain't right," Julissa said to me as we were getting out of the car. "He's going to try and rob you. I've got a real bad vibe about this."

At that point, I knew I was being greedy, but something told me Julissa needed to stay in the car in case these thugs tried to pull something. Just like I knew she would, she immediately started arguing with me once I told her to stay outside. I told her I wanted to get it over with, get in and get out, and then we could head out to a club and meet up with our friends. Her concern, though, was that with her inside they couldn't pull any bullshit on me because she could speak their language. Still, I refused.

Finally, she accepted the fact that I wasn't going to let her go in. To me it was going to be simple. I'd go in, set down the money, and pick up a few bags or boxes stuffed with drugs. Same shit as usual, just a different location. We had planned to go to a Latin club in Midtown that night, and I was eager to head in that direction, so I didn't want to argue. I just wanted to get the deal done.

I made my way alone inside and found the door that I had been told to enter. I rang the doorbell, and in just a few seconds Jose ripped it open and nodded for me to come inside.

Right away an uneasy, tight feeling settled into my stomach. The room was dark, and I could smell marijuana from the moment he opened the door.

"You got the money?" Jose asked me, closing the door behind me.

"Yeah, I got it," I said.

Before I could even finish my last word, I felt a deep, searing pain in the back of my skull. I dropped to my knees, then to my stomach, and my head suddenly felt like it was on fire. I rolled onto my back and looked up.

A short, fat, ugly motherfucker must have been standing right behind the door and struck me with the butt of a shotgun. He dropped to one knee, smiling, with the barrel of the gun no more than three inches away from my left eye.

Jose reached behind himself and pulled out a dull silver pistol and aimed it at my midsection.

"Give me the money, motherfucker," he said.

At this point, I was dazed, and my mind was foggy. I heard what he said, but I couldn't make my body act on it.

"I *said*," he yelled as he stomped on my right quadriceps, "give me the *fucking money!*"

Pretending that I was dazed and confused more than I really was, I rolled onto my side just enough so that my right jacket pocket was covering my hand. I felt around my side, trying to find my gun. I was thinking that I probably wouldn't make it out of that room alive, and I decided, if that was the case, that crooked cocksucker Jose wasn't going to either.

Then real fear finally set in. I didn't have my pistol. I had been arguing with Julissa and had forgotten to grab it. Now here I was, unarmed, my head feeling like an elephant was standing on it, a ruthless, good-for-nothing Dominican thug in an upper-class neighborhood of the Bronx threatening to kill me.

As I rolled back onto my back, I couldn't even close my eyes before the butt of the shotgun was rammed into my forehead. The crack I heard was so loud I would have guaranteed my skull had literally cracked. Instinctively, I tried to sit up, and as soon as I did gravity kicked in. My left eye started to sting as it filled with blood, and I felt the thick, red consistency of it stream past my nose, onto my lips, and into my mouth.

Jose kicked me dead center in the chest and sent me backward so hard that my head bounced off the hardwood floor like a tennis ball. It caused the already immense pain in my head to magnify, and I nearly vomited on myself.

With his foot now on my chest, just below my neck, and his pistol aimed between my eyes, Jose said again, "Give me the fucking money." He stepped back two half steps, smiled a dirty grin at me, and waited.

I reached into my inner jacket pocket to start grabbing money. This goes to show how dumb most gangsters are; if I had actually had a gun, they were offering me the perfect opportunity to shoot one of them. I pulled a wad of $100 bills from my pocket — they were rubber-banded together — and tried to throw it at Jose. But with the pain coursing through my skull and my chest, and with focusing on trying not to choke on the blood in my mouth, it made it only a few inches before rolling toward his feet. I felt like a child, helpless and weak. I repeated the process until there was about $10,000 in cash lying on the floor next to me.

And that, I just knew, was it. I was going to die in a house full of steroids, money, and guns. The very things that made up my life were now its undoing, and it was only a matter of seconds before everything would go black. I covered my head and closed my eyes, rolling again to my side. It was an instinctive position; I didn't want to see it coming, and I didn't want to give Jose the satisfaction of looking into my eyes when I died.

He kneeled down beside me and screamed for me to look at him. I opened my eyes, but I could hardly make out his face — all I could see was my own blood — until I wiped my eyes. I used my palm to cover the gash in my head to try to slow the bleeding.

"You're going to die now, you white piece of shit mother-fucker," he said to me, laughing.

I remained in the shape of a ball, covering my head. Suddenly, I heard a female voice screaming in Spanish followed by gunshots in rapid succession that sounded like bombs going off. I heard the shotgun fall to the hardwood floor behind me; as I quickly rolled over, I saw Julissa standing in the doorway, my pistol held in both of her hands, her arms extended forward. I picked up the shotgun, managed to get to my feet, and as off balance as I was swung it like a baseball bat right at Jose's head. He fell to the floor screaming like a girl as I felt the weapon vibrate in my hands from the impact.

The two thugs were on the floor now, screaming. Julissa had managed to open the door and pop off two shots. She was screaming something at them — something nonsensical to me

— in Spanish. I saw that the one who had been shot had only been grazed in the side of the ass. Like a child, though, he was rolling around and screaming bloody murder like a true coward.

"I've been shot!" he screamed. "Oh, my fucking God, I've been shot! I've been shot!"

I laughed and yelled back at him, "You ain't so fucking tough without a gun, are you, motherfucker! You little pussy, it's a fucking scratch!"

Julissa was standing there, gun now pointed at Jose, caught in a craze halfway between shock and crying. Her chest was heaving with deep sobs. "I thought you were dead," she cried. "I saw you lying there, and you weren't moving," she said. Her tears really started to flow now, her hands shaking uncontrollably and frighteningly fast while holding the pistol. "Why weren't you moving? You scared me so bad!"

I steadied myself, trying to find a semblance of calm in the hysteria, just in time to notice that Jose was going for the pistol he had dropped. I stepped between him and the gun and whacked the stock of the gun on his chin, sending him backward and screaming. I turned around to put my boot to the face of his friend and turned back to kick Jose three times across his face. I then handed the shotgun to Julissa, who stayed focused on the other thug, and I jumped on top of Jose. I punched him and beat him again until his nose was floating freely and blood covered his face.

Once I stood back up, Julissa took control. She started yelling in Spanish again and told them to quit screaming and take off their clothes. She made both of them get completely naked, and she made them throw their clothes out a window on the opposite end of the room. They limped around the room, leaving trails on the floor everywhere they went. I knew she had made them ditch their clothes so they couldn't come after us so quickly, but it was clear to me they weren't going anywhere except to the hospital.

Julissa then forced them to lie down while I tied their hands behind their backs. As I did so, she had enough humor left in her to make a joke. "Well, look at that," she said, gun still pointing between them. "Typical Dominican men. Big dicks but don't have any motherfuckin' brains!"

In hindsight, that was a prime example of the luxurious handle Julissa had on words and simple phrases. She lived for drama, and she was in the thick of it now, controlling the entire room and maintaining the very lives of two men literally in her hands.

Once I had them tied up, I collected all my cash, which still sat on the floor, and we bolted back out the door and into the car. As we tore off down the street, Julissa never once said "I told you so" or even got mad at me. She tended to my wounds, and her only concern was how I felt. There was something tender in her demeanor; she was totally selfless. She thought I was dead, but she stormed into that house anyway; she didn't know how many people were in there, only that I was. And that was enough.

Julissa told me that she had planned on shooting everyone in that house if I was dead. I knew she meant it. She told me that if she had enough bullets she would have shot an entire gang without a single question if I was in there dead. Then she told me something that scared me but truly made me realize how much this woman loved me.

"Gregg," she said softly to me that night in bed, tears starting to well up in her eyes. "If you had been dead, I would have shot them both until I knew they were dead. But I would have saved one bullet" — she paused, took a deep breath; I could tell she was building up courage — "for myself."

I didn't say anything, but I gave her a look that was obviously very curious, and concerned, about what she was saying.

"Because," she continued, a tear now dropping from the corner of her eye, "I would need one for myself. I can't live without you, and if you were dead I would want to be too."

I wiped away her tear, I put my finger over her lips to keep her from saying anything else, and then I kissed her. Despite my wounds and bandages, we made love that night, and it was as close as I have ever felt to anyone in my entire life.

Chapter 10
CARELESSLY STEPPING INTO THE DARK SIDE

Even with the ever-present dangers of being involved with the crowd that I was, I was finally making some very good money and feeling good about myself and my ability to provide for my family. Then it was suggested to me that Paul and I get back to opening up a gym, which we did, building the inside with our hands and sculpting it into a place we ourselves would want to train in.

Paul, with whom I was dealing shit, was just like me — natural — when we started working together. I was bigger than him, but over time he started getting bigger than me. On top of that, a few years earlier a guy named Bobby had started lifting weights and asked me for my advice every day. Fast-forward only a short time, and this guy was bigger than me and winning big bodybuilding shows. I was getting sick of it.

For years, I had been accused of using drugs even though I was as clean as a newborn baby. For twenty-three years, I was natural. Then, as guys like to call it, I made the choice to go over to the "dark side" and actually take anabolic steroids.

I remember popping some Anabolex to start, and I remember after swallowing them thinking to myself, "Oh, my God, I'm not natural anymore." They didn't even do anything to me at first, but the fact that I took them was like a complete mindfuck. Part of me felt so guilty that I might as well have robbed a bank.

I used to feel proud when guys like Rich Gaspari would compliment me on my physique, and I knew it was all built naturally. In 1982 and 1983, I trained with Samir Bannout, and he would compliment my arms. A Mr. Olympia complimenting me when I wasn't even touching the stuff they were was like the biggest compliment I could get.

After taking juice for the first time, I felt almost like a traitor. But at the same time, a new part of me was born. I was a bodybuilder, had trained more than twenty years, and it was something I felt bodybuilders did. I felt I had earned it. But for the first two months I was taking steroids, I denied it. I had a reputation as a natural bodybuilder, and I didn't want to lose that. My friend Bob Bonham would break my balls about it, but the fact was I liked it a lot.

Within weeks, my arms were getting veiny, and people started responding more than ever; I was to the point where I was cocky enough to wear tank tops in the New York winter. People were feeding my ego like never before. The bigger I became, the more I craved the attention. Well-trained muscle responds better than untrained muscle, and I had more than two decades of experience.

I would pop open bottles of testosterone, and it was like Christmas. I didn't walk around feeling angry or that I wanted to kick the shit out of people. Instead, I felt euphoric. I was jacked like a beast and loved every minute of it.

Steroids aren't addictive in the way heroin or coke is. You get addicted to the results. People think that somehow steroids make them bad. Addiction isn't bad when it's healthy. People like to watch television, so they do. People like to ride motorcycles, so they do. People like to eat chocolate, so they do. Are those all addictions? And, if so, they aren't hurting anyone —

what's the problem? My only problems stemmed from not being sterile enough. I'd reuse needles, I'd brush the tips off with my finger. Those were the problems — I didn't get angry, I didn't beat people, my attitude toward others never changed with steroids. My highs were higher, but my lows were never lower. Steroids enhanced my well-being but never caused a downswing.

Before I used drugs, people always talked about how girls loved jacked guys. And I was big before, but once I started using drugs I might as well have been Arnold himself. I'm 5'6", but on juice I felt like I was 6'5". It was like it gave me a Napoleon complex in a good way. Some guys need a Corvette or a fancy suit. Some women have to have a Gucci bag or plastic surgery or fancy jewelry. I didn't need any of that; I just needed the beef, the muscle.

I was getting the attention of professional bodybuilders. At the Night of Champions bodybuilding show one year, Kevin Levrone, one of the best bodybuilders in the world at the time, couldn't take his eyes off me even during an interview he was doing. Ronnie Coleman, the eight-time Mr. Olympia champion himself, couldn't believe it when he saw me.

I was big, and I was unbelievable. In retrospect, I was unbelievable in more ways than one. Things changed in many ways for me, both physically and mentally, when I started using gear. And every so often I put myself in a dicey situation. I didn't have "roid rage," but I definitely thought I was made of Teflon.

One example I can offer is when I did something very stupid in front of my then wife. On the Fourth of July 1998, I was at a big fireworks display at a high school where a couple thousand people were gathered on the football field. After the event, when everyone was leaving, there were five different lanes of traffic being directed out by a single police officer. After a while, the cop pissed me off. He let people in my lane go until I came up, and then he stopped me. Then he let all of the other lanes go time and time again. After fifteen minutes, he still hadn't let my lane go.

"What the fuck, bro'?" I yelled out my window.

"You hold on," he screamed back.

After a few more minutes of letting other lanes go, he finally let me out. I moved forward, and all the cars ended up in one lane being directed by a large redneck firefighter.

While I was stopped, this firefighter pointed at me and said to someone I couldn't see, "Look at this fucking asshole."

"You talking to me, bro'?" I asked him.

"You heard me, motherfucker."

"You're an asshole," I told him.

He laughed at me. "If you don't like it, get out of the car."

My wife was in the backseat with my one-year-old daughter Gina, and I jumped out of the car. The firefighter came running at me, and I cracked him in the jaw as hard as I could, reached out for his arm, and threw him down so hard I heard the wind leave him. I jumped on top of him, one leg on each side of his body, and started pummeling him in the face as fast as I could with shot after shot.

I felt a stiff boot hit my back moments later, and it turned out to be the first of half a dozen cops who jumped on me and started ripping my clothes apart as they beat on me. But I clutched my legs around the guy I was on top of and wouldn't get off until I was literally pulled off.

When I finally got up, I had no shirt on, my pants were ripped, and all the other cars around us started honking because their drivers knew the guy had been an asshole to everyone. Ultimately, the cops knew it too.

The lead officer came up to me and asked what the fuck was wrong with me. When I explained what had gone down, he said he didn't doubt me and told me to get out of there before he had to arrest me.

"I want more of that big *fat* fuck!" I told the cop.

Before he could say anything, my wife leaned out the window and said, "Gregg, what the fuck is wrong with you? Are you in high school?"

"Yeah, I'm in high school!" I hollered back.

I then started screaming for that asshole to come back. He never did, but a few of the cops came back and reminded me that my only options were to hit the road or go to jail. Naturally, I hit the road.

I got myself into crazy situations all the time. They followed me like a stray dog latching onto anything that shows affection. I hated it, but that was turning out to be my life no matter how hard I tried otherwise.

Even though I was making a lot of money, which I knew made me a target, and hanging with a very dangerous crowd, I wasn't as careful as I should have been. In the steroid business, you have to watch out for shady people, crooked dealers, and most importantly the police. They flock to guys with money when they sense it hasn't been obtained through a legit channel. But I felt like I was made of solid rock. What could touch me? And because of that I sometimes put myself in some situations I never should have been in. Luckily, I was able to save myself from some of my dumbest moves.

One time I had to do a mail-out of Sustanons. I tightly wrapped up a few hundred and placed them in a box. I took the box to the UPS store to courier them out. I didn't realize until I got there that you could hear the ampoules clanking around inside the box. The clerk asked me, very suspiciously, what was inside the box. I told him there was a bunch of stuff I was sending out to a friend. And he shook his head at me.

"Bro," he said with the typical New York accent, "there's something broken in here. It's like broken glass or something rolling around in there."

I shook my head. "No, there are some ornaments and things in there, but I just packed it up myself, and there's nothing broken."

"There's something else in this box," he said. "I have to open it to see if anything is broken."

Immediately, he took the box off the counter and set it on the floor, and then he took a box cutter out of his pocket. Naturally, if he thought something was broken, normal procedure was to check it out; they don't want customers shipping broken stuff and then claiming insurance on it.

As he reached to cut the box open, assuring me he'd tape it back up, I waved my hand at him. "Don't open that box," I said to him.

He gave me a slight grin. "Tell me what's in this box," he said.

"Bro', give me back the fucking box."

He wouldn't give me back the box and kept it behind the counter. "I'm going to open it," he said yet again.

"Fuck you," I said. "Give me the damn box right now."

"I can't do that."

Before he even finished his sentence, I hopped over the counter and yanked the box from the ground and jogged my way out of there. Had that box been opened and he'd seen hundreds of little glass ampoules, I can't even imagine how quickly things would have unraveled for me.

That experience taught me to start taping things up and together so they didn't roll around. That solved one problem. But even after that, after I started juicing myself, I didn't take the same care with my own body as I did with the products I was selling.

The Learning Channel did a documentary on me that has been very popular for a couple of years called *The Man Whose Arms Exploded*. It chronicled, among other things, a mishap I'd had with my arms, as if steroids had caused my arms to "explode," which wasn't the case at all. But when it came to steroids, I became lazy over time and did end up, on a separate occasion, with a very dangerous infection.

People ask me all the time, thousands of times a year, whether it's by postal mail, e-mail, or MySpace, at bodybuilding shows, or even on the street, "Are steroids really that dangerous?" They hear on television about how bad they are, the government freaks out about them being used in sports, all of that bullshit. And I tell them all the same thing: by and large, steroids in my opinion are not dangerous drugs for adult men. Stupidity is what is dangerous.

I was shooting so many grams of steroids over the days, weeks, and months that I started forgetting to do the most basic things. Most importantly, I started forgetting what not to do, like using a needle that had been dropped. For fuck's sake, I was dealing drugs, had thousands of syringes and needles in my house, yet I was dropping a needle and then brushing it off or wiping it with a wet tissue and then sticking it into my body. The surest way to get an infection is to do the stupid shit I did.

I have had a few abscesses over the years because of my lack of hygiene with injections. One occurred after I started spot-injecting Equipose directly into my biceps. For a while, my arm was hot to the touch, red, and swollen. I didn't think much of it and just started living off Tylenol and Advil.

At around 2 a.m. one night at my gym, I was feeling really run down, and instead of training with my friends who were there, who happened to be police officers, I lay on a bench face-down. Julissa started rubbing my back, and I was doing okay for a while. Suddenly, I felt something wet and warm on my right arm. I felt Julissa jump off me, and when I looked over brown and yellow pus was running out of my biceps. I sat up and squeezed this hole in my arm, and pus shot straight out, some of it even landing on Julissa even though she stood a couple of feet away.

She yelled and made a big to-do about my arm, and my friends joined her in trying to force me to go to the hospital. I refused at first; I usually drained my own injuries and took care of things myself. I started looking for an 18 g needle to stick in there and pull the rest of the pus out, but everyone insisted repeatedly that I just go to the doctor. Finally, I relented. Hindsight would later tell me I should have stayed at the gym.

When we reached the hospital, I was told that there would be no surgeon there for another four hours. I said to hell with that and started toward the door, but my cop friends held me inside. Eventually, I agreed that if I was going to stay the doctor who had checked me in would just have to cut it open and drain it himself. He said "absolutely not" at first, but once I insisted on leaving if he didn't, he relented. Big mistake for me.

The doctor cut open my arm and drained two glass containers' worth of blood and pus. What I would later realize is that he also cut my biceps muscle tissue instead of just cutting the infection out. The infection was very bad and very deep, but it wasn't necessary to take out as much as he did. He fucked up good, and my right arm has no peak (as compared to my left arm, which had the hematoma, as featured on The Learning Channel documentary and all over the Internet). It's flat after this hack job. Unfortunately, though, I brought it on myself and don't have anyone else to blame.

Chapter 11
TEARS OF MY LOVE

Winter came quickly during my time with Julissa. As usual in New York City, though, nothing stops just because the temperature drops below zero or the snow begins to fall.

In the midst of making loads of money and being caught up in puppy love, I knew that Julissa still hurt inside. I tried to fill the gaps in her life, but there was only so much I could do. She was so caring and so interested in the welfare of others that my reach was minimal. I took her from the streets and gave her a better life — at least financially and safety-wise — but she was a true street girl. She worried about her friends who were still hustling out there, every night not knowing where they were going to sleep. I think that was one of the reasons Julissa stayed with me no matter what: I provided a constant for her. I was there to ensure she had a warm bed and plenty of food, running water, and a place to come home to. No matter how apparent it was to me that she needed to leave me, something would always come up that, I feel, scared her so deeply she wouldn't even think of taking off.

One night, after we completed a deal in the city, we decided to stop by a Latin club on the West Side of Manhattan. A friend of hers, Venus, was there, and

Julissa hadn't caught up with her in a long time. They shared a bond; they had worked the streets together, kept an eye on one another, fought the battle of heroin addiction together, and even spent time in jail together.

When we walked into the club, Venus immediately noticed Julissa and came running up to her and jumped into her arms, hugging and kissing her. It was like watching two girls who had just got dates for the prom; they were giddy, jumping around and shrieking in that teenage manner. I could tell Venus was still on drugs and living the street life — she was about 5'4" and couldn't have weighed more than 90 lbs — but I still thought it was good for Julissa to reconnect with her old friend. It gave her something in her life that was good other than me, because I was still questioning how good I even was for her.

After we left the club, we stopped by a diner, where I bought Venus dinner. I would have bought that girl three hot meals a day if she would have let me because clearly she needed to eat. Her cheeks were gaunt, and her eyes looked sunken into her skull; her lifestyle and the drugs were clearly taking a toll on her. It was obvious to me too that, in a healthier condition, she would be an extremely beautiful woman. But *La Vida* ("The Life"), as Julissa used to say, had its way of making the very beautiful often very harsh.

Sitting at the table at the diner, I couldn't help but think I was looking at before and after photos. There sat Venus, pale and in need of love and food, and there sat Julissa, healthy and happy. It hadn't been that long since Julissa looked so fragile; it hadn't been that long since I held her crying, blood on her lips, having just been beaten by someone not worthy of being called a man. At this point in my life, I wasn't feeling good about a lot of things, but I did feel good about being able to help Julissa, at least physically, get healthy again.

After we finished eating, Julissa's sheer joy over being with her friend turned to sincere sorrow when it looked like we were going to leave her. My girl was happy, and I wanted to keep her that way as long as possible, so I offered to give Venus a ride home. At this point, we were in the city, and she was staying on Staten Island. With traffic and tolls, it was more than an hour-long drive, but to me that just meant hearing Julissa laugh and giggle with her friend longer. So off we went, heading to the projects of Staten Island.

Now, I knew Venus's brother was deeply involved with a Latin street gang and was very powerful. It's not an exaggeration to note that, if you mentioned his name, Hector, people would think twice about crossing you. He was known to be ruthless, especially to those who messed with people he cared about.

I had lived in New York all my life, I hung out with people every day who would kill me if they had the right opportunity or motive, but even I was uncomfortable heading down those streets once we got in the vicinity of her apartment. We slowly passed streets full of thugs and gangsters, drug dealers and murderers. It was below freezing outside, but for some reason these people were in hordes outside the buildings. And as we moved past, they all stared in my windows, and the first thing they noticed was a white guy driving.

Sure enough, when we parked and got out and started walking toward her building, the taunts and mocking began. I could hear and understand, in both English and Spanish, the callings about the "white boy." These weren't friendly streets for me no matter whom I was with. Knowing this, I took the pistol that I kept in my glove box and put it into my jacket pocket. The minute my foot hit the ground from the car, I kept my index finger wrapped tightly around the trigger. I had a bullet loaded in the chamber and wasn't going to hesitate if I had to pull the trigger.

"What the fuck, white boy?" I kept hearing. "What the fuck do you think you're doing here?"

Once people noticed I was with Venus, they started calling

out to her. "Venus, who the fuck said you could bring this white bitch to our hood? What the fuck is wrong with you?"

We hadn't been walking for more than two minutes before an ever-growing circle formed around us, all of them Latin thugs who clearly were not happy to see me. This was the type of neighborhood you read about every day in the newspapers: *Person Missing* or *Body Found* or *Woman Raped* went the headlines. And, from a life of hanging out with these types of criminals, I knew that rarely did the missing ever turn up. And when they did, they were always dead.

With this circle around us, we kept walking, and I remained as relaxed as humanly possible. I was scared as shit inside but acted tough on the outside. People are like animals; they will own you if you show them fear. You can turn and run and get pounced on from behind, or you can keep your chin up and your eyes narrow and look like you don't give a fuck and are ready to fight, and you might — just might — have a chance.

One tall, thick guy with dark, slicked-back hair stepped in front of me and started swearing at me. I tightened my grip on the handle of the pistol and pointed the barrel right at his stomach from inside my pocket. I mentally committed myself to firing that gun the second he lifted a hand to me. I told him he needed to mind his own business and that I was just taking Venus home and would be out in a minute. He kept mocking me, but fortunately for us both he stepped aside, and I quickly started moving again.

By now Venus and Julissa were yelling back at the mob of people, telling everyone to leave us alone. We made it into the building where she was staying, and I was ready to turn around and get right out of there as soon as we found her brother.

While we waited for the elevator, a new group of guys started in on us, and one grabbed Julissa. I was ready to end his life right there, but she showed her own strength and pushed the guy hard, sending him back into the wall. That got the crowd really riled up, and Venus started screaming she would call her brother down, knowing they wouldn't want that.

I stood at the elevator, waiting, feeling like the damn thing would never get to the ground floor. I kept adjusting my grip on the gun — my palms were sweating profusely at this point, causing the handle to get slick — and looking in every direction. I tried to keep an eye on every threat in the small corridor at once, but people moved around so quickly I couldn't even count the number of those taunting us, let alone quantify who were the biggest threats.

Behind me I heard a man yell in Spanish, and the crowd instantly broke up. I turned around, not sure what was happening, and saw someone with his arm around Venus. I found out right away that it was her brother, Hector. He pulled her into the elevator, and she told us to get out of there as quickly as we could. We didn't need any prompting; we headed straight for the door.

I pushed through a group of thugs with Julissa hanging onto my arm, and we reached the street, trying to make a beeline back to my car. Suddenly, seemingly out of nowhere, a group of six guys started walking up to us. In my right hand, I gripped the gun tighter, thinking, "Fuck it, here we go," and in the other I gripped her arm as tightly as I could to ensure no one could snatch her away from me.

But as quickly as the crowd had formed they scattered. Bright beams suddenly lit up the dark streets, and as I looked in each direction I turned right into a badge. A tall but skinny white cop was flashing his badge to me, and noticing I was white he told me to get my girl and get the hell out right that second. We started jogging to the car, and over my shoulder I heard screaming from residents as well as cops, saw people getting tackled, heard the familiar clicking of handcuffs over and over.

We made it out safely that night, but Julissa wanted to know what was going on. She made it a mission of hers to track down her friend Venus as soon as she could over the next couple of weeks and find out what had gone on that night. But schedules got busy, as they always do, people coming in and out of contact, and before she could get in touch again a phone call came that I'll never forget.

Julissa and I sat in her apartment watching television when the phone rang. We were on the couch, my arm resting comfortably over her shoulder. She leaned forward to grab the phone off the coffee table, and I just leaned back to rest my eyes. I never knew how long she would chat if it was one of her friends just calling to bullshit.

My eyes had been shut only a few seconds when I heard Julissa gasp. A few more seconds and her cheeks were soaked with tears. I could also hear the caller, a friend named Celeste who lived only a block from Venus, sobbing deeply.

Venus had been found dead in a hotel room in the Bronx. Her head had been found between the mattress and the box spring, the rest of her body beneath the bed. She had been prostituting and partying and wound up murdered by a trick she had been pulling.

She ended up buried in a state grave, just a number, with no funeral and no tears on the day she went into the ground. Her brother was locked up, and she had no parents. It was as if no one cared that another street girl had been lost.

Julissa sobbed in my arms for an hour after she hung up the phone. I just held her tightly, thanking God it wasn't her, praying it never would be, and thankful I had taken her out of that ruthless life.

Chapter 12
44TH AND 11TH

In the movies, a would-be execution always plays out the same way. The bad guy has a gun and puts it to someone's head. He screams for a while, rants and raves, and then he pulls back the hammer. The gun is usually a revolver in the movies because the director wants the suspense of that middle step between aiming and shooting. It can work with pistols too, it just doesn't look as good. In any case, real life isn't the theater.

I've nearly been murdered on more than one occasion. I'm an honest man, and if I had deserved it I would admit it. But I'm a good guy; I wasn't out mugging people or robbing their homes. My crimes were of a different sort. I always say you can't judge the character of a man by laws. One thing you have to remember is that nothing is universal. My selling steroids would have been legal in dozens of other countries. They're not addictive, they don't make you crazy; I never hurt anyone when dealing or using steroids. I wasn't out knocking off convenience stores to get my steroid fix. Dealing these drugs might have made me a criminal in the United States, but it didn't make me a bad person. Breaking a law doesn't necessarily make someone unethical; it isn't for the United States to judge who is ethically right or wrong.

But character won't save your life, unless you've also got something else: money. One time Paul and I ran into a problem when we changed our distribution channel, and it damn near cost us both everything.

After our time was up working with Reggie, we ended up in deeper with Remo, who was a very bad man and is currently doing time for murder. He knocked off a made man, a true member of the mafia. He himself is in very deep through family ties. These are the types of guys I dealt with, the ones who will whack you because they don't like you and just because they can.

Remo was at the top of our food chain. He got the gear, and we got it from him. And it was some of the best stuff out there at the time. European brands, Russian Sustanon, Omnadren, some sauce from Brazil — he was hooked up all over the place. Because he had so much product, and we could move it all, he started fronting us. Basically, it was a trust thing in that he would put up the cash for the product, he would get it to us, and once we sold it we would give him his share in full. By doing so, he was able to charge us a slightly higher price because he had to wait to get his funds. That's just how things worked, and we didn't mind.

During that summer, he handed off $35,000 worth of anabolic steroids to Paul. We weren't able to start moving things immediately, and Paul kept the gear stashed in his apartment. Unfortunately, he lived with a rather unscrupulous guy who ended up robbing him blind while he was away.

With no product to sell and no money to make up the loss, Paul and I knew we were in some hot water. At that time, though, we didn't realize exactly how dangerous Remo really was. We knew he was a little overboard on many things — like life — but we didn't deal with him outside business, so it was really hard to predict the kind of reception we would get when we broke the bad news.

Paul was the one who told Remo that the gear was gone.

Usually, if a guy is going to slit your throat because you lost his money, he's going to let you know straight up. Right away, just by his reaction, you'll know. Or at least you should know. Remo didn't seem too pissed off, though. He called a meeting instead. We figured the meeting was either to get us some more stuff to sell and make up the difference or to discuss how to pay back the money over time.

At 44th and 11th, there was a parking lot that always became empty after business hours. Remo asked to meet us there at 2 a.m., but that didn't scare us — it was the same plan we were used to. Act when the sun goes down.

As we rolled up and got out of the car, Remo was with another guy we knew, Piero Tempesti. Piero was a childhood friend of mine, also an Italian, who had taken a number of bad turns. He was an ex-NYPD officer who had ended up in the mob. At the time, he was also a very well-connected individual and not a man you'd want to meet in a back alley.

Remo got out of the car and still seemed to be calm. He gestured for Paul to get in the driver's seat and told me to get in the back. I sat in the back seat directly behind Paul, Piero was to my right, Remo sat in the front passenger seat. Right when the doors closed and we pulled out of the lot, the charade was over. Remo wasn't playing any games.

"You fucking morons!" he screamed. "How the fuck could you let someone steal my money?"

That's the way Remo saw his business. It wasn't steroids in this case. It wouldn't have been coke, heroin, ecstasy, speed, whatever. It was money. That's all the product was — just a solid or liquid form of cash waiting to be converted.

At first I figured we were going to be okay, that this guy just had to let off some steam. We had expected to profit from the sales of that gear too, so it seemed logical to me that he would realize we were both out. He didn't.

I think one of the reasons he reacted so harshly was that he and Paul never got along. You've got to understand some things about these guys before I go on here. See, Paul was a soldier. Not in the military sense but in the street sense. He had brains and the tools to make them work. He had thick musculature, and he knew how to use it. Simply put, the guy was an ass-kicker. Unless you had a gun, you didn't fuck with him.

The problem was that Remo did have a gun. The guy was a psycho thug with a gun, and that's not someone you mess with.

On several occasions, Remo and Paul got into some pretty heated arguments. They usually ended with Paul challenging Remo to a fistfight, an offer that was never accepted. The stipulation was hand-to-hand battle, and Remo knew he didn't have a chance, and that bruised his ego. A guy like that has an ego that you don't want to damage, but Paul wasn't going to be pushed around like a bitch.

It seemed like now all that hatred Remo had built up finally had an excuse to vent. And if the situation escalated beyond just yelling, I knew we could be in some serious trouble.

"That was my fucking money!" Remo yelled, as if we were some *momos* who didn't know that already. That's what he kept saying, "That was my money!"

I didn't know where we were going. All I knew was that Remo was pissed off, had a reason to be, and he was a crazy motherfucker. Piero and I were buddies from way back, and he would nudge me every time Remo became really loud, as if to say, "Don't say a fucking word, and maybe you'll make it out okay." One thing I didn't know was how Piero looked at business. If that was the line between friends, I wasn't sure. In any case, Remo was still the one with the gun.

So Paul kept driving, and Remo kept yelling. I knew it would soon reach fever pitch, and I knew from the next scream that the time had come.

"You guys are a fucking liability to me!" And with that, Remo put the pistol to Paul's head. At that point, everyone in the car knew that the trigger could be pulled any second. First I'd be down one friend, and if that happened it wouldn't take long to be down my life too.

Remo directed Paul to an empty lot down by the river. No one would be there, so I knew right away there was little hope of interference. The only people who hung out by this part of the river at this time of night were either whores or addicts who would just as soon rob a dead body as prevent a murder. As soon as the car was turned off, we were told to get out of it.

"Get behind the car, and get on your fucking knees," Remo yelled. He was yelling at the top of his lungs, but no one was there to hear it.

As I hit my knees and looked off into the pitch-black night, I felt the pistol shoved into my temple. It hit me so hard and fast I hesitated for a moment and thought I might have been shot.

Most people talk about cold steel when it comes to the barrel of a gun. Remo's gun had been pressed into Paul's temple for so long that it was warm when it touched me. As it did, I lost my ability to think, to stand, to speak. I felt my insides on fire with fear, and I can say I honestly thought there was no way we were going to make it out alive that night.

Paul tried to say something to Remo, but instead of a conversation he got the back end of the pistol smashed into the side of his head. Blood started gushing down his face, but he didn't stay down. He took the shot and got right back to his knees. As he did, though, that gun was right back against my head.

When we were in the car, I was more worried about my friend. I thought he was the one who was most at risk because of his past arguments with Remo. Then I realized what was going on, and I knew right then why I was going to be the one who died first.

It was obvious Remo figured he wasn't going to get his money. And if there's one thing these guys like more than killing a guy they think fucked them, it's making them suffer first. He didn't hate me more than Paul; it was the exact oppo-site, and that's why I was going to get whacked first. Remo wanted Paul to suffer through watching his friend get a hole in his head.

The depth of the whole situation was still sinking in. The irony too was close to killing me if the gun didn't. Less than ten years earlier my death would have been a tragedy. Now it would be written in the *Times* as just another thug getting knocked off from a deal gone wrong.

"You're a fucking liability!" Remo screamed again. He pushed the gun farther into my head, I could feel it pressing my skin back. The pressure was pushing me over, but I had to stay up straight because I was afraid if I made a quick move — falling to the ground — he'd pull the trigger. I accepted that I was about to die, but I didn't want to take a bullet that wasn't well placed. If I fell, he might put one in my shoulder, my chest, maybe my stomach. He'd probably let me bleed to death in agony. At least right then it seemed like he planned to put me down quickly. One in the head. Dead.

Spinning around quickly, Remo smashed Paul again in the mouth; I saw blood spew like it was a slow-motion movie. I wanted to tackle that motherfucker, but I had no idea where Piero stood. For all I knew, if I even put one foot flat on the ground, he'd pull out a piece and send me to my maker.

Remo turned back toward me and repeated that liability bullshit. It was almost like he was trying to convince himself that he couldn't let us live, but I knew better. This guy was going to off us whether we were a liability or not. Fact was, his money was gone, and even if he realized he could trust us to keep our mouths shut, unless he was getting that cash, it was lights out for us. As far as I could tell, he wanted to kill us so badly it would be worth the loss in money.

I looked over at Paul, and I saw his face completely covered in blood, and then I saw tears in his eyes — just as I had in mine

— that were now mixing with the blood on his cheeks. Then I seized up in fear again.

At first, I felt a gun being pressed back along the same place on my neck. Then he moved it slightly, and I knew it was all done with — no more fucking around. An inch left, just in front of the ear. He was lining me up. And he laughed.

I tensed up, my stomach felt like it was ripping itself apart, and I was on the edge of puking all over myself. I was praying inside, thinking of my son and my wife and my partner Paul. I wanted to see them all again in good health, I wanted to hold them. I had prided myself on being able to provide for and protect my family, and instead I was about to die from a bullet through my brain. With each person I thought of missing and being parted from, my anxiety grew. In hindsight, I was blessed my daughter hadn't been born yet, because if I had both of my babies running through my head my heart might have exploded.

Just then Piero told Remo he wanted to take a walk. I knew Remo just wanted to finish the job, I could feel his hatred, but he stepped away with him about ten yards from where I was. The two started talking, and I caught Piero's eye; he gave me a look that told me he was going to get us out of this mess. As they kept on, I could see Remo shaking his head no, but then I'd get another look from Piero to reassure me. I stayed motionless, afraid even to swallow; I watched as Piero got right in Remo's face and kept talking.

A few seconds after I turned my head away I heard the gravel crunch and knew they were walking back toward us. Sure enough, the gun went right back to my head.

"Fuck you, Piero. No way, fuck you!" Remo said.

Very calmly, Piero spoke up again. "Yes, Remo, you need to listen to what I just told you. I gave you a solution, now you need to let them go."

Whatever Piero had said pissed Remo off immensely, and

he yelled as he spit in my face and spun around, screaming, "Fuck you!"

Suddenly, the gun went off, and I felt my breath leave me. My blood pressure was so high my vision was blurry. Remo had shot Paul or maybe Piero for talking back — that's all I could think. That son of a bitch really was insane. At that point, I had nothing to lose, so I turned my head around.

Remo hadn't shot anyone. He was throwing a tantrum, ranting, screaming, swearing, and waving his arms all around. He had fired two shots right into the dirt. I still wondered if I would be next. I caught Piero's eye, and he was still completely calm, and that somehow told me it was going to be okay. He had taken care of us.

Remo walked over to Paul and smashed him again with the butt of the gun, screaming, "This is bullshit! This is fucking bullshit!" He then turned to me, pulled me up by the shirt, and I waited to get a beating of my own.

But it never came, and instead the deal hit the table. We were going to get "a break," he said. Piero had told Remo that, in exchange for our lives and letting us go, he would give him the $35,000. Remo was in a corner, he admitted, because if he killed us then he'd never see his money, and neither of our "useless lives" was worth that much.

But as things always seemed to, the proposition changed as soon as it had been made. Remo decided that he would still hold us liable for the money and charge us interest. So now, on top of what we already owed him, he demanded another $10,000. To make the money, Piero said he'd front us the drugs, and ultimately we could pay him back over time.

Finally, Remo put the gun away in his belt. "You've got two weeks."

Remo had just told us we had fourteen days to sell the same amount of steroids we'd sell in a slow two months. I didn't know how we were going to do it, but that bad news was the best news I had heard in a while. Before leaving, Remo spit in Paul's face and spit yet again in mine.

Remo and Piero drove off, leaving Paul and I to find our way back to our part of the city. No cab driver wanted to pick us up because my partner was so bloodied up. I carried him the best I could as we walked for more than an hour. I finally ended up offering a driver a $100 tip if he'd just let us in his car.

Money means more to people than someone's life, and finally the driver took us to Paul's apartment on 72nd in Manhattan. Sure enough, the thick-headed but gutsy partner of mine refused to go to a hospital. I took him into the shower at his place and washed him off with both of us still in our clothes. He had two huge gashes, one on his head and the other on his ear, and he clearly needed stitches but steadfastly refused to go to the hospital. To this day, he has a huge scar on his scalp.

We had fourteen days to put together $45,000, or we would end up in a ditch. We ended up doing it in just over a week, paying it all off and walking away free and clear. But we both knew that next time there would be no negotiations. Our game plan had to change, and it did so immediately.

Chapter 13
A LITTLE HELP FROM A FRIEND

Even though I've had more than my fair share of run-ins with people whom it wouldn't be wrong to call the scum of the earth, I've always had a few good friends who backed me up no matter what or no matter how much stupid shit I did.

On a cold night in New York, my partner Paul and I went to Show World, a famous spot for all things perverse in the city. It was the early 1990s, and a new generation was just finding its groove in the underworld. The kinds of debauchery that went on there would make the average person vomit and any truly straight-laced cats lose their fucking minds. It was the type of place that on one level you would have your relatively normal strip club, but on the next you could watch videos of things you'd never want to see, get one rubbed out for you by a transvestite, watch live sex shows, all kinds of things. The only thing you had to worry about was running into some old guy who had his dick out in the middle of the floor trying to get off. Luckily, you could at least smell disinfectant constantly hanging in the air.

At the time, Paul was seeing one of the girls there. Even though the majority of the girls at Show World were really ghetto trash, Paul had somehow managed to find one who seemed to have her shit at least halfway together. So on a whim one evening, we decided to go down and hang out at the stripper area.

When we got there, we found out his girl wasn't there, but we stuck around anyway. We watched as a couple of girls moved around on stage and took a few beers from some guys and stuck them inside themselves, touched each other, that sort of thing.

Off to the side of the room was a dark-skinned announcer who introduced a girl named April to the stage. We were sitting off toward the back on a ledge, trying to keep our distance from the action. Watching was fine, but we didn't want to get too close to the shit that was going down.

As April came out, she got right to business. She ripped her clothes off, danced around a bit, shook her panties off, then started playing with herself. After a few minutes of that — and men in the audience masturbating openly — she stepped into the crowd and started helping a guy jerk off.

The announcer then yelled out on the microphone, "Hey, get off the ledge, you two, and get out here!"

Paul and I looked at each other trying to figure out if she was talking to us. Just a few seconds later, sure as hell, she made sure we knew it.

"Yeah, you two fucking white boys," she called out as she pointed to us. "Fucking white boys, get down here."

Now, Paul isn't racist. He thinks everyone just needs to do the right thing, tolerate each other, and go on about their own lives. But he can't stand it when someone tries to drop his race into name calling. Paul and I just stayed seated, trying to remain calm, but the announcer came on again.

"I said," she called out louder, "the two fucking white boys in the back, get your fucking asses down here!"

Paul stood up right away and said, "Fuck you, nigger. Don't call me a fucking white boy!"

In an instant, the announcer dropped the microphone and started arguing with Paul. Right in the middle of it, this announcer took off her shoe and threw it at him. That was the catalyst for everyone to go crazy. Paul started in on her, she started in on him, and guys everywhere suddenly started throwing punches and getting wild.

From all corners of the floor, Show World security guys started flooding the area. Guys were drunk, not knowing what was going on, people saw these employees fighting, and it just grew and grew into a huge brawl. I ended up back toward the door where the cash box was, fighting guys who just came at me for no particular reason other than to fight.

I picked up the cash box and threw it at the wall, and it crashed open against all of the peep show booths. Like something out of a bad movie, all of a sudden several guys came rushing out of these booths with their pants down and their dicks hanging out, trying to figure out what was going on. All they heard was a loud crash — now there was money everywhere — and they went running.

I jumped over a turnstile back toward where the girls were still dancing naked and Paul was fighting. I saw a Coke can and watched Paul as he tried to get back out of there. While he was trying to pull himself away, this bitch pulled out a knife and took a slice at him. I threw this Coca-Cola can so hard at this woman that it literally knocked her backward and out onto the floor. Paul and I went back over the turnstile and tried to get out of there.

By now, the cops had shown up, and this bitch was back on her feet, and she was screaming and pointing at Paul. "That motherfucker threw something at me," she said. And it was clear she had been hit with more than a fucking soda, but by all means she had been nailed well with eight ounces of carbonated sugar water, courtesy of me.

The cops in New York, as can be expected, don't take a lot of shit. Right away they grabbed Paul and slapped cuffs on him. I heard what they were saying, and I jumped right into the fold and started telling them that it wasn't Paul who had thrown the can, it was me.

Paul — standing there with a black eye and bleeding — shook his head. He knew I was married and had a lot of things going on, and it would be very bad news for me to go down like that. Without hesitation, Paul spoke up. "Bullshit, he's trying to take the rap for me. I threw it. She cut me, and I threw the can at her."

I said again, "That's not what happened. Look, arrest me because I'm the one who threw it. I'm the one who hit that nasty bitch with the damn can, and, you know what, it still didn't shut her ugly ass up."

Paul told them, yet again, that he had done it, and he shot me a look that made it clear I was to leave it alone. He had my back so much he was willing to take this charge for me no matter what. Period.

At that point, the cops set him in the back seat of the patrol car parked out front. But after he reminded them that this bitch had cut him, they put cuffs on her too and put her in the same car. It didn't take long before they started going at it once more in the cops' rig, and they had to be separated into different vehicles.

Paul is a very good example of something positive happening to a guy who didn't deserve it. I thought I had done enough bad things in my life that no one would ever go out on a limb for me, but there he was, in the back of a police car, in cuffs, bleeding, just because he knew this situation would cause drama between my wife and me.

Many people don't look at friendship the way I do, and that's perfectly fine, but when you really sit back and look at it, it's the most important thing. I don't need a lot of friends; I don't want them. But what I want — and what Paul reminded me I have — are friends who are willing to do anything for me.

I didn't say those words to that announcer, and I didn't throw the first punch, but I had Paul's back. And in a much bigger way in the end, he had mine.

I can look back on that brawl and remind myself that, no matter how hard things got, no matter how bleak the situation was, no matter how many dark years I lived, all along I always had the most important thing: true, honest-to-God friendship.

Chapter 14
POLICE ASSAULT

One particular run-in with the police that startled me a great deal actually had nothing to do with me. Unfortunately, it occurred just hours after I picked up one of the biggest loads of drugs I've ever carried.

Julissa and I stopped by an apartment building that was, at the time, occupied by quite a few members of a very dangerous Latin street gang. I had my pistol in my pocket as usual, and she was carrying a pistol in her purse, "just in case." We had talked on the way over that if something went down the goal wasn't to try to get out alive — because we knew that wasn't an option — but to take out as many of them as possible.

Fortunately, nothing came of the meeting, and I picked up many thousands of dollars in steroids, placed them in the back of my Yukon, and left. My ride was high enough and the travel direct enough that I didn't think to pay special attention to make sure they were all covered up. The casual observer wouldn't know what the boxes were, and soon enough they'd be off-loaded at my gym. That was the plan, at least until Julissa got hungry.

As we drove through the city, I stopped at the corner of 47th Street and ran over to grab some things from a street vendor. When I got back, Julissa was standing outside the vehicle, and I handed over a shish kabob to her.

We stood there eating, and I noticed that down the block the cops had two people detained. There was a man in a tuxedo and a woman in a long white dress, both of them looking as if they had just come from a wedding. It was one of those passive but quaint "Oh, good for them, I don't give a fuck" moments.

I turned around and was bullshitting with Julissa while we both ate. I heard a ruckus coming from the area where the cops were and didn't pay any more attention to it than that. This type of shit happens in New York City all the time, it comes and it goes, and when it's none of your business you learn to stay out of it.

Suddenly, the commotion grew, someone screamed, and I heard gunshots. Julissa dropped her food and grabbed on to me. We looked over and saw the man in the tuxedo lying on the ground in a pool of blood.

The scene just exploded from there; cops seemed to come out of nowhere, a crowd grew around the body, and the woman in the white dress started screaming and crying. She kept screaming, "You killed him! You killed him!" and "Why would you shoot him?"

I didn't see the shooting, but people up and down the block had come out with what they claimed to have seen. I overheard a woman telling another what had just transpired. According to her, there were two cops arresting the dressed-up man and woman, and one directed them to place their hands on the wall. Both of them complied and didn't seem to be causing any trouble when all of a sudden the guy turned quickly as he started talking, and like in a bad movie the cop shot him in the back. He immediately dropped to the sidewalk, and blood began pouring from his back and pooling around him.

People all around were yelling at the cops now, screaming that the man hadn't done anything to provoke being shot. As other officers showed up, the one who had done the shooting was whisked away, and before I knew it the entire area had been blocked off as part of the crime scene. My Yukon was pinned in by cop cars, and Julissa and I were soon pulled away for questioning.

Cops were streaming up and down the street, and dozens passed the Yukon with the steroids just sitting open in the back. I eyed every cop with the same amount of caution I would eye a pissed-off gangster with a loaded gun.

When we were being questioned, I tried to keep my back to the crime scene so the cops would face that direction instead of my vehicle, but the cop doing the questioning kept peering back as if he knew something was going on. Looking the way I did, I was used to one of two reactions from cops: either they were extremely nice to me and wanted to be very buddy-buddy, or they were complete assholes who were dying to catch me with steroids so they could make names for themselves. The officer talking to us wasn't letting on what he thought of me. My guess, and hope, was that he was preoccupied with the idea that one of his brothers of the badge was going to go down, and shit would hit the fan at the department, but I wasn't certain.

When the cop would get on the radio or step away to talk to another cop for a minute, Julissa would pull me in close and talk to me. I could hear the terror in her voice. "I'm not going back to jail, Gregg," she said to me repeatedly.

I was scared when she said that because I knew she had that pistol in her bag, and I knew she was serious. I didn't worry about her going after the cop, I worried about her hurting herself. That terrified me more than anything. "Just relax," I told her. "We didn't see anything. They don't have any reason to search us. We were just passing through."

The cop came back and asked us a few more questions: why we were in the area, where we were coming from, where we were going. And then he asked what we had seen of the shooting. Julissa immediately shook her head. Then he looked at me.

I looked over at the scene, medics having already taken the

guy away, the girl still sitting there — in handcuffs no less — crying on the curb. "Is he going to live?" I asked the cop, ignoring his question.

He glared at me. "He should be fine."

I breathed a sigh of relief. There were enough witnesses to make sure a no-good rookie cop would learn the hard way. "I didn't see anything," I said.

Again, almost instinctively, the cop looked at my Yukon and surveyed it for a long moment. He took half a step toward it, Julissa gripped my arm tightly, and I saw her right hand moving about in her jacket.

Oh, God, no . . . , I thought.

And, by the luck of the draw, that cop stopped in mid-stride and looked back toward the blood on the sidewalk. Without a word, he walked away.

I learned to do little things more carefully at that point. To just cover things up, to pack things more tightly, not to make stops no matter how badly I — or anyone else — wanted to. Like anything else in life, it is the little things that make the difference, but in the end we all find out that, no matter how well we plan things, one little mistake can cost us everything.

Chapter 15
THE MOST IMPORTANT THING

Many people look at me and think I have to be completely self-absorbed; no one believes that a guy with big arms or who sells steroids could ever be a family man. But no matter what mistakes I've made or the bad things I've done, my family has always been my number one priority. I would die for my children, and I'd kill for them without hesitation.

Even as time passed and things with my wife were going further and further south, I still tried to take my son Paul out with me as much as possible. He was almost ten years old at that point, and I liked to take him to Yankees and Mets games, depending on who was playing in New York that week. My daughter, Gina, was still a baby, but Paul was a regular baseball aficionado. He loved going to the ballpark, and for a while we were at games two and three times a week. It was a time for me to connect with my son, and no matter how far removed I was at night when he was sleeping, during the day I felt whole and complete when I could be a real father to him.

One warm day during the 1999 season I took Paul to a Mets game. It was July 18, and they were playing the Dodgers. We had front-row, box seat tickets by the left field foul pole. This was near the peak of my size, and my arms were nearly thirty inches at this point. Clothes never fit me, so I was wearing a sleeveless shirt.

During the fifth inning, I heard a guy whistling at me, and my son noticed it was one of the guys in the Dodgers bullpen. I looked down in that direction and noticed that one of the relief pitchers was standing there posing a front double biceps and staring right at me. He kept flexing his arms at me and nodding in my direction, and I realized he wanted me to do the same, so I did. A few other guys in the bullpen had also been looking at me, and after I flexed an entire group formed down there. I flexed again, and suddenly they looked like an ant farm down there, everyone moving about jockeying for a better position to see me, pointing at me, nodding their heads. Soon enough the players in the Mets bullpen started hollering at me, and I realized the giant Jumbotron screen above the scoreboard was showing me and my son. In short order, it sounded like the entire crowd in Shea Stadium was chanting "flex, flex, flex!" So I stood up again and squeezed out another front double biceps pose and smiled as the crowd roared.

We were between innings by this point, and the Dodger players were running out to take their positions on the field. One of them had brought a ball with him and tossed it toward me and pointed to my son; the ball was for him. Just as it came toward me, a woman seated behind us reached out and grabbed the ball away from my boy. He was heartbroken. He knew that ball was for him and couldn't understand why someone would take it from him.

I went to the woman and offered her $50 for the ball, and she said no. Then I offered $75, and she still said no. I explained that it had clearly been tossed to my son in the first place, but she merely gave me a disgusted look and said, "It doesn't matter, I caught it." After offering her $100, to no avail, I finally told her I'd give her $150, or she could get lost. Obviously being a greedy bitch, she took it.

When I gave that ball to my son, his face lit up, his eyes grew wide, and his tiny hands grasped that baseball like it was all the money in the world wrapped up into a ball. That look was worth any amount of money to me, and I would have paid it too.

That wasn't the only time I ended up on the big screen at a baseball stadium. On another outing to the ballpark, this time watching the Yankees play at Yankee Stadium, I had box seats next to the Yankees dugout. It was a great day for baseball — as every day is — but it was one of those hot, muggy, miserable days in New York City. It was 100 degrees, and the sun was beating down harshly; everyone was sweating, and it felt like every minute just grew hotter.

After we had been sitting down for a few minutes, my son noticed the Yankee bleacher creatures section in the outfield and became very adamant about sitting there instead. That section was known for being rowdy, and, though it seemed to me that it might be a fun place to watch from, the important part was that was where my son Paul wanted to go.

I knew many of the cops at the stadium who arrested ticket scalpers, and they were very good to me and would give me their take for free. I held on to the box seats and went and picked up two bleacher tickets from one of my NYPD friends.

The moment our asses hit the bleachers in the outfield, the bleacher creatures started chanting "steroids, steroids, steroids!" At this point, I realized that with every chant more and more people in the stadium started looking at me, and, sure enough, the Jumbotron pointed down right at me.

Paul tugged at the hem of my shirt and looked up at me. "What are they saying, Dad?"

As he was asking me this question, the chant changed to "juice-head!"

I told Paul we needed to go sit in our real seats, and at first he was a little upset with me, but in time his passion for the game took over. That day David Cone pitched a perfect game, and we avoided any fights in the bleachers. Not a bad day.

Baseball did a lot for my family in those years when Paul was growing up. It was a time for us to connect and to take our minds off the drama at home and the divorce that would soon come. Home life was ugly at times, but the sport of baseball was also beautiful — always something to look forward to and escape with.

In the summer of 1999, I ended up being my son's hero. There was a local kid, Joey, and his father, Joe Sr., who used to practice baseball every day. Even in the winter time Joe Sr., in the hope of turning his son into a professional ballplayer one day, would clear out his living room to make room to do baseball drills. As the story goes, the nut-job had made a killing in the 1980s from Intel stock, so he had a lot of money, didn't need to work, and instead spent his time being an obsessive parent.

One day my son Paul and his friend from school, Chris, were out hitting balls on a local play field. I pitched to the kids as they hit, and they played the field for each other. That day Joe Sr. and Joey came and asked if they could play against the kids. I hadn't really felt like playing anyway, so it worked out.

At first, my son and his friend held their own, but over time Joe Sr. started throwing fastballs as if he were trying to be Nolan Ryan or something. He started taking things way too seriously and just became a complete jerk. He mocked my son and Chris, and it took everything I had not to step up to him. I didn't want to start a fight, but I didn't like what he was doing.

Finally, my son begged me to take an at-bat. He knew I was a good hitter, and he wanted me to show up Joey and his pinhead father. I finally gave in and used a small T-ball bat. Joe Sr. clearly wanted to strike me out, and his first pitch — a fastball right down the middle — was exactly what I wanted. I drilled it over the fence and into the tennis courts next door. My son and his friend were ecstatic, cheering and hooting as I ran the bases like Reggie Jackson.

My son looked at me with pride and tears in his eyes and gave me a huge hug. He then turned to Chris and said, "See, I told you, my dad is awesome!" This instantly became one of the greatest father-and-son moments I've ever had.

Chapter 16
SAMANTHA

As the summer was coming to a close, I was starting to feel pretty good about how things were going. My gym was running smoothly, Julissa and I were more in love than ever, I was spending quality time with my children Paul and Gina, and I was finally feeling like the hatred from their mother was simmering down. My life had its issues, to be sure, but for me they were falling into a nicely laid puzzle that I was able to manage. Most importantly, I felt like a real father. I was doing what God intended fathers to do, and it just amazed me at the warmth and love I felt when I looked at my two children. They were so precious to me, and I could not fathom anything that could happen to change that. To me it was simple: parents loved their children no matter what. That's how things worked.

It wouldn't be long, though, just weeks after I hit that home run for Paul that made him so happy, before I realized some people don't deserve to become parents. Julissa and I had just completed a big deal outside my gym and dropped a couple of duffel bags full of drugs off with some relatively put-together gangsters. They almost looked too normal to be in their line of business. Usually, guys in the game have murdered-out suvs or sports cars, but these guys were wearing tucked-in shirts and designer jeans and drove a family sedan. It certainly didn't bother me any; it wasn't often that I got to do a deal with guys who I didn't feel were ready to put a bullet in my chest.

With ten grand in my pockets and jacket, I went with Julissa to find her friend Samantha after we went to the East Village to grab a bite at the Around the Clock diner. It's a gritty diner where the food tastes best in the early hours when no one else will serve a hot plate and somehow it became a favorite for post-deal meals. Julissa couldn't stop talking while we were eating, and it took forever to finish our food.

Samantha was another one of her working-girl friends, and Julissa was excited because she was trying to help her get off the street. A friend of mine was a porno producer and was always looking for good-looking girls for his videos. It isn't glamorous work by most people's standards, but it beats prostitution, and the most important part to Samantha was that it was legal. Julissa had got his phone number last time we were with him and told him about her friend, and he was looking forward to meeting her.

When we left the diner, we made our way into Midtown and right away saw that the cops had the road blocked off between 8th Avenue and 42nd Street. That was right about where we needed to go, and when you live the lives we did, and had the friends we had, you always get a gut check when you see police strobes.

I parked my Yukon, and we slowly made our way along the street. It was a magnetic scene: we were attracted to it whether or not we wanted to be, but all along our minds were running through the worst possible scenarios. Was Samantha hurt? We saw an ambulance. Was another of Julissa's friends hurt? A few people were crying, everyone looked shocked and in disbelief. It was a very somber moment, and we didn't know who it was; we just knew someone was on the ground in the middle of the street.

When we got closer, we saw groups of people huddled together hugging and crying. They were consoling each other because, it was apparent, something awful had just happened. And when we reached the police tape, we realized that the situation was far worse than we had imagined. Julissa rushed her hand to cover her mouth, to stop herself either from screaming or from vomiting, I didn't know which, and I felt my breath leave my body.

Lying in a pool of her own blood, being attended to by medics, firefighters, and police, was Samantha. She had a wound across her neck that started at one ear and led to the next, deep and wide and full of her blood.

Julissa started screaming and ran toward the body, nearly making it before two police officers grabbed her and pushed her back. I took her arm and tried to drag her away; she resisted every step. My right hand gripped her right arm, and I was forcing her back toward the gathered crowds when she dug her nails into my hand to try to make me let go. Blood started to ooze out of my hand, and she looked at me, her eyes narrow and full of tears, and I shook my head. She realized then that I wasn't going to let her go.

We found a group of familiar faces — not friends, just familiar faces — and asked what had happened to Samantha. They told us that her boyfriend was unhappy that she was talking back to him in front of his friends, and, directly in front of those people, he slit her throat with a box knife. And so it was, another street kid lying dead on a city street, not a family member around to care.

Julissa cried in my arms and told me stories of how she and Samantha had been on the streets together, protected each other, cried with each other. We talked about how unfair it was for her parents to have thrown her out when Samantha was young, just like the trash, never for a moment giving a damn about their baby. And that was what hurt most, that these street kids were misguided souls who got swept away and buried as if they had never existed in the first place. But at one time they were all newborns, innocent, perfect. They didn't ask for this life. They became victims of circumstance and by-products of a life lived without love.

Through her tears, Julissa sobbed that Samantha was only twenty-six. "Only twenty-six," she cried. "Twenty-fucking-six years old, and she's gone, Gregg. She's gone! It's so unfair, it's so unfair, it's so unfair . . . it's bullshit. Where is God for those of us who need him most?"

I held her, a familiar scene, feeling sorry for her loss yet thanking God it wasn't my Julissa who had left this world. I didn't know that not long after that night I would, horrifically, lose my love at the same age. And in that sorrowful moment, I had no idea that I would be the cause of my own torture.

That night we just embraced and felt the cruel injustice of the world, that night caused by a worthless street thug with a temper. May he forever rot in hell.

Chapter 17
LOSING MY PILLAR OF STRENGTH

Not a full hour had passed into June 13, 1998, when I received a phone call from my father telling me I needed to rush down to the hospital. My mother had fainted, he said, and he quickly hung up. When this call came in, I was in the gym with Julissa and a priest, Father Mark Rosetti. Father Mark had just finished his workout and told me to drop Julissa off and then to meet him at the hospital.

I learned that earlier that night my mother asked my father to help her to the bathroom because she wasn't feeling well. I guess it was the drones of death upon her. My father walked into the bedroom, helped her out of bed, and started walking with her. They took three steps together when my mother just let out a loud gasp and fell backward into my father's arms. They both went to the floor with my father's arms still wrapped around her. Blood began to come out of her nose and mouth, and despite his best attempts my father couldn't get her back to her feet.

In the call to me, my father said only that my mother was unconscious. In actuality, she was already gone. She died there, in his arms. I believe that ultimately he was grateful to be holding her as she took her last breath, to make sure she didn't die alone in a hospital.

When I arrived at the waiting room, my father had been joined by my sister. I looked at them both, watching the concern in their eyes grow with every passing minute. Father Mark had gone back with the doctors to see my mother.

Moments later a doctor came out through the double doors that led to the interior of the hospital, accompanied by Father Mark. The priest walked straight to my father, placed his hands on my father's shoulders, and with genuine passion and regret said words to my father that I'll never forget. "I'm sorry, Mr. Valentino," he said softly. "She is gone. She has passed away."

Father Mark was a family friend, and over the years after my mother passed away he would be involved in many life-altering moments. I knew this was hard for him, for my father, for all of us. My mother was the pillar of our family, full of strength and love, and now we were told she was gone.

My parents had been married for forty years. From the day I was born, I had never seen my father cry, but he could not suppress his tears at that point. He is the strongest, best man I have ever known in my life, like all of the amazing comic-book heroes wrapped into one, but he had lost the love of his life, and his tears were well deserved. Even in his sorrow, he looked masculine and strong, but I knew what he was feeling inside.

The moment I found out that I had lost my mother, the world might as well have ended for me. I heard a loud ringing in my ears, and a hot flash surged through my body. I started walking toward the emergency room, and as I did so I told the doctor I was going to see her whether it was allowed or not. No one tried to stop me, and I quickly pushed through the doors. As I stepped through, a nurse, knowing where I was going, actually pointed me down the hallway to a bed that had curtains closed around it.

I pushed back the curtain and saw my mother. Grabbing her hand, I knew she hadn't been gone long; she was still warm. But the longer I held her the colder she became. I wrapped both of my hands around hers, and I pressed them against my face. I tried so hard to keep her warm, but as time passed I simply lost the battle. Her hands grew slightly colder. Then a little colder. Then colder.

I was crying loudly, yelping like a puppy. This was my mother; I would have done anything to have her around for even one more minute. This wasn't happening to me, I told myself. This had to be a dream. But when I begged her to talk to me, when my tears hit her cheeks and she didn't so much as flinch, my real nightmare began. I didn't know at that point that this was the beginning of a whirlwind downfall for me; I had no idea what was yet to come. I thought that moment was as bad as life could get; it was the worst pain I had ever felt several times over. It was physical, and it was mental, and it was extreme.

People talk about love and what it means, but the bond a son has with his mother is inexplicable. It often takes until we are grown that we realize how much our parents truly mean. I knew no matter what I did, no matter how bad things got, my mother would always be there for me. She was the one woman who wouldn't leave, the one woman who wouldn't push me out of her life. I could not screw up badly enough, could not say anything so horrific, that it would cause her to stop loving me. And now I was leaning over her lifeless body, crying like I had never cried before, because she was gone. I would never hear her sweet voice again, never feel her love in a hug, never again see her approval of me in her eyes.

Losing my mother was a major turning point in my life. After she passed away, I started closing people out. I didn't want to lose more people in my life, and I wanted to keep those who were close to me even closer to try to protect them. My mother was the strongest woman I've ever known, and I took what she taught me, her strength and character, but had no idea how to use it. She was so strong it was almost mythical. She had a lifetime of experience that made her so tough in so many ways.

My mother once had an operation that required her entire chest cavity to be cut open. From the minute she woke, she refused to take pain medication. The doctors warned her that refusing the medicine would leave her in unbelievable pain while the wounds healed and could do more harm in the future. They warned her that she would hurt so bad she might start vomiting uncontrollably and might even wish she were dead. Still, she steadfastly refused. And she never puked and never wavered from her decision. There was never a complaint from her, not one, throughout her recovery.

In this particular situation, my mother felt she was protecting herself, and those of us who loved her and relied on her, by taking the hard road. She had a rare blood disorder and feared that pain medication would prevent her blood from clotting, so she turned every medication down, one after the other. Whenever I whine about a headache or stomach pain, I think about how much she must have endured. Ultimately, the doctors praised her for her courage, and I wanted to prove to her that I was even half as brave as she was. But the courage I exhibited was in the heat of crime or danger, all the wrong things.

While the fighting I endured over the years leading up to my mother's passing was all strictly brought on myself as a result of decisions I made, my mother survived abuse at her childhood home and persevered. And she learned how to parent, what not to do, and tried to teach me the difference between right and wrong. Growing up, I learned that my mother accepted her suffering, and she became the most wonderful mother to me as a result.

When my mother was a kid, her stepfather used to beat her and her mother. She would constantly take beatings and watch as my grandmother got knocked out by this man. She grew up in the Bronx, and over time this abuse hardened her and made her tough. It led to a day when, after her stepfather had once more knocked out my grandmother, my mother ran into her room, grabbed a radio, and smashed it over his head. She then grabbed a butcher knife and stuck it under his chin, just into his skin, and made it clear that if he ever touched either of them again he would die. No matter what, my mother told him, even if it meant getting the worst beating of her life in the process, she said she would make sure she killed him. After that, her stepfather made an overnight move. Even though she was so young, my mother did whatever it took to protect her family.

She could have become cold and guarded as a result of this abuse, but she didn't. She met my father and was the most loving, caring, and genuine woman I've ever known.

I learned so much from my parents. In a time when everyone from children to the government are looking to blame mothers and fathers for the wrongs their kids commit, I take full responsibility for all of my actions. If I had lived my life from the start acting on even a quarter of the values that were presented to me, I might be president right now. My parents were good people: they were lovers, best friends, and soul mates from the start. From my mother, I learned courage and strength; from my father, I learned what it was to be a man, I learned what it meant to be a devoted husband and father, confidant and provider. From watching them together, I learned what true love really is and what it's like to lose the one who makes you complete.

I also learned from my father, too late for my own good, how to treat your soul mate. Even after she is gone. Every day since her passing, my father has visited my mother's resting place. Whether there's snow on the ground or sheets of rain falling from the skies, he will set up a chair and umbrella and talk to her or read her a book. To this day, he won't look at another woman because, when he gets to heaven and is reunited with my mother, he wants to be able to tell her everything he kept himself busy with while she waited for him. And he knows she's looking down on him every day.

The loss of my mother affected me in countless ways. I knew everything would change in my family, but it wouldn't be for the better. I was comforted at home by my wife, to whom I was a worthless asshole, and by Julissa in what I called my second life. Instead of getting things back in order with my wife and my children, I turned up the intensity on my cheating and lying. I became greedier than ever. I wanted more money, more sex, more muscle. I wanted to be so muscular that everyone in the world would know my name. And, most important to me, I wanted to be so strong that nothing could ever hurt me like this again.

God, I was an asshole.

Chapter 18
COMPLETE BETRAYAL

I grew up with a guy named Kurt. He has been there for so much in my life, including the day I met Julissa. He was the one hanging out in the booth with a girl he had picked up, making out while I went outside and rescued Julissa.

He and I grew up together, and in time he started working out at my Powerhouse Gym in Yorktown Heights. Parts of my gym I rented out, including a space for a tanning salon to a woman who later sold it to Kurt. For a year, I gave Kurt free rent because I wanted to give him time to get going with his new business, because he was my friend. What he inherited when he bought the place, though, was just amazing; it has marble floors and ornate decoration everywhere, top-of-the-line equipment, just an immaculate business. Even though I was asking only $900 a month for rent, and he would sometimes make $1,000 a day with customers tanning and buying products, I still gave him his space because I knew what it was like getting on your feet. I knew success was fleeting, and I wanted to give him time to build his name, his reputation, and his bank account for whatever life would throw at him later.

Over time, because he was a close friend, Kurt came with me on little drug deals here and there. He wasn't a great guy in general, though; he had been in and out of prison, and he bragged that he had even had a shootout once with the NYPD. To people whom Kurt didn't consider his friends, he was a pretty ruthless gangster. For the most part, he had always treated me like a brother, but when it came to his business, after the year was up, he still didn't want to pay me. Despite what he was making at the salon, he somehow conjured up that paying for that space in a building he didn't own was too much for me to ask. I told him, though, that the bottom line was he needed to pay me $900 a month. That was it. But he didn't like that and quickly started tripping out about the whole situation.

The thing is, I considered Kurt a close friend. And when I considered someone a friend, I considered him a member of my own mafia. When I called someone a friend, he was essentially "made" to me; I had his back through thick and thin and would give him the shirt off my back if he needed it. Because of this, Kurt knew where I kept everything — my money, the drugs — that had value. He knew at this time that I had just done a big deal, and he thought the money was at my house, so he actually sent guys to my home to try to find the cash.

Early one morning, at about 4 a.m., I got a call from my wife, who was hysterical. She said to me, "You have to get home, they're trying to break in the house." She was so afraid when she heard people trying to break in that she grabbed my son out of bed and took my daughter, who was still less than one year old, and huddled in the bedroom bathroom. They shook in fear and tried to sit quietly in the locked, dark bathroom, afraid that each breath would give away where they were. Then she took the kids and ran to the back of the building and this time hid in a closet, doing whatever she could in whispers to keep the kids quiet in case these thugs managed to get through the door.

I had no idea whether they would hurt my kids or my wife, but I ran out of the gym, got into my car, and went tearing down the street. When I reached the house, I jumped out and ran to the door and saw no one. I tried the door, and it was locked. I called out for my wife, and after she opened the door, and I saw that she and the kids were okay, I took out my gun and ran into the middle of the street. At the top of my lungs, I screamed, "If I catch you motherfuckers, I'll kill each and every one of you cocksuckers!" And I would have too. Without question, I would have been in jail for murder because I would have shot them without hesitation. God was looking out for me because, had I found them, it would have been a bloodbath.

Next thing I knew Julissa was on the phone telling me I had to get there right away. I jumped back into my car, and when I arrived at her place the door was literally off the hinges and lying on the floor. They had robbed her blind: her jewelry, more than $10,000 worth of drugs, all of the cash, everything of value at her place.

When I calmed Julissa down, got her door back in place, and helped her to clean up, I made my way back home as quickly as I could because I hadn't even told my wife where I was going. I knew she would have assumed I was driving through the streets shooting out my window at anything that moved and remotely resembled a man.

As soon as I stepped through the door, my heart sank, my stomach tied itself in a knot, and every part of my body carried a hot, tingling sensation. Physically my family was fine, but mentally a new level of distress was kicking in. I instantly realized these motherfuckers weren't just after my money or my drugs, they were trying to destroy my life. I stood there taking in fast, shallow breaths and shook my head.

My wife was sitting on the couch with a picture and cards and handwritten notes I had written to Julissa laid out on the coffee table. I later found out that they had been slipped under the door while I was at Julissa's, where they had been stolen from. I probably would have dwelled on the testicular fortitude that someone had to have done this, knowing I could have returned at any minute and shot him dead, but I was preoccupied with the realization that I had finally, officially, been busted. It wasn't that Veola hadn't known something was wrong before, but now this was proof. The picture wasn't sexual, but it was of Julissa and I together, and the notes and cards I had written to her over our time together added more nails to my coffin.

Now, at this point, I didn't know who was doing all this. I didn't know for certain who was betraying me like this, but I couldn't focus on that at the moment. I did what any guy would do and told my wife that Julissa and I were having a fling but that it was over. I told her that the notes were old, that it was all behind me, that I had made a mistake, that it was over. I never really believed that Veola accepted that as the truth, but it got us past the moment and through the night, which had already been full of anxiety and adrenaline.

Two days later two guys came into the gym for a free day, which we offered to let people try the place out, and they went into the locker room. I walked in there to take a piss, and by the time I came out they were gone. As soon as I noticed they were gone, I got a bad feeling; something was off. I ran straight to my own locker in the back, and sure as shit the lock was cut. Another $50,000 in steroids were gone. I ran out the front door of the gym and looked in every direction for them, but they were nowhere to be seen.

A week later I got a phone call late at night from the police and was told my gym had just been robbed. Shit was stacking up — everywhere I slept or worked had been targeted. At the gym, we had a big bay door in the back, and someone had backed up a truck and stolen equipment from me — treadmills, stair steppers, Hammer Strength equipment — and all the money and drugs I had left in that building. At this point, I knew it was Kurt because his salon opened right into the gym.

Anyone else would have had to break windows to do what had been done.

In the course of just over a week, I was out more than $100,000 in cash, drugs, and equipment. My house had been under attack with my wife and kids inside, Julissa's house had been ransacked and robbed, and now my gym had become a target. I didn't know what these guys would try next, and I felt my only option was to send Julissa down to Atlanta, Georgia, to stay with some friends for safety. I could be with my wife and kids, but I couldn't be in two places at once.

I started looking for Kurt as soon as Julissa left. I was on the lookout for him, and I was absolutely certain that when we met something would go down. It crushed me that someone I considered such a close friend would betray me like this, and I would absolutely not accept my family and loved ones being harassed. And I had partners in the gym, it wasn't just mine, so now they were also messing up the livelihood of other people just to get at me.

A friend of mine who lived upstate called and told me that a guy in his area was selling very specific drugs, including Parabolan. At the time, that particular drug — also known as Trenbolone — was very popular, in part due to Dan Duchaine writing about it in his *Underground Steroid Handbook*, but it was also extremely difficult to get. No one but me had it, and everyone knew that. The steroid world is funny like that; when you're in the game, you always know who can get what. All of my Parabolan had been stolen, and somehow these guys out of nowhere were selling it just upstate.

"A friend of mine owns a health food store," my friend told me. "And two gangsters came in and tried to sell him shit."

"Find out who those motherfuckers are," I directed him.

And very quickly I found out that the two who had gone into this health food store were Kurt's nephews, the same two I had seen in my gym that day who robbed my locker and ran. At that point, we called the police, not because they had stolen steroids, but because they had broken into Julissa's home as well as my gym.

Kurt not only violated my property and stole my belongings, but he fucked up my family life too. And that isn't to say what I was doing was justified, but when things went down — and I always knew at some point they would — it wasn't supposed to happen like that. I knew that Kurt and I would have it out at some point, and I knew that the cops were well aware of what was going on. So I kept Julissa down in Georgia with a friend of mine who was attending Life College. If there was going to be a gunfight, or if I was going to get arrested, she didn't need to be a party to that.

Ultimately, Kurt had a run-in with the cops before he had a run-in with me and ended up in jail. At the same time, even though Kurt and his nephews were screaming tattles on me and making sure everyone knew I was dealing drugs, the cops didn't come to take me down. They knew that steroids had been involved, and they knew that tens of thousands of dollars of them had been stolen. But the lead investigator decided that I had been a victim of crime, and the drug dealing was entirely a separate matter.

In time, I brought Julissa home, and life went on, albeit very differently. Even though the cops didn't come after me right then, I knew that anywhere I went now I'd likely have unfriendly eyes on me. And in the end, I'd find out there were more people on to me than I had imagined.

Life was becoming very uncomfortable for me.

Chapter 19
THE END OF ONE LIFE

Since her friend Samantha's death, Julissa had been very much on edge everywhere we went. She was tired of hurting, tired of finding her friends murdered or beaten or strung out on drugs. I had felt that life was just starting to turn out right, but then things slowly started to unravel.

As the days, weeks, and months clicked by, my nerves became more and more raw and exposed from what I kept seeing on the streets. I finally just started expecting things to get worse because, at least in that respect, I wouldn't be let down. But my life took a whole new twist when I found out my wife had been following my every move without even leaving our couch.

My wife decided she'd dealt with enough of my bullshit, of my deceit. She knew I was dealing drugs, and I figured she knew I was hanging out in the strip clubs, getting laid, and living wild. I knew she had a pretty good feeling that things weren't over with the girlfriend either. But I thought I was a master of lies, an ace at spewing bullshit, and I thought that would keep things calm. I was wrong in every sense.

I was in my gym with Julissa and a few other friends, well after business hours, when my wife came storming in with a wide grin on her face. I almost dropped dead when I saw her. She came right up to me and told me that she had been following my second life through a private investigator she had hired, and she slapped a stack of papers against my chest. I knew what they were: court papers. After sixteen years, two kids, and mountains of my bullshit, she wanted a divorce.

It hit me later that it had been going on right in front of me, literally, but I had been too dumb to realize it. I had seen a familiar face around at random times, and I had felt like he was following me. But I didn't know if he was a cop, a gangster, or what. A PI would have been my last guess until my wife used the words herself. I remember a guy following me after a fight Julissa and I had when I brought her flowers and candy. When she and I were fucking, I'd sometimes see weird flashes outside the window. At the time, I assumed it was a car driving by, but it wasn't. It was this investigator stalking me.

With my wife there in the gym telling me she wanted a divorce, as selfish as it sounds, I was devastated. I had always felt that she could never say goodbye, that we were meant to be no matter how much I fucked up. My heart sank as low as it could go, and it felt as if life was leaving my body. Being without her wasn't me, yet I couldn't bring myself to change my transgressions. I loved her, but it wasn't enough to change my ways. Yet I still felt robbed. I was the one doing the cheating and the lying, and I still felt like the victim. I wanted both of my lives, and I wanted things to stay the way they had been. I knew it wasn't fair, but I was greedy at that point in my life, and it was that greed that brought me down.

I thought that all I had to do was give my wife money and buy things for her and the kids and that doing so would make everything else I was doing okay. I thought that, if I provided a life they couldn't get elsewhere, it would buy me her love. It took me until she put the divorce in print to really understand that all along I had merely been slowing down the sinking of my own ship.

In the end, in hindsight, I got what I had coming to me. I was a very bad husband, and Veola deserved far better than me. She made the right decision for her, and she more than deserved to be happy. I couldn't change even if I wanted to, and even if she would take me back my demons had such a hold on me that I knew divorce was for the best. The damage had been done, and it was time for me to pay the piper.

My wife had come to me and said she wanted a divorce, and I knew I was the bad person, the one who had done the cheating and the bad things, so I agreed. I put up no fight. I told her she could have whatever she wanted, whether it was money, our possessions, the house, she could have it all. I asked only that she not try to prevent me from seeing my children. "No matter what happens you'll always be able to see your kids," she said. "We'll still raise these kids as a team, and I'll never give you trouble. Anyone who comes into my life will have to understand that you and I are still a team and doing this together." I liked what I heard, and essentially I gave her an open contract to decide as she saw fit.

The divorce changed me a lot. Because of it, I became a better father. I make sure that my kids are put first and that everything we do together is quality time spent. There's no just sitting around when I'm with my kids, watching television and just letting time pass. I make sure they get to do whatever it is they want to do, not what I want to do, and even if I have only one dollar left in my pocket it's theirs. I pay my child support, and I still buy my kids everything they want. It makes me sick to hear fathers tell their kids, "I give your mother money; she needs to buy you things you need." That doesn't happen with me.

Ultimately, my wife and I grew apart; we just weren't close anymore. She met someone new, which I found out through my son, who came to blame me for what was happening to his parents. She had her life, and I had mine. I kind of lost it after my mother died, and I was making so much money and getting so big that I just drifted into creating my own world where I couldn't get hurt. I had been living two lives, wanting the world to live by my rules, and the decision my wife made at that time put things into perspective and signaled the end of one of them.

If I hadn't been cheating on my wife, I doubt we would have got divorced, but though I regret many things I've done I can't change them. We can't change the past; what's important is how we move forward after we've made mistakes.

I knew I had made mistakes, and in the underground world I had made myself a resident of I was used to focusing on the future and not worrying much about the past. My wife was telling me to move out of our home and her life, and I followed her demands. And I put more time into my body, my work, and my Julissa.

Chapter 20
JULISSA PUNKS A PUNK

What I want people to understand is that Julissa was an entirely selfless person. She had the biggest heart of anyone I have ever met, and it all came from her past, a very dark, a very wretched, past.

Julissa was a bad drug addict, and often she was homeless. She told me stories of how she would walk miles in a blizzard with no jacket or sneakers, wrapped only in a quilt, if that's what it took to get her heroin fix. Sometimes she had no money for drugs and would beg for cash on a street corner or give the dealer a blowjob in exchange. And sometimes the dealer would just take her money and not give her anything except a beating. Julissa sometimes slept in old buildings and on newspapers; she had nothing steady. Her life was a nightmare. But all of this caused her to have a big heart.

At times Julissa and I were together, if we were eating in my car and we passed a homeless person, she would make me stop the car, and she would get out and give her food to whoever it was. Seeing homeless people or drug addicts on the streets is common in New York City, but she would give her food and money away. One time she even took her shoes off and gave them to a homeless girl. She loved the street people, the down-and-out addicts, the people who were like she used to be.

I asked Julissa once why she gave these people money, because I felt she was feeding their habits. I said they weren't going to use that money for food; they were going to use it to buy drugs. And she simply said that was fine with her because it would give them at least a moment, at least a few seconds, where they would forget about where they were or just fly away from their reality. She said there were many times when she wished she could have had someone show her a moment of kindness when she was down and out, and when it finally happened — when she and I met — it changed her life forever. But for all of her kindness, for everything she learned on the streets, Julissa walked away with not just compassion but also a complete street sense.

After partying at a club one night, Julissa and I cruised toward the Eastside of Manhattan. We stopped and ate at a diner as usual, but she was still craving one of her favorite things: Cuban sandwiches. Nightlife was my favorite pastime, so I had no problem staying out and heading toward Alphabet City and her favorite Cuban bodega. We planned to stop quickly and pick up a few snacks for her for the next day; she just loved these things.

As we sat at a stoplight in the Alphabet City section just a couple of blocks away from the bodega, in a very Spanish area of the city, Julissa jolted up from her seat and stared out the passenger window, one hand now on the back of her seat and the other outstretched to grip the dash. I looked over and immediately saw what caught her attention so quickly.

On the sidewalk was a heavyset Spanish man beating up a girl, clearly a hooker, and another girl who was probably also a hooker trying to pull him away. The man was yelling at the girl he was hitting, and both girls were yelling and screaming at the tops of their lungs.

I knew seeing this hit home with Julissa, and it struck me in my heart too. This was nearly the exact situation that I had met

Julissa in, and she always felt for her fellow girls on the street. I put the car in park before Julissa had even told me not to budge.

She rolled down the window of my Yukon and stuck her face outside and yelled at the guy in Spanish. He ignored her, and I watched and listened as he struck this poor girl on the side of the head so hard I could hear a cracking sound. Julissa repeated herself and added more of what I had no doubt were insults.

Finally, the guy let go of the girl and looked at Julissa and pointed. "Shut your fucking mouth, bitch!" he yelled. "Mind your own fucking business, bitch!"

Both of the girls, the one on the ground and the other standing, were yelling toward my car in both Spanish and English; the part I could understand was "Please help us."

I yanked on the door handle to step out, and as soon as I did Julissa grabbed my leg. She didn't say anything to me, keeping her gaze fixed on the asshole on the sidewalk, but she made it clear she didn't want me to move. She kept yelling at the guy, Spanish swear words rolling off her tongue fluidly.

The man took a step so that he stood at the edge of the sidewalk. "Listen, bitch," he yelled. "Mind your own fucking business before I beat you and your man's ass too."

The moment this bastard threatened my girl I was more livid than I had ever been. I wanted to get out and punch him in the mouth and make him eat his teeth, but Julissa just gripped my leg tighter to keep me in place. I complied, but the minute that prick made one threatening move I was ready to take care of business.

Julissa shot off at the mouth again in two languages now, telling the guy that he wasn't man enough to beat her ass, that she could fuck him up herself. Surely one thing Julissa did not lack was a smart mouth or a huge amount of courage. She was clearly getting under this guy's skin and enjoying it.

When he looked clearly fed up, he nodded toward me. "Hey,

my man," he said to me. "You better keep your whore's mouth in check, or I'm gonna do your job for you."

At this point, I knew what was going to go down because I saw Julissa's hand behind the door. I just smiled at the guy and said not a word.

"Yo *maricona*," Julissa hollered. "What the fuck did you just call me?"

The guy repeated himself, calling her a whore.

"Come say it to my face, Papi. I can't hear your coward ass from back there."

The guy came to stand in the street about three feet from my Yukon. "I called you a whore," he said, emphasizing the last word. "You're a cunt."

Julissa smiled. "A little closer," she said, her voice sounding as if she were trying to suppress a laugh. "If you're man enough."

The asshole took another giant step forward and stuck his face directly in my window, so close I could see the sweat on his fat forehead. "I said —"

Julissa cut him off in one quick motion as she lifted her hand and stuck the barrel of my silver .38 pistol right under his chin.

The man's eyes went wide, and I heard his gasp.

"I'm gonna blow your fucking head off. Are you ready to die, motherfucker?" she asked him. And then she laughed, and I joined her in that.

The man began to tell Julissa how crazy she was, and she told him she was just crazy enough to blow his brains out all over the street. "I'm a crazy *boriqua* bitch, motherfucker, and I hate cowards who beat on my sisters. It's filth like you who give Latin men a bad name, and now you're going to die, motherfucker!" I could tell he was pleading with her, but now they were talking in Spanish, and I couldn't understand a single word.

As they went at it, I watched as the two girls on the sidewalk finally made the smart decision to run away. Once the girls were out of view, Julissa, in one smooth motion, smashed the handle of the gun into the guy's nose, spewing his blood onto the black paint of my suv. The asshole fell to the street holding his nose, and Julissa spit on him before yelling, "Piece of shit woman beater!" Then she told me we could leave. As we did, she yelled at him some more in Spanish, and I knew at that moment she had killed one of her personal demons. She needed to do that, and I was very proud of her.

As we went about our way, she was in a great mood and as hungry as ever. She made me stop at another place, where I bought her two more Cubanos for the road. Not long after we stopped again at another Cuban bakery, where I bought Julissa her favorite desert, flan, for the ride home.

Chapter 21
A COUPLE OF CHARACTERS IN MY DRAMA

I used to deal a lot of drugs to a Polish guy named Dominik. For quite a while, I also gave him shout-outs in my column in *Muscular Development* magazine because he also did time, like me.

Dominik was my hook-up for European drugs. When I first met him, he was broke, in this country as an illegal immigrant, and driving a beat-down Vega that had one of the headlights duct-taped to stay on. He had absolutely nothing to his name and no hot prospects. After we started working together and I introduced him to some people, he ended up with a fleet of fancy cars and a house that cost him over $2 million.

I met Dominik at an eatery in New York City one time to pick up a few thousand ampoules. When he walked in, I could tell immediately that something was wrong. His face was usually drawn up into a smirk — he was a strong guy with a defined jawline — but this day he looked white and drawn as if he'd just seen a ghost. He sat down in the booth I was in, across the table from me, and explained to me what had just happened. The police had pulled him over and gone through his car, searching through everything he had.

The police, as he knew they would, found thousands of ampoules in his car. They were single doses of

Winstrol that were white. Dominik managed to convince the cops that the drugs were actually samples of hair products. I don't know if the cops actually believed him or not, but it seemed clear that they were looking for harder drugs — crack, heroin, methamphetamine — and even if they really knew what they were holding they didn't seem to care. Or so he thought.

It wasn't but five minutes after Dominik told me what had happened that the same cops who had pulled him over walked into the eatery. Dominik went corpse-stiff that instant, and I took a pen out of my pocket and started scribbling on a napkin. Julissa was with me, and I turned to her, slipped her the napkin under the table, and nodded toward the door.

On that napkin I had written the name of a club for her to meet me at and that, if I wasn't there in one hour, she should run home and start cleaning house because my absence meant I had been busted. The cops were staring at us, looking in our direction repeatedly, and something didn't seem right. My first thought was that they had let Dominik go because they had determined he wasn't the pick-up guy and was just bringing the drugs to a bigger player. That was the truth, of course, but I was praying the police hadn't actually figured that out.

After twenty tense minutes, we managed to get out of there without a word between us and the police, and we ended up laughing about it for a long time afterward. Today the vision of cops holding anabolic steroids in their hands and thinking they were shampoo samples is as hilarious as it was back then. Maybe we should have taken the irony of the cops coming into the same place to eat as a sign that things were getting a little too hot, but ultimately it was just another day for us.

Before Dominik ended up going down and eventually being shipped out of the country, he became a very rich and danger-ous person to deal with. One time I met with him he had just come back from whacking two guys down in Florida. The story goes they were waiting for him and for a while had their way with him. As I looked at Dominik, I could tell he had taken one hell of an ass kicking. He had bruises from baseball bats over his body, and he walked with a serious limp and hunched over. But, without telling me exactly how everything had gone down, he did assure me that the guys weren't around anymore. I let it be.

Another guy I hung out with often and did some work with was named Hector. Usually, I'd meet him in a particular parking lot to do our transactions. Across from this lot was a place called the Land and Sea Diner. One evening I was there waiting for him, and he was very late. When he finally showed up, he was agitated and restless and explained that he had just been pulled over by the NYPD. The cops ended up searching his vehicle and found the drugs he was supposed to be bringing to me. He was packing about $10,000 worth of Steris drugs. And they took them, every last vial, then told him to get the fuck out of there.

Here and there Hector would get into something we weren't comfortable with or knew wasn't a good idea, but no matter what we always had fun when Hector was around. One evening we had gone out to the Sound Factory and then to a strip club. We ended up picking up a bunch of the dancers and taking them back to my gym. After I dropped them off, I ran to get Julissa, who hadn't come out that night, and we headed back to the gym.

In general, it was like Animal House. We partied there, we trained late, sometimes we'd watch Yankees games, anything we wanted. It was like our own little playground. I had great times there, and some of my favorite memories stem from there.

Julissa, who always dressed very well, would hang out with her friend Trina Nunez, a professional bodybuilder. While Trina was training for a show and doing cardio on a treadmill, Julissa would get on the treadmill next to her and walk in high heels. And she'd smoke a cigarette while doing it.

On this particular night, as soon as I walked in, I could tell the party had already started. A couple of the girls were doing their thing on a bench press station, one of my friends was banging a girl on my dumbbell rack, a couple other girls were playing around in the stretching area, just a good time all around. But I couldn't find Hector.

I walked to the back and still couldn't find him, then checked the locker room, and there he was in the shower fucking three strippers. Julissa couldn't believe it. "Look at these filthy pigs," she told him. They didn't even pay attention to her and went on about their business.

Hector ended up coming out to hang with Julissa, me, and another friend of ours while the girls cleaned up in the locker room. At this point, the other guy we were with asked about some money from a deal we had done not long before. It was more than $100,000 in cash, and we had put it in a duffel bag.

"It's in a locker, I think," I said.

Hector's eyes lit up. "Wait, that's in the men's locker room."

All three of us ran into the changing area to see whether or not these girls knew that just a couple feet away from them sat six figures in cash. Needless to say, we all smiled widely when we walked in to find three very naked, very slutty girls and our bag of cash untouched.

That night we had all taken just a couple of cars to my gym, and Hector had ridden with me. When we finally took him back to his own car, his girlfriend was waiting for him, and when we parked she saw him kiss a couple of the strippers. Before he even got out of the car, she was standing there with a baseball bat, waiting for him, because she knew he had been cheating on her. The strippers ran, and Hector ended up having to deal with a very angry woman who carried a big aluminum bat.

Chapter 22
WHEN THE WORLD ENDS

When I returned in the fall of 2000 from the trip to Howe Caverns with my ex-wife and my children, Julissa was very upset. When I walked into her home, she was sitting at the table, surrounded by thousands and thousands of dollars she had been collecting for me while I was away, yet she was completely unhappy and in tears. She sat at the round oak dining room table with her arms folded over it and her head down. I could hear her crying.

Julissa was upset with me for leaving to go on the trip. She couldn't understand why I would leave her and take my ex-wife anywhere, and she just couldn't comprehend the parental aspect of what I was doing. I didn't expect her to because she didn't have children, but at the same time I was angry that she would come down on me the way she was. It was a guilt trip; her tears and her accusations that I didn't love her or that I was trying to get back with my ex-wife were ridiculous. I didn't know what to say to her, and I was offended she would even think those things. I had risked everything for her. I understood it was an awkward situation as my new living space was only a block away from my old place, where my ex-wife still remained, but I needed that. I saw my kids every day, I took care of them, I loved them, and

I needed to be near them. It wasn't about my ex-wife, that was over, but it was impossible to get that point across.

Julissa was unhappy, and when she was sad she liked to spend time with her friends. She asked me to take her into Manhattan to visit a friend of hers named Jade, who worked as a very high-class, highly paid prostitute. Movie stars, directors, agents, sports stars — this girl had been bought by all of them.

After I picked up Jade, we went to an S&M club in the city. Julissa looked as if she were coming down with a cold, and her voice had started to get very scratchy and light. Normally, she partied pretty hard, but this night she just didn't have the same enthusiasm. I offered to take her back home, but she was adamant we stay out, and we partied throughout the night. By the time we called it in, it was 10:30 a.m., and I had to get to a baseball game where my son was starting as pitcher.

At this point, Julissa was again upset with me because she wasn't the absolute first on my list every moment of the day. She was angry I wouldn't go back to Jade's place and catch some sleep with her. I argued with her a bit and ended up leaving her at Jade's with a promise that I'd be back when I could.

When I reached the game, I called her just to check in, and she ended up pursuing another argument, still upset about the vacation I had gone on. She was very hurt, and I understood that, but she wouldn't let it go no matter what I said to her or offered her.

I realized that much of what was transpiring had to do with her lack of sleep. She was getting sick, we had been out all night and nearly into the afternoon, and I just wanted her to get some rest before we tried working everything out. I told her to stay at Jade's, get some rest, and I would pick her up the next day. But, of course, that wasn't good enough, and she kept nagging me, on and on. Finally, I had had enough. "Fuck you!" I screamed into the phone, causing other parents around the field to stare at me, and I hung up.

Me at 19, 100% natural.

Two weeks after this photo was taken,
I started using steroids.

Another Gregg and MD Fan

What's up! I just wanted to say that your column in **MD** has kept me and my homies over here in Iraq laughing our asses off, even during scary scud and mortar attacks. To take our minds off being bombed or being killed we would sometimes wonder what would "Valentino" be saying during one of the skirmishes. This helped us forget about the immediate danger we were in and kept us all laughing. We all thank you and **Muscular Development** for keeping us sane over here in Iraq. By the way, I too have a Latin fetish and even married "The little jalepeño." We've got four beautiful half-Mick/half-Spanish rugrats together and we couldn't be more blessed. Keep up the honesty and keep it real.

Spc. Brian Fahey, Camp Anaconda, Iraq (Dec. 2005)

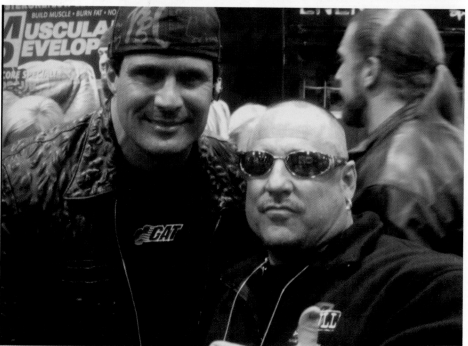

Jose and Gregg.

Gregg and Triple H.

Ice-T, Gregg, and Grandmaster Melle Mel.

The Governor and Gregg.

Fan For Life!

I have been reading your column for some time now, Gregg Valentino, and I always found it entertaining.

However, for the December 2006 issue, when you let the haters have it, I had to give you an ovation. I've seen the pictures of you in the magazines and wondered what kind of person you would be if I happened to meet you on the street and that article told me. You are a stand-up guy, a role model and an overall cool person. Fuck the haters and keep on steppin' with your head held high. Also, glad to see you and Lee Priest squashed your differences.

MA Hill, e-mail (Aug. 2007)

Daughter Gina.

The Ramblin' Freak Fan Club

I just wanted to say briefly that awhile ago, I was going through some very difficult times, not being able to go to college for my senior year and having to take
off due to financial issues, and not having the money to eat and especially being
away from my family; I was a mess, to say the least. I had to work cutting grass,
picking up garbage, washing cards, but I did it. I always cut out your writings
and carried them with me, and just when I felt depressed or broke and about to
give up, I would reread your old writings about your hardships and how you over-
came them and the funny bits. It always made me smile and I'd pick myself up
and carry on. I appreciate you reading this. By the grace of God, I'm now able to
head back to New York City and will continue my education in Staten Island.
I've been able to get some money for food and I've made it up to 240, relatively
lean. God bless you and your children; keep up the excellent work. I'm hoping
one day to be able to see you once I get back to NYC soon.

Akram (Nov. 2008)

Later I learned that what I said to her made Julissa so upset she started taking whatever pills she could find, looking for something — anything — to calm her down. She didn't know what she was looking for, and it was a recipe for disaster.

Julissa loved to go out and have a good time, but when I say party I don't mean drugs. She was recovered from that part of her life, and her way of partying was spending time out with good friends and enjoying the crowd. She was high on life, crazy cool, and as clean as the driven snow.

What Julissa was swallowing and putting into her small body was absolutely ravaging. She took Tylenol with codeine, Sudafed, and NyQuil for her cold. Because she was upset with me, she took Prozac and Valium. When she couldn't sleep, she took Percocet, Xanax, and Vicodin. She was so distraught because of me that she wasn't thinking clearly.

When Jade noticed that something was wrong with Julissa, that she was abnormally lethargic and groggy, she merely put her to bed and went out instead of calling me or staying with her friend to make sure she was all right. Of course, she also could have taken her straight to an emergency room. Instead, with my girlfriend lying in her bed with a dangerous cocktail of drugs in her blood, Jade left with her other friends to go have a good time out at the Sound Factory night club.

When Julissa woke up later and realized she was alone, she panicked. She knew something was wrong and tried to call me, but I was sleeping. I didn't answer the phone.

The next day I was running around the gym taking care of day-to-day business and finally noticed she had tried getting a hold of me. I was busy, though, thinking there was plenty of time to call her later. A couple of hours later my phone rang again, with her name on the caller ID, and I picked it up. I heard a man's voice.

"Who is this?" he asked me. "Who am I speaking to?"

I suddenly thought that Julissa was in some kind of trouble, that maybe something had gone down, that now she and her friends were in jail or that her purse had been stolen. Immediately, I was defensive. "You're the one calling me," I said. "Who the hell is this?"

He explained to me he was a detective and demanded to know who I was.

"Gregg Valentino," I told him. "I'm Julissa's boyfriend. What's going on? Put Julissa on the phone right now." I could hear police radios in the background.

"You need to come down to the police station right now, sir," he said.

"Why? What happened? Put Julissa on the motherfucking phone right now."

"There has been a drug overdose. You need to come down here right now."

I heard camera shutters snapping in the background. I was in complete shock. "Where is she now? Is she in the hospital?"

"You don't understand," the cop answered. "She's gone," he said coldly.

"Where did she go?" I asked in complete disbelief. "Where is she? Is she in jail?"

He sighed, sounding as if he were frustrated with me. "You don't understand," he said. "She's gone. She passed away."

My ears suddenly felt like they were burning, and my head took on a piercing pain. I felt my body tense up and a burning rush flow through me. I gripped my phone tightly, and I felt like I was going to vomit, right there, standing in the middle of my gym floor. Warm tears started flowing down my face, and my throat was so tightly constricted it took me long pauses between words to say anything to this detective. "Has anyone called her mother?" I finally managed to spit out.

"No," the officer said without sympathy. "No one has called anyone."

And I knew right then that I would have to make the hardest, worst phone call of my entire life. I told the cop I was on my way down because I needed to see Julissa's body, and I hung up. I then dialed her mother.

Maria, her mother, picked up the phone, and my emotions just took over. I couldn't speak and started bawling.

"Who is this?" I heard her say. "Who is calling my phone crying? Who is this?"

It was so hard for me to catch my breath. I needed to tell this mother, a woman who was practically *my* mother, that her baby was gone. Her precious child was no longer of this earth. It took me what felt like minutes to finally speak.

"Mama," I cried out. "It's me . . . Gregg."

I needed to say no more. Maria knew — a mother's instinct — that something was wrong, that something terrible and unfixable had happened.

"Oh, Gregg, no," she said. I could hear her voice leave her in three distinct gasps. "No, no, no!" I heard her scream, followed by the sound of the phone hitting the floor, then the dull thud of a body collapsing to the ground. I could hear her sobbing and pictured the sight of her weeping on the floor.

"Mama, who is it?" came the voice of Julissa's sister from the background. "What happened? Who is it?"

Linda, Maria's other daughter, picked up the phone and at first was very angry. "Who is this?" she demanded. "Why is my mother crying?"

"Linda, it's Gregg," I whispered softly. I couldn't draw the courage or the strength to put any audible volume behind my voice.

"Gregg . . . ," she said, leaving her sentence open.

I swallowed hard. "Yes, Linda," was all I had to say. She, too, knew what had happened without a single word more. In seconds, I heard her crying, and mixed with her mother's sobbing and my crying it was more than five minutes before anyone said anything.

"No! No! No!" Maria kept screaming. It was her worst fear, I knew. All of our nightmares, our greatest, deepest, darkest fear, was now reality. Her screaming, her sobbing, still haunt me at night.

As I listened to the sobs of Julissa's family, I wanted to end it all. I remembered at that moment that my last words to the woman I loved more than life itself were "fuck you." She deserved better than me, she should have left me, I should have left her for her own good. But she didn't, and I didn't, and every day of my life it haunts me that I swore at her and that those were the words she took to the grave with her. For that I can never forgive myself.

Maria and Linda agreed to meet me down at the precinct, and I headed that way, my head and heart full of sorrow and anguish.

I ended up meeting Linda at the morgue to identify the body, and we were warned that there were severe physical changes due to the way Julissa had died. She had very bad lividity; her whole head was huge and purple. Because of that, we were shown pictures first in case we decided not to go view the actual body.

As the morgue technician flipped through pictures of a body that was swollen everywhere, Linda gripped my arm tightly as if there were hope. The body we were viewing made it hard to determine any identity; the lips were thick, the skin was very pale, and the head was extremely swollen, nearly beyond recognition.

"That's not her," Linda said. "Gregg, that's not Julissa."

I wanted to believe her. I wanted to agree that it wasn't Julissa, that it was a mistake, that somewhere in New York Julissa was still out and about, maybe trying to reach me but having forgotten her cell phone. I imagined that maybe she was eating the Cuban sandwiches she loved so much or waiting for me at home. But I had to face reality.

"It's her," I said softly. "That's my Julissa." Even though badly bloated, I knew that it was my love on that cold table.

We agreed to go see the actual body, and Linda and I headed downstairs behind the technician, holding hands tightly. When we reached the lab area prior to where the bodies were kept, a nurse warned us that what we were going to see was not pretty. But she told us that, if we were sure we wanted to see her, she would give us time alone. We nodded, and she directed us toward the door as Linda took my arm.

As we pushed through the double doors, we saw one body wrapped tightly in pure white sheets, only the head exposed. It was worse than the pictures; more time had passed, and it was absolutely real now. I couldn't pretend the pictures were someone else, because her body was now right in front of me. I knew her hair, her eyes, her nose, her neck.

Linda and I stepped up to the body and started crying, kissing Julissa's cheeks. I kept kissing her but was broken down that now, for the first time, she wasn't kissing me back. My tears flowed down onto her cheeks, and I apologized. Time and time again I apologized to her. I was sorry for the life I had brought her into, I was sorry for the things I had said to her, for neglecting her, I was so sorry for having ruined her life.

"I love you," I said, looking at her face. I wanted her to say it back, that she loved me too. I wanted her to kiss me the way only she could, and I wanted to see her big brown eyes stare at me in that amazing, adoring fashion they always had before. I stood up straight and took Julissa's hand from under the sheet. I held it between my two hands as if somehow I had the power to warm it up.

Linda was in hysterics now, climbing up next to the body and screaming, sobbing, trying to wake Julissa up.

After Linda stepped back down, I leaned into Julissa's ear and whispered that I would always love her. "I will make sure you are never forgotten," I promised her.

I rested my head next to Julissa's and looked over at her cheeks. I was caught off guard because for a moment I thought she was crying. But it was my tear glistening off her face. It was poignant to me; as always, it took two of us to be complete. Here lay her dead body, and it took my tear to make her appear alive. She was my love, and she completed me, and as I said my final goodbye I knew I would never be complete again.

After my promise to Julissa, something clicked inside of me like a switch. I knew clearly at that moment that she was no longer there, that this body we grieved over was just a shell. My Julissa was full of life, always excited to see me and overflowing with love for me and her family. My Julissa would kiss me back, would hug her sister.

"She wouldn't want to see us like this," I said to Linda.

Suddenly, I felt a strength I hadn't known before. I felt as if Julissa's spirit was there telling me to stop the tears and know she was somewhere else. Somewhere better. My Julissa was very vain, she wouldn't want us to see her looking like this, and instead she would want us to remember how pretty she was. She was with us — very much so, as she always will be — but she wasn't in that body any longer, and we needed to go.

I took Linda's hand, and we both leaned in together and kissed Julissa's forehead. I knew it was time to go.

Linda tried to be strong, but she broke down and jumped onto the table with Julissa's body. But something told me to pull her off, take her away, and remember everything that so was wonderful and amazing about Julissa. I felt something telling me not to remember her like this. So I leaned in to Julissa's ear once more. "Rest in peace, my love," I said. And I bent down, picked Linda up, and carried her away.

I looked over my shoulder and watched as the morgue attendant put the sheet over Julissa's head, and I watched as he wheeled my Julissa away. Even to this day, I know that Linda cannot get the image of Julissa's dead body out of her head, and in some ways she regrets having seen her like that. For me, that voice I heard in my head might have been Julissa, but I rarely think about that day in the morgue. In my head, I see the woman whom I knew and loved, and the one on that gurney wasn't her. Not in that body.

For days I learned more and more about what had happened the night Julissa died. She had mixed many different medications, and I couldn't even imagine how scared she must have been when she woke up and realized no one was there to help her. I tried to wrap my mind around it, but it was so far beyond my comprehension I kept failing and failing and failing.

I learned that when her body was found she was trying to crawl out of the room, and that was the position she was discovered in: reaching out for help. In her other hand was the phone, with my number as the last one dialed. She took her last breath with the phone still in her hand, my name still on the screen. I was eventually told that the police dialed my number not merely because of the recent calls in her phone but also because of her tattoo. Julissa had a tattoo on her back with two hearts and my name that read *Two Hearts That Beat As One – Gregg and Julissa Forever.*

So many things about her passing inflict pain on me every day. Foremost are my last words to her. And following are all the things that could have changed the outcome. If I had been awake to answer her call, if I hadn't left her there in the first place, or if her careless excuse for a friend Jade had come home as promised . . . but instead she picked up a john and stayed out all night.

Julissa had gone to see her childhood friend Jade — who was once a street kid and still a prostitute — the day she died, and Jade wasn't even the one who found her body. Jade and a few other girls lived in an apartment and worked out of it. The owner of the whorehouse had sent a guy friend back to this place to pick something up, and when he got there he saw a girl he didn't know, naked and unconscious. He called the house owner and said none of the other girls was there, but a girl he wasn't familiar with was passed out and didn't look right. The owner simply brushed it off, said it was a girl named Julissa who was staying with Jade, said to throw cold water on her and wake her up. After doing so, this guy realized it was a dead body and called the police.

Julissa died in Jade's bedroom, and Jade never even went to the funeral. To this day, she has never called the family and not once paid her respects.

Not long before she passed away, Julissa spoke to me as if she knew something bad was coming, as if she had had a pre-monition that her time on earth was winding down.

About a month before Julissa died, her mother went to Costa Rica to visit her friends. While there, her mother played the big shot, the hot shot with all the money. But in actuality she didn't have the cash. She would call Julissa and Linda and ask them to send money down. Eventually, Linda had enough and called Julissa and asked her to quit sending money to their mother as well. Regardless, Julissa sent the money, and it made her sister very angry.

"Why would you keep sending her money?" I asked Julissa.

"Because I feel bad for her," Julissa told me. "I know how much my mother loves me, and I'm going to break her heart."

The first part of that claim was true. Her mother did love Julissa more than anything else in this world. So much so that she would even tell the other kids "Julissa is my heart." She made no bones about it. "Julissa is my favorite," she'd say in front of anyone.

"Why would you break your mother's heart?" I didn't understand.

"I'm going to die early," Julissa said matter-of-factly. "I'm going to die young, and it's going to kill my mother."

I couldn't comprehend what she was saying.

"If this is going to make my mother happy," Julissa said, "I'm going to do it."

"Bullshit," I told her. "You're going to live to be a hundred."

A couple of short weeks later she was gone.

I'm still lost without my love. The closest I get to her now is leaving flowers and a burning candle at the building where she died every September 10th, the anniversary of her passing, and at her burial site for her birthday and holidays. At one point, I even spray-painted a message to her on the sidewalk outside the apartment she died in. I wrote that I loved her and missed her and wanted her to rest in peace.

Chapter 23
RUNNING ON EMPTY

About the time that Julissa passed away, my picture was really starting to get picked up by magazines and put into different features. I had never looked for publicity or gone after photo shoots and things, but I latched on to whatever I could in those days. I felt lost. I didn't have what had been most important to me anymore; I didn't have my partner.

Because my girl was gone and my wife had left me and taken the kids with her, I really put myself into my body and my business. I started taking more steroids than ever before, and I started selling more than ever before. On account of taking them, I was blowing up. My arms were getting even bigger, and I loved to train more than ever. I was smart enough to clean up my act, too, and didn't have abscesses to worry about. But because of the dosages I was taking, I was holding so much water that, like a fat man, I had trouble breathing. It was a means to an end, though. My motto was "drop the reps, up the dosage." I even showed up to the Mr. Olympia contest one year and walked by the champion, Ronnie Coleman himself, who looked at me in amazement and swore. "Jesus Christ, look at the size of this guy!" he said. I loved it.

But on the front of selling drugs, I was having trouble.

I had lost my business partner and, perhaps equally as important, my translator. I was still working with many of the Latin street gangs, except now I couldn't talk to many of them. I was Clyde without Bonnie, and it put me in some very dangerous positions. I wasn't thinking clearly, because I missed her so much, and more and more I realized how many sticky situations she had kept me out of.

I knew quickly that I was very vulnerable in the drug-dealing game now. I ended up in Washington Heights in one instance when working with a Latin gang member who eventually became an NYPD cop. We used to joke about not knowing how he ended up an officer because he was completely whacked, a real nut-job fuck-up. Before he joined the force, though, he was a regular scam-and-eggs type of guy, always into something to try to make some money. He was so shady that Julissa never liked him and never wanted me to get involved with him. With her gone, I was stupid and started doing some transactions.

One of these deals led me to work with a gang member who tried to rob me. He knew I had money on me because I was supposed to be picking shit up from him. He was introduced to me in Washington Heights not far from the GW Bridge. I was sitting in my car when he walked up to me and stuck a gun right to my head and screamed, "Give me the fucking money, and I won't blow your brains out. Get stupid with me, and I'll blow your brains all over the inside of your car. Give me the fucking money!" I started shaking and thinking about ways out. I'd nearly have rather had him shoot me than be the little bitch who got robbed by a coward fuck who had to use a gun. That said, it didn't make having a loaded weapon next to my head any less scary.

As he was threatening me, a loud crotch-rocket sport bike cruised by with a high-pitched, noisy exhaust. When the guy turned around to look at the bike, I floored it and took off in my Yukon. I heard two shots fired from behind me, and I crouched down, but neither hit my vehicle. In my rearview mirror, I saw the guy and two friends get into a car and speed after me.

I floored it right up 181st Street to the entrance of the Parkway, but they seemed to stay right in line with me. Their car was more agile than mine. Finally, I turned onto the Cross Bronx Expressway and hightailed it like a madman until I reached Jerome Avenue in the Bronx. As I turned off, I thought I had lost them. I was breathing like an obese man, and my hands were shaking as I directed the wheel.

I was trying to go straight onto Fordham Avenue and was stuck behind a car also waiting at a red light. Moments later the car full of thugs pulled right up next to me, the gangsters screaming in Spanish. They stepped out and started kicking my vehicle, and two of them had baseball bats. I couldn't go forward because of the car there, and I couldn't turn to either side; on my right was their car, and because we were under the L tracks there was a giant steel beam on my left.

On either side of my Yukon now, they were trying to open the doors, pulling on the handles. I looked to my left and saw a heavyset Dominican with dark hair yanking on the door, swearing at me. I could tell by looking into his dark eyes that, if he got it open, I was dead.

"Julissa, grab my gun!" I yelled. "Julissa —"

I caught myself. I looked over and saw the empty seat rather than Julissa. That's how lost I was. In the middle of a gang trying to kill me, I kept thinking she was there to have my back. I reached over and popped the glove box and saw that my pistol wasn't there. Julissa had moved it a while back.

While I was still leaning toward the passenger seat, the window shattered, sending glass shards over my head and back. A hand reached in to try to find the door handle, and I grabbed the hand, wrestling with it to keep the guy from getting the door open. As I struggled with his arm, I saw that behind him was the guy with the gun coming toward me. He had an evil look in his eye, and I felt a warm rush to my head. I thought, if I delayed one more second, I would be dead for sure. Still holding on to the arm, I hit the gas and heard the guy scream, followed by a gunshot that didn't connect.

I turned into oncoming traffic and let go of the arm so I could sit up straight. When I looked in my rearview mirror, they were following me, also driving the wrong direction. I was screaming and yelling for Julissa, scared as hell, and weaving in and out of the steel beams, hoping they would lose control and hit one.

I was going crazy at this point, realizing that Julissa had been my strength through all of the crazy shit I had been doing. And now she was gone, and one of my first moves without her I was nearly getting myself killed.

No longer did I stop at lights, and I blew every stop sign I came to. I ended up on Deegan Parkway, traveling over 100 miles per hour, and in time I lost them. Afraid to go back to familiar streets, I just drove for an hour, not wanting to risk turning around too soon.

Late that night when I returned home, I took a flashlight out to look at my Yukon. The panels were deeply dented, the passenger window was smashed, with only glass remnants, and in the framing of the back window was a bullet hole. As I stared into the blackness, the cold night overcoming me, it finally hit me that I was truly, in every practical direction of my life, alone.

After that night, I made a determined effort to approach situations with more caution, often bringing along a partner, but even that wouldn't prevent having the life nearly stripped from my body yet again.

Chapter 24
LITTLE DEATH

My partner Mikey and I had gone into Brooklyn to the Brownsville area for a deal. It isn't the type of neighborhood you just happen upon; it's designated for low-income housing, and it's nicknamed "The Hill." The place has a hell of a history, and over the past couple of decades it hasn't been the place you want to get stuck in if you're a pair of white guys. But there we were, and we knew the history of the place so well that our stomachs started turning before we even drove into town.

Over forty years ago, the Pulitzer Prize winner Jimmy Breslin said that Brownsville was like "Berlin after the war; block after block of burned-out shells of houses, streets littered with decaying automobile hulks. The stores on the avenues are empty, and the streets are lined with deserted apartment houses or buildings that have empty apartments on every floor." That was 1968. Not much has changed since, only the faces.

The place breeds hatred and anger, and everywhere you look there's a tough guy. A lot of them are legitimate with their fists too. Former boxing champions such as Zab Judah, Riddick Bowe, Shannon Briggs, and even Mike Tyson were born in Brownsville. To top off its mystique, Brownsville was the home base for Murder, Inc., the infamous crime group that carried out countless murders on behalf of the mob. Because of the record of the area, Murder, Inc., was also known as the "Brownsville Boys."

Mikey and I had been called into town to meet a pair of guys at an old, worn-down, two-storey brownstone in the center of the city. Initially, we said no; we didn't know the guys, and we weren't comfortable heading into a part of Brooklyn we weren't familiar with. After we declined, though, the offer started growing.

First our contact said he'd buy an extra ten grand worth. Since we'd often jack up our sale price to double what we had bought the drugs for — and sometimes even more — that was a significant amount to put into our pockets. Still, money was already coming in strong on a regular basis, and a dead man can't make use of a single dollar. We said no again. Then our contact cut the bullshit and offered to buy an extra six figures in product, which more than doubled his order. That, we decided, we couldn't turn down.

We grabbed a pair of .45 caliber pistols, tucked them into our jackets, loaded the drugs into the car, and set off at midnight.

The guy who had called us was supposedly well connected to a Latin street gang we dealt with. When he got in touch with me, I had heard his name only once in passing. When I started looking into who this guy was, I was initially put off; someone described him to me as "a short, fat Mexican fuck with a big mouth who waddles." I had been robbed and threatened by many gangsters over the years, and all of them had at least looked the part of a bad-ass. I was put at ease at first by the description I had heard. I couldn't imagine this guy being a real player in the drug game, especially steroids. It occurred to me that he was probably trying to make a play and that because he was small — in more ways than one — he couldn't cut it in the street drugs the gangs normally dealt with.

A few hours before we packed up to leave, I made a small drop to one of my Latin connections, Manny, and learned a little more about the person I was heading into Brownsville to meet. Manny confirmed the first description but added a little clarity. This "short, fat Mexican fuck" was nicknamed Little Death. The subsequent descriptions I was given about the way this guy had supposedly disposed of people he didn't like nearly made me lose my breath.

I took this information back to Mikey, who made the simple suggestion that we just not go. We both knew right away, though, that this wasn't really a viable option. You can't change plans on guys like this because they fear you're working with the cops. They look at everything in a worst-case scenario. Even if I were to get deathly ill and bedridden, they would think I canceled because the SWAT team couldn't get into position to raid them. It was a no-win situation.

To make matters worse, Manny said that, as far as he knew, Little Death didn't know a damn thing about steroids. Manny had no clue why he'd be buying them, let alone so much, but did say at least that money wasn't an object for this guy. Sometimes, he told me, Little Death just liked to buy things merely to say he had them. Still, something about him not knowing steroids was very unsettling. Manny also said Little Death was the closest thing possible to a real-life Scarface when it came to cocaine. That was a huge red flag.

I've maintained since I first entered the steroid world that what sets apart the people who buy, sell, and use steroids is the fact that they aren't junkies. They aren't a detriment to society, and they shouldn't be treated as such. You don't have the problems with steroid users that you do with the type of people who buy, sell, and use drugs like crack, heroin, and cocaine. Until this point, I had made it a rule to try to avoid people who dabbled in both, let alone people who seemed to run a drug empire.

In any case, Mikey and I knew we were fucked and had to go

through with the trip. Almost everything I had heard about this guy told me we'd be better off taking our chances by canceling on him, but for better or worse we took the Manhattan Bridge out of the city, and I kept a white-knuckled grip on the steering wheel.

When we reached Brownsville, I pulled off the road a block before the address we were supposed to meet at. We watched the building and saw every light on inside. Just as I put my hand on the keys to turn off the car, the front door opened, and a Latin guy and a black girl came out, yelling back and forth with someone inside. The door finally closed, and I let the car idle as we kept watching, waiting for a clearing before heading in.

At the same time the two people we were watching went out of view, an older, big-bodied Cadillac pulled up behind us. The light was so bright in my rearview mirror that I couldn't see who was driving or how many people were even inside. Nearly a full minute passed, and, just like us, the car sat there. High beams on, motor running.

"Drive around the block," Mikey told me. "I don't like this."

I put the car in drive and slowly crept down the street, soon passing on the passenger side the house we were supposed to be going to.

"What the fuck is that?" Mikey said, looking past me to my left.

I had passed whatever he had seen. "What are you talking about?"

"Bro," he said as he turned to adjust his body so he could look behind us into the night. "I think there are a couple guys wearing fucking ski masks in that car."

A hot flush came over me. "Are you sure?"

"It was dark," Mikey said. "But I'm pretty sure."

"Fuck!" I yelled. "What do we do? If we leave and something goes down, we'll be dead by morning."

Mikey shook his head. "We got to get this done. Get in, get

out, and hope that if something goes down we'll be long gone."

I quickly sped around the corner and parked on the back side of the block. I reached into the back seat and pulled up a duffel bag and a backpack that were both bursting at their zippers.

"Ten minutes," I told Mikey.

Little Death never asked me if I was coming alone or with someone, and I never told him either way. With the unknowns of the situation — not just the actual motives of this guy but also some potential gangsters waiting outside — I thought it best for Mikey to come up behind me. If something went down, I'd need him to be able to get in and hopefully get me out instead of potentially being ambushed right along with me.

I threw the backpack over my shoulder as I got out of the car and gripped the handles of the duffel bag tightly. I hustled up the block and paused at the corner to look to my left and my right as well as across the street. I didn't see anyone sitting in any of the parked cars, and the Cadillac also seemed to have moved on.

The house I was heading into was set up high on its foundation. There were four brick-laid steps that led to the front door. I took a deep breath before I started to ascend them. When I reached the door, I placed my ear close to try to get an idea of what was going on inside. It was silent. Almost eerie.

I set the duffel bag down and reached into my jacket and grabbed the handle of my pistol. I slid my thumb up the grip and found the safety latch, pushing it up into place. Something had come over me, and I felt this was going to be the type of guy who would ask me to empty my pockets, and I didn't want to explain my gun. I quickly pulled it from my coat and pulled up my pant leg. I stuffed the barrel into my laced-up boot, allowing my baggy jeans to cover the handle.

When I stood back up, I knocked on the door. After a long wait, I heard a lock turning and the handle twisting. The first thing I saw was a green T-shirt; the next was a hand coming straight for me. I was caught so off guard that I had no reaction. Two hands gripped my jacket and pulled me in, throwing me to the ground. I felt my pistol jostle upward, and I was afraid it would fall out of my pant leg. I tried to push myself up but immediately felt a sharp pain between my shoulder blades as I was kicked back down.

"No, no, nigga," a deep, muffled voice said. "Don't fuckin' move." Then I felt something cold gently press against the back of my head. I knew it was a gun. "Keep your face to the floor, and you might keep it," I was warned.

Seconds later I heard the door click shut lightly. I felt my entire body shudder. My heart was racing, and I was breathing as if I had just run a marathon; I couldn't catch my breath. I could only take in short, fast gulps of air that couldn't satisfy what my body was craving.

Eventually, the voice told me to stand to my feet but to keep my head down and stare at the floor. I was pushed through an open doorframe and into a room where I saw new faces. Sure enough, just as Mikey thought he had seen, I could see from my peripheral vision a tall man standing in the back of the room with a ski mask over his face.

"Motherfucker," came a voice thick with a Spanish accent. "I thought this was you setting me up."

I lifted my head, and sitting in a chair with his hands tied behind him was the guy I knew had to be Little Death. His face was bruised, and he had a gash above his left eye that was causing blood to run down his face. Although I had never met him in person, my arms surely gave me away.

"That's good for you, though," he said. He was actually smiling at this point despite blood having run into his mouth and causing his teeth to turn red. "Because whoever did me like this is going to fucking pay, homie." I could see little red specks of blood fly as he spoke.

The guy who had me at gunpoint grabbed the back of my jacket at the collar and placed the end of his gun behind my right ear. "Lie on the floor and put your hands behind your head," he directed me.

Slowly, I lay down and looked toward the side wall, where the mantel of a built-in fireplace was covered with drugs. I saw scales, mirrors, gloves, and at least a dozen wrapped squares of white powder.

Shortly thereafter the man who had been standing by Little Death stepped behind me, out of sight, then came back into view with my backpack in hand. He unzipped the bag and looked inside. Although I couldn't see his face, I watched as he shook his head disapprovingly. He pulled a box out of the bag, and I heard a muffled "Testosterone, what the fuck," and he dropped it to the floor. He then turned the backpack upside down, and dozens and dozens of boxes and vials of steroids fell out and littered the floor, a couple bouncing to just inches in front of my nose. Once the bag was empty, he turned toward the fireplace and started filling the backpack with the bricks of powder.

"What do we do with this guy?" the one watching me asked the other.

"Don't matter" was the answer.

"We need to do him too?"

The backpack was quickly zipped up. "Think he'll talk?"

Before any answer could be given, I heard the front door crash open and heavy footsteps over the hardwood floors in the entry. "Nobody fucking moves!" I heard Mikey scream. I couldn't see anyone move but imagined the guy behind me tried to make a move, because Mikey yelled even louder this time, again directing, "Nobody fucking move! Put your gun down!"

I jumped to my feet and ran to stand next to Mikey. I reached down and pulled my pistol from my boot. Once I had it centered on the asshole who had put his own gun to my head,

I stepped forward and used my foot to pull his weapon away.

"Hey, homie," Little Death said. "Kill those motherfuckers and get me the fuck out of here."

Mikey shook his head. "I don't know you, bro'. This isn't our problem."

"Like hell it isn't, fool. He just tried to do your boy!"

I shook my head at Mikey and placed my pistol in my waistband. I stepped over to Little Death, behind his chair, and I untied the knot that was binding his wrists.

"Stay sitting down," I told him, then stepped back over to Mikey.

"Kill these fools!" Little Death yelled. "Do them both!"

"Shut the fuck up!" Mikey screamed. "This isn't our problem."

I looked over to Little Death. "You got any other guns in here?" He shook his head at me. "Good," I said. "Maybe no one will get shot tonight."

Mikey and I slowly made our way back toward the entryway. He kept his gun out, slowly aiming around the room to ensure that no one moved. I saw the duffel bag I had brought in with me sitting by the door, which was still open from Mikey's entrance.

"You want to just leave them?" Mikey asked me.

I nodded. "We don't need the drama. Let them figure it out," I said.

And with that we ran down the steps, around the corner, and toward our car. In the distance, we could hear the sounds of a brawl and figured that Little Death was catching the worst of it merely because it wasn't a fair fight. Mikey and I got into the car and sped out of Brownsville as fast as we could without drawing any undue attention to ourselves.

We were out several thousand dollars in drugs, but we were alive. Another close call averted and a clear lesson in the future to always go with our gut instincts. We stopped at a diner that night and ordered some food, but neither of us ate much. We just shook our heads occasionally in disappointment that we had put ourselves in such a predicament.

I never heard from Little Death again, but a few months afterward I ran into Manny over the normal course of business. When I told him about that night and asked him if Little Death had made it out alive, Manny looked at me like I was crazy.

"I never heard anything about that, man," he said. "He never mentioned it to me. But he's locked up now, man. He got caught up. He's gone for a long, long time."

I didn't tell Manny how good that made me feel, but my drive home that night was a more comfortable one than I'd had in as long as I could remember. I had wondered whether or not there was the proverbial blood on my hands; had I run out and let a man die at the hands of another? It had torn me up for a while, but knowing now that he was alive — still somewhere in the world and breathing — did me a lot of good. Better yet, he wasn't anywhere that he and I would ever happen to cross paths.

Chapter 25
JULISSA'S GHOST

For months, I had been told that the cops were on to me and that they were following every move I made. I was on an ego trip and didn't pay any attention. I had friends on the force, and I dealt steroids to everyone from cops to actors to athletes to big shots on Wall Street who was going to touch me? The way I figured it the police knew whom I was dealing with and probably assumed that sooner or later I'd get myself killed, and they would be done with me.

By March 2001, my gym was still running strong. One of my employees was an old friend of Julissa's named Nicole. She lived off 139th and Broadway and took the train to Westchester and then a cab to get to work in Yorktown Heights. When her shift was over, it was late and very dark, so rather than worry about her taking public transportation home I would drive her myself. From her area, I'd meet up with my friend Gary, and we'd go out to the clubs and enjoy the nightlife.

One night, very cold with not a cloud in the sky, I parked down the street from Nicole's place, and we sat and talked for almost an hour. Nicole had always been a very cool girl, and since she had known Julissa we liked to talk about memories. As we were talking, we watched as this thug made his way up Broadway and then down the block we were parked on. He had a bleached blond crewcut, wore a Walkman, and was drinking from a pink Nehi soda bottle. The way he stumbled around made it clear to me he was either drunk or fucked up on some drugs.

I watched as this guy passed us, and I went back to talking with Nicole, who had her back to the passenger door. A few minutes later, just like in a horror movie, I saw a face come up from out of nowhere and press against the window. Nicole saw my eyes, turned around, and screamed when she saw the same guy's face separated from her only by glass.

Her scream startled this guy, and he tried to pull himself quickly away but wound up smashing his elbow into my mirror. As he grabbed his elbow, he stumbled around the mirror and fell over into my front right quarter panel, then rolled onto the ground in front of my Yukon. He somehow made it back to his feet and started to stare at me.

All the while I was clutching the door handle, ready to get out and confront this guy, but something told me "No, stay in the car." It almost felt like I had hands pushing down on my shoulders. I wasn't one for bullshit, let alone people touching my ride. I was ready to get out and throw this punk the beating of his life, but something kept me seated.

The guy started laughing and lifted his chin like a real tough guy. Then he nodded at me, as if he was challenging me.

I tried to lift the door handle, but it felt as if my hands were stuck in place.

"What a punk," Nicole said to me. "He's lucky you don't kick his ass."

Again I tried to push the door open, but it might as well have been welded shut. I just couldn't do it. I was like a child trying to lift a Ford. Something was holding me back, and I just could not, no matter how badly I wanted to, get the door to open.

The guy laughed louder now, really playing it up so I could hear it. He was taunting me, pointing at me, and looking as if he was having a wonderful time. He smiled at me and displayed a full set of gold-capped teeth.

"What an asshole," Nicole said.

I took a deep breath and was determined to get out and rock this motherfucker. I squeezed the door handle once again and pulled it, stopping just a click short of causing it to fly open. Again I heard that voice, "No, stay in the car. Do not get out of this car."

"What the fuck!" I screamed. I smashed the steering wheel with both of my hands.

Nicole looked at me as if I was losing my mind, and I felt as if I really was.

The asshole in the street held both of his arms out, standing right in front of me, as if to show everyone he was there and ready to throw down. I tried to stay calm, but seconds later he blew me a kiss and then threw up his middle finger.

"I'm going to kill this son of a bitch," I said.

I turned my body so I was squared up with the door, put both of my hands on the door handle, and pulled. I heard it unlatch. All that was left was to push the door forward and step out, then beat the piss out of this cocky son of a bitch who had scared my friend, cracked my mirror, and scratched my car.

No.

Don't.

Stop.

Let him go. Do not get out of the car.

Do not get out of the car.

I kept hearing those words over and over in my head. Something was holding me back, and I could not, with all of my might, get my muscles to do what my mind was telling me. All I wanted was to push the door open, but my mind refused to pass along the message to my arms. Finally, I screamed, swearing again, hitting the steering wheel with my right hand balled into a fist, and leaned back into my chair, shaking my head.

The punk started laughing again and this time started walking off. I felt like a coward. I was also the macho guy, the first one to step up to anyone who pissed me off. But for some reason, I was relegated to being glued to my seat as I watched this guy walk off.

After three steps, though, he stopped. He whipped around and looked me dead in the eye, reached into his jacket, and pulled out a shining, nickel-plated, .45 caliber pistol. He pointed it directly at me. In a strong Spanish accent, he said to me, "I dare ya, before you get out of the car, I will shoot you in the fucking head. I dare ya, watch what happens when the door opens. You die right there, motherfucker."

I swallowed hard and sat very still, listening.

"If you take one step out, I will blow your fucking brains out before your feet touch the fucking ground. Then I will kill your bitch too."

Still I sat silent and immobile.

"Want to try me, white boy?"

I looked him right in the eye and just shook my head and nodded, as if to say, "Hey, you got me."

He laughed again, put the gun away, and once more walked off, but now with a cocky strut in his step.

Nicole sat in shock. "I can't believe you didn't get out right away," she said.

"I tried," I assured her. "I kept trying. I just . . . I don't know, I couldn't get the door open. I kept hearing voices telling me not to, and I just . . . couldn't."

Before I even finished speaking, her eyes lit up as if she had just figured out all of the world's problems. Things looked clear and distinct to her now. "It's Julissa, Gregg." Nicole smiled at me.

I shook my head. "What do you mean?"

"She stopped you. She knows that it isn't your time and that you and I both still have things to do in our lives. Julissa just saved us, Gregg."

At the time, I was reluctant to believe Nicole, but she was absolutely right. Julissa had been there for me when she was alive, watching my back, and she was still doing the same thing even after her death.

Under normal circumstances, I would have been out of that car as soon as that man's face touched my window. But I had been held back by something, and I now know it was, with certainty, my Julissa. Without a doubt, she had saved my life once again. And even though she couldn't save me from what would come in the near future, she later saved someone else who was, for a long time, very close to me. A good friend of mine and Julissa's, a young guy named Matti, was also saved by her death.

After Julissa died, he was devastated by her passing as much as everyone else. He was close with her, and she helped him out a lot with business dealings he was doing; she was also there to talk with him, whatever he needed. As great a lover and soul mate as Julissa was to me, she was just as great a friend to everyone else she cared about. And that was one of her most lovable traits; if you were her friend, you were her friend for life. Whether that meant giving you her last bite of food or taking a bullet for you, she would do it. If she trusted you, then you had the best friend you could ever have for life. And Matti knew this. So when she was gone, he cried as hard as all of her other friends who knew they had a true angel taken away from them.

A short time after Julissa passed away, Matti was away on vacation and in a nightclub. He was sitting at the bar and saw an extremely gorgeous woman. She was exactly his type; he used to joke to me about the type of woman he wanted — tall, fit, tanned skin, big breasts, and a great smile — and this girl had everything. It was like he had met his dream in the flesh, almost too good to be true.

And they hit it off. She was talkative, she was into him, they were flirting and just having a great time in general. After a bunch of drinks, he asked her what she was up to.

This girl looked at him and said, "There's a hotel next door. Let's go get a room and have some fun."

Like any man, Matti smiled and was suddenly attached to this girl at the hip. But as much as he wanted her, he looked off into the distance, and in an attached room he saw a very familiar face near the pool table. He squinted, having to jostle for position in the massively crowded club to see that far away. He saw Julissa. He swore it. She was standing there and frantically waving to him to come to where she was. He later told me that he would have bet his life at that moment it was her, even though he knew she was gone.

Now, when Julissa passed away, everyone was shocked. No one could believe it. I had seen her body, cold and lifeless, so there was no doubt to me. I couldn't even hold on to that bit of faith that everyone else had that told them she was just on vacation. For me, that was only a dream. In fact, I used to dream that she was out there somewhere, just hiding from me. Every time I woke up, though, I knew for sure she was gone. But some people wanted to believe she was still out there somewhere.

And so here Julissa was, to Matti, in this nightclub, waving to him, frantically trying to get his attention and get him to come to her. And in a completely uncharacteristic move for any man, but especially my friend Matti, he blew this girl off. She was talking, and he told me later it was like the whole place suddenly went quiet. The place was so crowded you could hardly move, but this gorgeous woman, to him, suddenly went silent.

Matti ignored her and got up from his seat at the bar, shoving his way through the crowd and toward the pool table. When he was just feet away from where he thought he had seen Julissa, he heard four gun shots ring out. *Bang-bang-bang-bang!* He whipped his head around and looked toward the seat he had just left moments before and saw the girl he had been talking to, and another guy who had taken his seat, lying on the floor in pools of blood. They had both been shot to death.

Just a few feet behind them a group of patrons had tackled the shooter, who turned out to be the girl's estranged husband. It was a "crime of passion," as they're known. The man had come into the bar looking for his wife, she had been talking to a man, and he had killed them both. Matti, had he not got up, would have been that second victim.

Once he realized what had happened, he turned back toward the pool table area, where people were running around frantically now, and he started to look for Julissa. He looked and looked and looked, and she was nowhere to be seen, but he swore she had just been there, beckoning him toward her. He fought against the crowd that was rushing toward the door and made his way to the back wall of the bar. He stood up on a stool and peered out over the crowd, searching in every direction for my Julissa.

And then it hit Matti. She had never been there in the flesh. It had been her ghost. The same ghost who had saved me had saved him. And this was after my arrest, after he had turned his back on me. He and I hadn't spoken a single word or seen each other in the interim. Later he and I would reconcile, and he would tell me it was that tragic night that led him to come and ask for my forgiveness. Because he knew Julissa had saved him, and he knew that she had forgiven him even though, wherever she was in the afterlife, she must have hated him deeply for turning his back on me. But now she was letting go of that hate, and she did so to save his life.

Chapter 26
THE END OF LIFE AS I KNEW IT

There were always risks attached to whatever I did. When it came to the drug dealing, I had felt for a couple of years that I was probably being watched by the local police or, worse, the DA Task Force. Then for a few months the rumors really started gaining traction, but still I didn't really pay them any mind. I was king of the mountain, on top of the world. Nothing could touch me. Nothing, of course, until the right people came along.

The night I went down I was in my gym. My friends had left for the night, and I was getting ready to go out and meet up with some other friends, maybe go to the clubs, whatever came up. As I was getting ready to leave, I heard loud banging on the front door of the gym. When I reached it, I had barely placed my hand on the handle when the door came crashing back into me.

A team of police officers pushed through the doors, extending guns at my head. "Freeze!" they yelled at me.

I didn't move.

"Get on the floor!" they screamed.

I listened.

"Get your hands behind your fucking back!"

I complied.

As these officers rushed around my gym, kicking over benches, knocking over stacks of weights, and ripping the doors off lockers, I felt the barrel of a pistol snuggled neatly into the back of my head.

People seem to think that there's a single, nice, procedural way to arrest someone. The general public, for some reason, seems to think that, if you don't give the police any reason to harm you, you'll be fine. If you listen, there won't be any problems. Unfortunately, that's bullshit. The police get extremely aggressive, and a few of them that night had choice words for me pertaining to what would happen if I resisted. None of them involved me walking out of that building.

During the mid-1990s, cops used to come to my gym; from street cops to state troopers, they'd show up and shoot juice in my gym. It wasn't uncommon to see four or five cop cars at one time in my parking lot. They'd come in, take off their gun belts, and train a little, and often they'd put some juice in their bodies. All in a day's work. In the back room of my gym, I had officers of the law, even in uniform, taking steroids right in front of me. These guys were my friends, and as far as I was concerned they should be on steroids. Police officers have to fight off some of the nastiest, meanest motherfuckers in the world, and often the criminals are on drugs that give them superhuman strength. There is no reason a cop shouldn't be able to use anabolic steroids, which are proven to be safe, to try to level the playing field a little.

Ultimately, the irony that I was getting busted by partners of the same people who bought the very steroids I was going down for wasn't lost on me. When the cops seemed to have satisfied themselves with wrecking my gym and collecting all the juice I had stored there, they hauled me off to jail. Once I was given my phone call, I immediately dialed a partner of mine with whom I had a standing deal. If one of us got caught, the other one would take care of it.

As soon as he picked up the phone, I told him that the worst had happened, that I was busted. I needed to get bailed out. I didn't expect any hesitation whatsoever on his part; we had made a lot of money together, we had been partners for a long time. But to my total surprise, he hung up on me. Later I found out he went around telling people I ratted on others to reduce my sentence, which was absolutely not true.

Getting betrayed like that stung very much. Making the pact to bail one another out had been his idea, which I had agreed to merely because I believed that, if it came down to it, he would take care of business. Instead, when shit hit the fan, he decided to cover his own ass. That he would try to add insult to injury and tell other people who knew us that I was a rat was just unforgivable.

Chapter 27
UNLIKELY CELEBRITY

Never in my life have I been comfortable with celebrity. Being recognized makes me nervous, and being asked for my autograph makes me embarrassed. For many years, I had been the fan, the kid who showed up to the bodybuilding shows and waited hours to meet his idols. Arnold Schwarzenegger, Sergio Oliva, Frank Zane, Boyer Coe, Reg Park — they were just a few of the world's top bodybuilders whom I looked up to. Even today I'm much the same way; I don't look at myself as worthy of having my picture taken, of putting my signature on people's property. But that said, if people want to honor me that way, I am very grateful, albeit with a deep degree of apprehension. I didn't build my arms to appeal to the media, so once they came knocking at my door it was a shock, and I still can't believe it all these years later. And the fact that so many people just want to take a picture with me, just want to meet me, still floors me.

Despite having my own monthly magazine column, having documentaries about me, having appeared in movies, I have never become any more comfortable with fame. The first time I was asked for my autograph I felt my chest tighten and my face get hot as if I were a kid caught with his hand in the proverbial cookie jar. In spite of that, when I first started appearing in magazines for having the world's largest arms, I developed a following, including at the gym I trained in.

While I was familiar with the regular crowd at the gym and talked to new people every day, there were certain people I remembered more than others. Some didn't like me, which never bothered me, and others seemed enamored with me. I was used to giving training tips out on a daily basis, but one particular guy always took it up a notch. Sometimes he wouldn't ask me for help, and I would just see him trying my versions of exercises. Often he would bring me a stack of pictures or muscle magazines and ask me to sign them. Far more than I wanted, he usually tried to get off the topic of training and really get to know me, which at times became very strange and awkward.

This kid was young, rail thin, with fire-red hair. He wasn't a natural athlete, but he worked hard, and I respected that. Too often a person comes to me talking big and bad but has the work ethic of a toddler. This kid was different, and for better or for worse he idolized me. If I started wearing a new line of clothing, he'd pick up a few pieces himself. If I started doing only a couple of specific exercises for arms, he would follow suit. We didn't train together, but he was practically my shadow. He was always talking me up, telling people about me, telling me how much he wanted to be like me, to be huge like me. When I walked into the gym, his eyes would light up like it was Christmas morning, and he even had a tendency to wait around the weight room just to say hello to me on his way out. It made me uneasy even though the kid was harmless.

Every magazine I was in, this kid bought it and brought it to the gym. Before long he had to have owned more than thirty magazines with my signature on them, only God knowing why he had me sign each one. One time he came to me and told me how I was his hero, and he wanted to buy a big photo of me to hang on his wall at home.

Throughout the long period of time this kid latched on to me, I was always very good to him. I never pushed him away, I never cut him off, and I always answered his questions the best I could. But it was becoming too much, and though I didn't show it outwardly inside I was far beyond frustrated. I was tired of the constant question-and-answer sessions, tired of him trying to be my friend but looking at me as if I was a god. It was awkward, and I was getting close to being pushed over the edge.

"Gregg, I want to be just like you," he would tell me time and time again. And each time I would tell him how I appreciated the sentiment, but he should make his own way, be his own man. I knew the other things I was doing — dealing drugs, hanging with the wrong crowds — and didn't want that for him. I knew the things I had seen — the junkies, the prostitutes, the blood — and they weren't things I hoped he'd ever see.

"But, Gregg," he'd reply, "you're my idol. I really do want to be just like you."

"Look, you don't want to be like me, kid," I would finally say when I was frustrated. I'd look him in the eye, hoping he would catch a glimpse of what I couldn't tell him and understand that I was not everything he thought I was. I wanted to tell him, and everyone who looked up to me, that my life wasn't all photo shoots and television and endorsement contracts. My life was dark: I was living two lives and countless lies. I was involved with dangerous and bad people, and I knew that very bad things were going on around me. But there was this damn kid, over and over again.

"Gregg, I want to be just like you."

Finally, when I felt I was reaching my boiling point — the end of my rope, you might say — he was gone. It was like the kid had just disappeared not just from the gym but off the face of the earth. I never went into the gym more than a couple of days without seeing this young guy and his unmistakable hair. But for whatever reason, I didn't see him even once again as the weeks passed. Not thinking much of it, I was actually relieved that he wasn't following me around and practically attached at my hip. I never thought he'd be gone for good, so I was enjoying a break from him.

And then, suddenly, my world crashed completely down on me, and I ended up being forced to take my own extended vacation from the gym and life as I knew it. I was arrested, my belongings were confiscated, my money was stolen, and I was on my way to jail. I went from being that guy everyone knew on TV and in the magazines to being just another nobody locked up behind bars.

It was night when I was locked up. I arrived at the jail, was strip-searched and booked, and gave up the very clothes on my back. I was sent through a line to pick up my bedding and followed a group of correctional officers to what would become my new home, being taunted as I walked, my head hung in shame. I had never thought of myself as a bad person, I hadn't done the things I considered so horrible. I had never killed anyone, I had never pimped a girl out for cash, I had never sold crack or heroin or any drug that could actually hurt someone. Never in my life have I drunk alcohol or let a parking ticket lapse, yet I was being booked next to people who had raped women and children, assaulted their wives, killed their enemies, and sold poison on school corners.

"Those muscles are useless now, aren't they?" a CO asked me, laughing as he led me through the jail. The lights were off in the cells, and I could hear the echo of this officer's boots hitting the concrete as if it were coming out of a loudspeaker.

Most of the other COs were good to me; they were kind and understanding. Some of them agreed that I shouldn't even be in jail for steroids; hell, some of them were probably using the exact gear I had been selling. They could have been clients for all I knew.

"Leave him alone," another officer would say.

The asshole co would just laugh again. "Mr. Muscles isn't shit in here," he kept saying. "He's just a little fucking bitch now. Ain't that right, Valentino? Ain't you just a little bitch now?"

As we walked through the facility, I could hear sheets being rustled around, and through the darkness I could see the heads of other inmates press against the bars to see who the new guy was. I tried not to pay attention, but with the lack of excitement in jail a new neighbor was news that it seemed no one could miss. Every few cells I could hear a whisper because someone had seen me in a magazine or recognized me from TV. I was embarrassed.

To get to my six-by-nine cell, we had to go up a flight of stairs to the second floor. We stepped off the landing and made our way down a long concrete aisle with cells on both sides. All the while this particular officer was getting his kicks from talking down to me, from belittling me. When we finally stopped walking, once we had reached the outside of my cell, I looked him straight in the eye.

"Fuck you," I said to him. "Look at you. You're talking all of this bullshit because you're jealous."

Before I even finished speaking, I saw a light go on inside a cell three down from mine and across the aisle. A few seconds later I heard a voice scream, sounding almost as if someone was hurting the guy in some sort of horrible manner. The cos and I looked over at the man, and instantly I recognized that face. It was the red-headed kid from the gym. He was grabbing the bars of his cell now and screaming at the top of his lungs, pulling and pushing on the bars and using his left foot to kick at them.

"*No!*" he screamed. "What are you doing? *Let him go!*"

A guard barked at the kid, but he just kept screaming. I heard him yell my name between his shouts and his swearing and his banging against the cell door.

"Why are you here?" he called out to me. "You can't be here!"

As an officer opened my cell door and grabbed me by the arm to pull me inside, I looked at this kid's face and felt a great deal of remorse. His cheeks were wet, and his eyes were welled up with tears.

"You can't be here!" he shouted again and again. "Gregg! Why are you here?"

As I was pushed inside, I could hear a guard take his nightstick and rail it against the kid's bars. He threatened the kid with punishment if he didn't quiet down and turn his light out, which after a few moments he finally did. I was quickly left alone, my light also turned off, and I sat there listening to this kid cry.

I felt angry. I was angry for so many reasons. I was mad at myself for getting into this situation, I was mad at the kid for getting himself here, I was mad at him for ever looking up to me, and I was mad that I had let him down. I didn't want to be his idol, I didn't want to be a celebrity, but for whatever reasons I was those things, and I felt it was my responsibility to live up to them. Yet I had failed. My heart was beating as if it were going to jump out of my chest, my mouth was going dry, and my head started to throb. No matter how sick I was beginning to feel, I couldn't calm my anger, which just kept growing and growing, all while I heard this kid slapping the concrete wall and crying.

Unable to contain myself any longer, I stood up and walked to the cell door. I stuck my face as far through the bars as I could, and I yelled at that sobbing kid across the way whose heart I had just broken. "Now do you want to be like me?" I yelled at him. "Huh? Now do you want to be like me? Look what happened. You wanted to be like me, and here we are, we're both in hell now!" I waited and then punched the cold steel door. I steadied myself, punched it again, and yelled. "Yo, you wanted to be like me, *just like me,* and look where it got you. Now you're really *just like me.*"

I drifted away from the door and sat on the cot I had for a bed. In the darkness, I could still make out the wrinkles in the orange jumpsuit I was wearing, and I could still see where the ankle shackles had left an imprint just above my feet.

As I sat there, slowly but methodically my chest started feeling tight. Soon after I felt like I couldn't breathe. Here I was, sitting now in my own private hell, and I didn't know what to do. I started hating everything I had believed in. I suddenly hated bodybuilding — it could keep the big arms and the muscle magazines — I didn't want any part of it anymore. I cursed myself for picking a sport that required that I use drugs to reach the top; if I had never found bodybuilding, I would never have been near any illegal drugs. I've never drunk alcohol, I've never smoked cigarettes, I don't even drink coffee. But bodybuilding had led me to steroids, and now because of hormones I was sitting in jail. *Fuck everyone,* I thought to myself. Fuck Arnold, fuck Lou, fuck all of it and every one of them.

I sat in misery. I didn't know what tomorrow would hold for me, but at that moment I thought back and remembered everything my love Julissa had told me before she passed away.

"Gregg, you never want to go there," she had said. And she had known all about it, she had been in prison nearly a dozen times. "There is no God in jail. Time stands still. It is hell, Gregg." And she had been absolutely right.

I suddenly felt so low that I considered what would happen if I made a run for it as soon as the door opened in the morning. I wondered if I jumped over the railing headfirst if I would die when I hit the ground; I wondered if I would be that lucky.

That night I found myself talking out loud, speaking softly to Julissa's ghost. I felt Julissa was standing right there in that cell with me. Not the dead body of the girl who had committed suicide just months earlier, but the girl I had loved. The smiling woman with the dark hair and athletic body who had loved me despite all of the wrong decisions I had made in my life. I felt as if she were standing there, shaking her head in disappointment, saying "I told you so."

Julissa had never approved of my lifestyle, the drug dealing, the gangsters I associated with. "You're going to lose everything one day," she had warned me. And she had been right. And I had taken her down with me, destroying her and everything else I had touched during that period of my life.

And there I sat in the darkness thinking about everything I had ever done, every decision I had ever made. I had this kid sitting across the aisle from me staring through his own cell bars at me. I had disappointed him beyond words, I knew. I had lost everything: my homes, my money, the Yukon I had just paid $42,000 in cash for — everything was gone.

I sat up all night, my head in my hands. I had nothing left. I had not one material possession left to my name. The only thing I had left was time. I had time to think about what I had done and how I had ended up in that place. Mostly, I thought about my children.

Chapter 28

ON THE INSIDE

As I sat in jail, even though in the grand scheme it was a short time, I had much time to ponder my life, the decisions I'd made, the wrong I've done. I had loved and lost and had done it all over again, and somewhere along the way I had done things so stupid that I was now behind bars. It became front-page news in the papers, it was the top story on the nightly news in my city, and later Jon Stewart made fun of me himself on his popular cable television show, *The Daily Show*.

In jail, I was amazed at how some people seemed to be too comfortable there, how others almost looked like they enjoyed being locked up. And just like among the population, some of the guards were cool, while others were assholes. Day by day, though, the experience weighed on me and made me feel like less and less of a man.

The most heartbreaking part of being in jail was hearing my kids cry when I got the chance to call them. My son would cry and tell me he wanted me to come home; when I told him that daddy had made some bad decisions and now couldn't come home even though he wanted to very much, he would cry harder. The worst part was listening to my then three-year-old daughter ask me if they, the police, had me tied to a chair. She wanted to know if that was why I couldn't come home. She was so young, but she knew something was wrong with her father. That was bittersweet for me; she knew that I loved her so much that nothing in the world that I could control would keep me from her, and that told her I wasn't doing well. And the separation nearly killed me. But I had done the crime, and now I was paying for it.

I wrote my son Paul a number of letters during the time I was locked up, many of which I sent, some of which I didn't. For me, it was a way to stay sane because I could feel like I was speaking with my son even if he wasn't there to give me an immediate answer. He was in my mind, he was in my heart; it was my way of talking to him, and it made me feel so much less lonely. My cell was solitary, and the walls constantly felt as if they were closing in, but in my heart I had my son with me always.

Many people assumed I was given the "Club Fed" treatment like a lot of high-profile businesspeople or athletes. And I wish I had been, but the truth is I was treated like any other newly labeled felon. While many guys get to lift weights, eat often, and even get their weekly juice shots as part of their plea agreements or "medical need," I had none of that. It was lockdown for me most of the day.

As anyone who has been in jail can tell you, time passes slowly there. There's nothing but you, your thoughts, and a whole lot of time. When I was locked up, times were bad. I felt down all the time, and I was severely depressed being away from my children. But, in hindsight, there were some times that people find very funny. Since I have somewhat developed a comedic following, I do like to share those stories.

From jail, the correction officers would transfer convicts to court in shackles. They would have six of us in a line, each with ankle cuffs, and we would be attached to each other by a long chain that went around each waist. They would load us into a small van, no bigger than a regular-sized work van, that had a wall down the middle. They would put six of us on one side and six of us on the other, cramming us in like tuna in a can. There would be twelve of us jail *momos* in a work-type van that wasn't meant for half the number. It was ridiculous; the average American would get ticketed to hell if he carried twelve friends around like that, but if you're the local law enforcement you're free to cram as many "bad people" into a sheet metal box as possible.

On one of the days in court, we were all given warm, putrid-smelling bologna sandwiches for lunch. The bologna was full of slimy white fat chunks, and it was pressed between two pieces of dry, crusty, whole-wheat bread. Ask anyone who has been to jail about the bologna sandwiches, and I swear he'll have traumatic flashbacks. In any case, I hate whole wheat; I've always considered myself a very healthy person, focused on living the bodybuilding lifestyle, but something inside me does not let me enjoy whole wheat. I never have, never will. So when you dry it out and add the fattiest chunks of bologna you can find, it's a recipe for disaster with me.

Now, after this lunch that I unwillingly swallowed to get the few meager grams of protein it might have had into my body, and the day in court, my gut wasn't feeling well. To be blunt, I had a bologna-sandwich-on-whole-wheat monster-shit tsunami waiting on tap. My stomach felt like it was ready to erupt like Mount Saint Helens, and I was getting seriously dizzy trying to hold things back. Not ironically, several of the other inmates were complaining of the same gastrointestinal distress that I had. But some of them, unlike me, were able to hold it in check. I knew things were going to get messy very quickly if something didn't go down the pipe.

In the average home, going to the bathroom isn't a problem. Walk into the facility, do your business, flush, clean up, get the fuck out. Unfortunately, in this jail cell we were all in, there was only one toilet. With no walls. It was right in the middle of the cell, out in the open for all to see. And the worst part was that there was no toilet paper. It was a metal throne and nothing more.

I couldn't hold it. I was suffering. I was sweating, my body was cramping, I was hunched over from the pain in my stomach. Bottom line was it had to go down whether there was toilet paper or not. Mother nature was calling desperately, and I had to answer that call.

I told my fellow pinhead convicts, "Guys, it's going down, or that van is going to be a real nightmare on the way back home."

In unison my jailhouse brothers said, "Oh, hell no, fuck that."

So, like gentlemen, my fellow inmates turned their heads as I sat on the stainless steel convenience and went to work. Life felt better for me instantly, but I still had the problem of no toilet paper. So, doing what I had to do, I asked a cellmate for a bologna sandwich that had been thrown on the floor by a less-than-hungry resident. Once I had it in hand, I proudly took the bologna off and used both slices of that wheat bread for what it was really worth and probably originally meant for. That, my friends, I call survival.

When I finally got hauled down to the courtroom itself, I was ridiculed all the way by people who had never seen me before. Even inside, everyone in the courtroom gasped when they saw me walk in. It was like suddenly something interesting was happening. Minutes before I had been just another criminal locked up and surrounded by other convicts, and now I was the center of attention in a previously sleepy courtroom.

Inside the courtroom, I had it better than I knew at the time. I was blessed with a judge who took into account two very important facts: I had no prior criminal record, and the drugs I sold were not addictive, nor did they do horrific things to the bodies or minds of people who bought them. I don't know how many judges pay attention to the facts, but I was given to one who did, and he was very fair to me.

I remember standing there, feeling so small and insignificant, feeling like a complete failure. I looked over my shoulder and saw my father sitting there with perfect posture and a stone-cold look on his face. He was wearing sunglasses. I knew that inside he was crying, and I knew I had broken his heart. But, always the strong one, he covered his eyes because he didn't want to look weak.

My father has never drunk alcohol or smoked a cigarette. I always wanted to be just like him, as strong and honorable as he has been since the day he was born. Because of that, I've never taken a single sip of beer or hard liquor, and I've never once tried tobacco or marijuana or any other recreational drug. All because of the man who was sitting there, drastically disappointed in his son. I just hoped he knew that I was standing there not because of anything he had done but because I had fucked up. Because I had made wrong choices. I hoped he knew that, when I had made these choices, I knew they were wrong, and I knew they were wrong because of what he and my mother had taught me. I couldn't have asked for better parents, and it was tearing me up that one of them had to watch his son stand as a criminal.

The judge ultimately ruled in favor of essentially giving me a second chance. I was given five years of probation and no additional jail time or prison sentence on top of what I had already served. But he gave me a stern warning that if I made one more wrong decision he would gladly send me upstate for many years.

I'm grateful to that judge, and I'm grateful to my father. He put up his house to bail me out, and no matter how ashamed he was he was always there every step of the way.

Overall, jail changed my view of the entire judicial system and not only because I was there. I really don't think any logical person, when he or she looks at the facts, can honestly believe that a steroid user should be put in jail. When I was in jail, I sat in a cell sandwiched between real scumbags. To my left was a Crip who would serve many years because he had murdered some members of the rival Blood gang. To my right was a man who had slit his own wife's throat; in cold blood, with murderous intent, he had held down a woman he had promised to love and protect as long as he lived and ended her life with a single swipe of a blade. And there between them was me, a guy who had never hurt anyone in his quest for bigger arms. The guys to either side of me were headline news because of their vicious crimes, and my "crimes" got me on the covers and in the pages of countless bodybuilding magazines.

Chapter 29
EUGENE BARBAGALLO

One of the most bad-ass guys I've ever met was a guy I grew up with named Eugene Barbagallo. He was an absolutely crazy motherfucker who was in and out of prison like clockwork. Inside he was a very caring guy, but when it came to the law he just couldn't stay on the right side.

Eugene was already in jail when I got locked up. I remember running into him and seeing him with a cane because his leg had been broken. He didn't look nearly as energetic and vibrant as I always remembered him being, but just seeing him was like a little piece of home to me. It was a comfort to see a guy I had known for so long. Jail was just a pit stop for him, no big deal, but it was my first time behind bars, and I was scared as hell. But Eugene took me under his wing in a way, and it relieved many of my fears.

"Don't worry about anything," he told me. "You're going to get out of here."

I remember correction officers yelling at us at certain times when everyone was supposed to be quiet, and Eugene would just yell back, ever so nonchalantly, "Fuck off, can't you see I'm talking to my boy here?"

There were only two people who helped me to get through jail. One was Eugene. The other was also a familiar face outside my cell, someone who had been there for many years in my life. A priest named Father Mark Rosetti came to see me every day in jail. In general, you couldn't get visitors like that, but because he was my religious leader he was able to come see me beyond the allowed two visits per week. And it was great for me that he was there every day. For years, he had been a source of strength during my toughest trials. He was so integrated into the life of my family, in fact, that it was almost as if he had a sense of when I needed him.

On one occasion, before I got locked up, he said to me, "What does today signify?"

I couldn't figure out why he was asking me this.

"Something big happened today," he said. "I know this."

In actuality, it was my son's ninth birthday. Additionally, it was the same day my wife had her first big melt-down. She was known by everyone to be very calm, very even tempered. She was so relaxed and well liked that people would later ask me when they heard of our divorce, "How could you fuck that up?" She was just that laid-back. But on that day, I knew something just took a turn for the worse.

Veola asked me to go to Dunkin' Donuts to pick up these things called Dunkin' Munchkins. She gave me a really off number to get so my son could take them to school, but when I got to the shop I found out they came only in packs of 50 or 100. I ended up just getting the bigger pack so the kids could have some extras if they wanted them. I didn't care if the extras were eaten or thrown away or fed to someone's dog; I just made sure the kids had enough, and the rest were inconsequential.

For whatever reason, when I returned home with them, my wife bugged out. It was such a small issue, but it was the catalyst for sinking the ship that was our marriage. I told her to take the extras and throw them out, or eat them herself, what the fuck did I care? But she couldn't handle it.

"You fuck-up!" she screamed at me. "How could you fuck

this up? You're just a fuck-up!" It was bizarre and so uncharacteristic of her that it could only have meant bad things.

In any case, the priest said to me that my mother had appeared to him during mass that day. She had appeared to him as clear as day. This was the same priest whom my mother had gone to for years for confession, whom she had listened to each week on Sunday. And he was a good man who, I will add, was jacked like a bodybuilder. My mother had always confided in Father Mark, and he felt she was doing so again. He swore that in this vision she looked very upset by something. He told me that she didn't speak to him, but she had a very concerned look on her face that just screamed to him, "I need your help."

That story made me think that, if my mother could come to Father Mark, then she could come to me. And I started feeling as if it wasn't just my son there with me in my heart but also my mother. And they were coupled with Eugene and Father Mark in the flesh. They were my support group, the ones who told me I would get out of that tiny, cold cell, that I would turn my life around. I felt like I had hit rock bottom, like I couldn't get lower, but then I realized all of the people — and the love — I still had around me. And none was more vocal than Eugene. If I even looked more down than usual, he had something to say to prop my morale back up. And he helped me through every single day until it was time to go.

When I got out of jail, it wasn't but a couple of weeks later that Eugene got out too. He'd stop by my gym just to ask how I was doing and check on me. He treated me like his little brother.

Unfortunately, a month or two later he took a hostage in a house and held off the SWAT team for quite some time. He ended up going to prison yet again, but this time it was his last time. After he was given the wrong medication, he had an anxiety attack and became very unruly. He got in a fight with a bunch of the officers in the prison, and they ended up beating him to death.

I'll never forget Eugene. For years, every June, I put a rest in peace column in the magazine. He was like a guardian angel to me when I was in jail and a guy to whom I owe a lot. He had my back in jail, and he made me feel good knowing I had a friend there. He gave me strength through his words and through his faith. He is gone now, or free as I like to believe, and just like he had my back I've now got his. I'll never let the world forget him or the immeasurable value of what he gave me in my time of darkness.

Chapter 30
BEGINNING ANEW

It felt like my life was over when I was arrested. Everything I had known and loved was either taken away from me or dead. My mother had died, my girlfriend had died, the police had taken all of my money, they had seized my brand-new Yukon, and my business suffered. All of the computers I used to run my business were taken, and on top of that the gym was hit with nearly a quarter million in taxes. When I couldn't pay them off, we had to liquidate everything.

To make matters worse, my decisions were also costing other people — those who worked for me and counted on me — their livelihoods. In the end, I couldn't keep my gym. The Powerhouse Gym of Yorktown Heights, once one of the top gyms in New York, was sold off in a deal for which I saw not a penny.

Along with my mental anguish, I was physically torn up. I felt a constant burning pain in my head and my heart from watching my world crumble. Physically, too, I was deteriorating. I had gone from administering myself 3,000 to 4,000 mg of testosterone weekly to absolutely nothing. After you begin injecting exogenous hormones, your body quits producing its own. Unless you come off properly, your natural production of male hormone is next to nothing. I was living with about the same amount of testosterone as a nine-year-old girl, a serious medical condition for a man. But with steroids, you don't get anything in prison or in treatment like you do if you're on heroin. For heroin, they give you methadone; for steroids, they laugh at you.

I had gone from a sense of complete control in my life to a sense of absolutely no control, to total weakness. My sex drive was nonexistent; my desire to be productive in any manner was fleeting. I was constantly tired, constantly sad. And during this period I realized, for the first time, that I had never actually been in control. It had all been a lie and at the time just a beautiful façade. I had been hiding in a world that wasn't reality, just a myriad of lies and disbelief.

Losing everything was the rudest wake-up call I could ever have received. It was as if God sent one of his angels to blow a trumpet in my ears and to tell me that, for some reason, I had been spared. Maybe I had lost everything, maybe people around me had suffered and paid the ultimate price, but for some reason — one I still don't understand — I got a second chance. I made it through. I was still living, still breathing the New York air I had for so long taken for granted. But the same angel that gave me the proverbial slap in the face warned me that this was my last chance, that I had better not screw up again.

Getting my life back on track wasn't easy. My hormones were off for a long time, and the imbalance affected everything from my thoughts to my joints. I felt like I aged twenty years over the course of just one. My inner self was hurting more than my outer self, and everything was a wreck. But, again, I was given a second chance. I just didn't know for quite some time where I needed to start.

For months on end, I was literally unable to do the things I had done before, things that had been part of a lifestyle that ended up being my self-destruction. I couldn't get my dick hard for a year, and while I wouldn't wish that on my worst enemy it kept me away from that life of sex and money I had been so used to. It caused me to change my ways out of sheer necessity.

To this day, my testosterone is in the toilet, my estrogen is sky high, and my growth hormone is close to nil. My doctor tells me I could be put on hormone replacement therapy and get steroids — in much smaller doses — the legit way now. But time and time again I refuse. I want to do things differently this time around. Legal or not, steroids were a part of my life for a long time, and I don't want to be on them no matter how good they might be for me in the right amounts. I'm just done with them, period.

For ten months, I also attended a drug treatment program. At first I was very angry that I had to sit around and talk about my supposed problems with people who were addicted to alcohol and cocaine and heroin. I wasn't addicted to steroids; my body might have been used to them, but I wasn't knocking off 7-Elevens or any less of a friend or father because I was taking them. In hindsight, though, I learned a lot from that program. It helped me to shape my approach to things.

Many people know the quotation and use it in some form, but I truly learned "that which does not kill you only makes you stronger." People write to me every day and tell me how bad they feel for me, how bad they feel about what I've gone through in my life. They don't agree with the laws against steroids; they can't believe I've had so many people close to me die for no good reason. But I tell them all the same thing: please don't feel sorry for me. I made it through, and I have been given a second chance I'm taking full advantage of.

Countless people go through their entire lives and never experience true, honest love. I have. I've had a few women in my life love me more than anything. Two of them broke themselves against me. My ex-wife was suicidal for quite some time, living in fear that at any moment a drug dealer would break in her door and kill her and our children. But she loved me anyway, my selfishness and greed be damned. These days she can't stand me. She wouldn't care if I stepped out into the street tomorrow and got hit head-on by a semi. And I don't blame her. She was unconditionally in love with me, devoted and honest and everything I wasn't. I took sixteen years of her life, and I'd do anything to give them back to her, but I can't. And she hates me for it, but I completely understand.

As for my Julissa, I was very lucky to have been loved by her for five years. Those five years were our entire lifetime together, and I experienced and felt things I never thought existed. She showed me that it was possible to love someone so much it caused you to hate yourself. I was her poison, her new addiction. She hated my ways and my drug dealing and all of the wrongs I did, but she didn't stop me and instead became part of my lifestyle because of how much she loved me. She saved my life on more than one occasion, and even in her death she saved me. In a way, she died so that I could live. My biggest regret is that it wasn't the other way around. She came from the streets, and I took her out of them, I made her reconcile with the family from whom she had been an outcast. But I can't help but feel she would have survived so much longer on those streets than she ultimately did because she chose to give her life to me. My life in a word was an *ordeal*, and she didn't make it out alive. I hate myself for that, and I think about her and my choices every day.

It has been a battle every day since my stint in jail and the loss of everything to get my life back on track. And, I've come to find, the drama never stops. It's only different.

Chapter 31
THE SYNTHOL MYTH

I have always had thick skin. I'm from New York; every-one here is blunt and honest with their thoughts and opinions. If they like you, you're treated like family. It's an Italian thing. But if they don't like you, they'll make sure you know it. The Internet is a lot like that too; people who otherwise in the real world have no courage to say anything to your face will trash you. They'll talk big as if they were really someone special. They'll put you down and act like they're holier than thou. I've taken my fair share of lies, I've taken my fair share of non-sense being spread about me. But sometimes it just goes too far.

For years, people have loved to tell the world how my arms got so big. People who actually know me also know the truth: I worked hard for them. I busted my ass in the gym and in the kitchen to ensure that my body was getting everything it needed to grow. From the proper training to the proper nutrition, I did what-ever it took to get the physical exertion and the right nutrients to my muscles. But then you have these haters on the Internet, these nobodies out in cyberspace, who have nothing better to do than sit on their out-of-shape asses and spread lies.

A number of people have made it their mission to

get the world to believe that I used Synthol to grow my arms to their massive size. Synthol is a nonhormonal, oil-based compound made up primarily of medium-chain triglyceride fatty acids. It gets injected into a muscle and causes localized swelling that, when done properly, makes the muscle temporarily rounder and larger.

Most of the time Synthol use is obvious. You see it with competitive bodybuilders all the time in the form of ugly lumps in their muscles or abnormal peaks. Despite not containing any steroidal hormone, it isn't even necessarily safe. And I think it's a disgrace to bodybuilding even though just about every pro uses it in at least one area of the body before a contest.

Rumors have swirled for years that I was a Synthol abuser. Let me set the record straight once and for all: I have never used Synthol. I have never once injected an oil that did not contain steroids.

My methods were simple, and I find it hard to believe that people don't understand or accept the truth. Synthol is mostly made up of fatty acids, whereas steroids are usually grapeseed or another type of purified oil in which the drugs are suspended. I injected — abused, I admit — massive amounts of steroids in oil into my arms. I site-injected the biceps and triceps. Over time, doing so stretched the muscle fascia. Some people say that would have a Synthol-like effect, and that's fine, but every drop of oil I ever put into my body was with the intention of delivering more testosterone or equipoise or whatever drug I was using into my system — never for the purpose of site enhancement or size. I received the stretch of the fascia from the oil and the localized growth from the drug; it's the one-two punch. Synthol is commonly used in bodybuilding to stretch the muscle fascia and cause local swelling, but it does nothing for real growth. Oil-based steroids such as testosterone and equipoise do the same thing but also offer true muscle gains by putting the drug into the muscle. All bodybuilders today use some sort of localized injections, and some use Synthol because they are already on high doses of drugs. In that case, it's a great way to get swelling without the added stress on the endocrine system of more drugs, but in my mind it was out. I had no problem with super-high doses.

But the bullshit doesn't quit.

Drugs, Synthol, the haters, the lies in the media — all of it together has changed my entire perspective on the sport of bodybuilding. It has changed so much since I fell in love with it years ago. If I didn't have my own column, if I didn't work for Steve Blechman, I wouldn't be at the shows, I wouldn't read the magazines, I wouldn't be involved nearly as much as I am now. I used to love this sport so much, but the ignorant few out there, those daily keyboard warriors, just don't relent. And it quickly becomes very tiring. I'm sick of it. The rumors have to stop. To an extent, the Internet is largely to blame for the misinformation pertaining to my arms. YouTube is especially huge for spreading lies.

I had a hematoma and a floppy biceps, made famous in the TLC documentary on me, and people blame that on Synthol. What really happened was that I was hit in the left arm with a bat during a Little League practice, causing the arm to fill up with blood, which in turn makes people who watch the videos of me say, "Oh, my God, that doesn't even look real, that's not muscle." They're right, it wasn't in those clips, it was blood, but it definitely was not Synthol. Near the end of 1999, my son accidentally hit me with a baseball bat. I used to go behind the plate when my kids practiced and helped out by acting as umpire. When he swung, he hit me on the side of the biceps. My arm started swelling and swelling. The blood kept pooling there, so I would stick a needle in my biceps and drain the fluid. I had no fear of needles and already used myself as a pin cushion, so it made sense. Why not?

People claim that the blood shown in the TLC show is proof I used Synthol, but it's the exact opposite. If it was an infection, it would have been pus, not blood. If it was oil, it wouldn't have be red. And it would have been both arms, not just the one. If you watch the video, there is no oil and no pus. If it was an infection, I would have been dead because no one can live with half a quart of pus in his body. What was in there was dead blood, like boxers get. When you see in the *Rocky* movie Sylvester Stallone tell his corner man "Cut me, Mick," he's referring to a huge swelling that has closed his eye and needs to be drained. Like my arm.

I've always been known for having huge arms, and ever since I got my first picture in a magazine people have hated me for it. They hate what they can't have.

Lee Haney used to say that you take your strong point and work it, shove it in everyone's face, and it becomes your money maker. Lee used to tell me that if he had Tom Platz's legs he'd be on stage posing them to no end, because they would be his money makers. That's what I was doing with my arms. I'd stand there with a tank top on, and I'd pose my arms. But I've always been big everywhere — my back was huge, my shoulders were wide, my waist was small — it wasn't strictly my arms.

You can't compare me to Synthol users. It isn't even close. It's a totally different build. Just because my arms were huge means nothing when trying to pin Synthol use on me, because I was built in every body part.

Guys have always done site injections with real steroids because doing so causes the site to swell. That's what I did. I knew that the site would swell, that the fascia would stretch, and I chose to put oil-based steroids locally into my arms. The same effect works everywhere; I have a friend who does his shots in his ass, and he walks around with the biggest ass anyone has ever seen on a guy.

My theory is that people shouldn't even waste their time with Synthol. I used to tell guys that, if they were going to inject oil, make sure it has hormone in it. Synthol is a waste, it's worthless, and it's a disgrace.

A huge criticism I've gotten for years is that I've sold Synthol on my personal website. People somehow think that because I sell it I must use it. That's not even close to the truth. I used to get questions all the time from guys about where they could get Synthol, so I decided that I could make some money selling it. That's it. Nothing more, nothing less. People looked for it and, thanks to all the bullshit, found my website, so because it's legal it made sense for me to sell it for a while.

For better or for worse, whether people feel I deserve them or not, I have countless supporters around the world. I still get thousands of letters every year from every part of the globe. Some people want to know about training, some people want to know about drugs even though they should know I can't answer those questions, and most people just send me their support. They love my column, my freaky size, my attitude, whatever it is. People support me, and I love them for it. Sometimes, though, people don't understand me, and they act on these misconceived notions. And at least once it has cost someone his life.

Chapter 32
MEDIA SCANDALS AND COSTLY MISUNDERSTANDINGS

In 2002, the Internet was flooded with messages about my death. Message boards and websites lit up with news that "Gregg Valentino Died," and the reasons were as varying as they were laughable. Some said it was a drug overdose, some said it was related to Synthol (even though I never used it), the list went on and on.

The rumor started when my picture showed up in a Swedish newspaper, a shot of me hitting a massive back doubles biceps pose, one of my trademarks, if you will. The article, though not in English, was "interpreted," if you can even call it that, by someone who thought he knew the language well enough. In hindsight, he didn't. He did, though, correctly interpret words like *injection* and *steroids* and *death*. This interpretation quickly spun itself until it was posted on American bulletin boards that I was dead.

Eventually, I received a phone call from someone in the industry who was smart enough to actually try to contact me to see if it was true. When it was verified that I was still alive, much to the chagrin of some haters, I took the time to step back and look at everything that was being said about me. It's a very interesting experience to have the world think you're dead and watch as people go off on tangents they think you'll never read. Some people really let their true selves be known to me. A lot of it was hurtful, and some people who I thought were my friends said some nasty things. But I'd rather know about it than not, and ultimately life goes on. Our true friends have our backs in life and death, while the leeches will step on you as soon as they can. I adjusted my circle of friends and was prepared to live my life as usual.

Soon thereafter the article was correctly translated, and the truth turned out to be much worse than the fiction it had spawned. To this day, what I found out haunts me.

A supporter of mine bought into the hype and lies about me that claimed I used oils to build my size. He believed what the jealous people around the world had chosen to write about me, and he truly thought that I was using an array of oils, injected into my muscles, to get my arms to the size they were.

What this young man did — he was only in his early twenties, from what I understand — was inject a combination of motor oil and vegetable oil into his arms. It entered his bloodstream and ultimately killed him. As the story has been told to me, after this happened the young man's parents entered his room and saw pictures of me all over his walls. They tore them down, and when the media got wind of it I became the man to blame. It was so disheartening to me that I was speechless. I don't mind if people talk about me, I don't mind if they spread rumors, but this had crossed the line. People's unfounded hatred of me confused a person so much that he wound up killing himself. Inadvertent suicide. All because he wanted to be like me.

It's something that will always be with me and something that I'll never understand. It makes me as angry as it does sad because I'll never know why he didn't contact me. He could have e-mailed me, he could have written me by postal mail, he could have hit up a message board I posted on. He had so many avenues to actually speak with me and ask if that is what I really did, and I could have set him straight. I could have told him the truth, and ultimately it could have saved his life. But he bought into the rumors. He saw past the hatred some people hold for me enough to idolize me and to want to be like me, but he didn't take the next step and confirm what I really did. He didn't ask me how I trained, he didn't ask me about the drugs. He just went ahead and injected himself.

I have a lot of trouble with people looking up to celebrities. I have a lot of confusion about "heroes." I appreciate what people do, great athletes or great actors or even great politicians. But *hero* is a word that is so overused today. You have to be very careful when you give someone that label, because it sets you up for the possibility that you will be let down. People call me their hero, and it's as much a struggle as it is an honor. How do I maintain that position without letting them down? How do I live my life yet stay on a positive platform for someone else? And in a way I feel responsible for someone already having paid the ultimate price.

It's true I couldn't have stopped what happened. I had nothing to do with that young man losing his life. I know that, I remind myself of that, but I don't believe that anyone could hear such a story, know that someone wanted to be like him so badly he was willing to do such crazy things that ended up killing him, and not be affected.

I close my eyes sometimes and think about my own children and wonder who they're looking up to. I wonder what they might be willing to do to be like their own "heroes." Because of that, I spend every day of my life now trying to be that guy for them, doing my best to be the hero my kids look up to. I'm not perfect by any stretch of the imagination, but for my son and my daughter I'd sacrifice everything, and I believe they know that.

The entire ordeal makes me reflect on every interaction I have with people today. When people send me mail and ask questions, I am very aware of the power my response might have. It is a responsibility I didn't sense before that ordeal in 2002. And it truly does make me angry that someone might be willing to waste his life to be like someone else.

I crack a lot of jokes. I love humor. I have a persona that people see, I'm called a "freak," and I enjoy it every time. But don't try to be like me. I've suffered through so much because of bad decisions I've made, and I carry an incurable pain with me every day of my life. If I can be an inspiration to someone, I consider it an honor. If I can be used as an image of what to do or, perhaps in some cases, of what not to do, I'm okay with that. But I don't want people misinterpreting me again and having another life wasted. The best thing I can do is help someone to become the first of himself or herself, not the "next Gregg Valentino." Don't waste the gifts you have.

Hearing about the loss of that young man reminded me of a song from a band called Staind. They have a song called "Waste" that speaks bluntly but truthfully to the decisions that someone makes in life that ends it. And this, in retrospect, is all that's left. It can't change anything, and knowing that still weighs heavily on me.

It seems that, even after getting out of jail and putting the steroid and huge arm part of my life behind me, drama still tends to follow me no matter where I go. I guess it's just my nature, a magnet for abuse of one type or another.

In 2006, a former producer of Maury Povich's talk show filed a $100 million sexual harassment lawsuit against Povich. Ironically enough, I knew this girl, as did my close friend Bob Bonham, and I ended up catching a lot of heat for some things I didn't actually say, and I was essentially kicked off the show. Years ago, this girl, Bianca Nardi, had a friend who was dating Bob. Because of this, I ended up meeting Bianca a few times. To me, she was cool enough, a crazy type of factory girl who liked to have a good time. She was a bigger girl, blonde, definitely the type of girl a lot of guys would be into.

When Bianca was around me, she was definitely forward and a little frisky with me. I didn't think anything of it because it certainly didn't bother me. When we weren't all hanging out, I never really thought of Bianca. But once shit hit the fan and she sued Povich, the *National Enquirer* started poking its nose into the case, looking to make a scandal out of the story.

In short order, the *Enquirer* found my boy Bob. It's worth mentioning that Bob knows Bianca far better than I do. Not only was she Bob's ex-girlfriend's best friend, but she was also a member of the gym Bob owns called Strong & Shapely. Not thinking much of it, Bob told the truth to the *Enquirer* writers when they started asking about her; he's a straightforward guy, and he had no reason to shy away. He just said she was a little crazy, liked to party, nothing out of the ordinary. Because of her friendly ways with me in the two times I had met Bianca, Bob passed my name and number to the magazine reporters. The *Enquirer* paid Bob for talking, and he probably thought I could use the money and, in looking out for me, thought they might offer me some cash too.

I was contacted by the same people who had spoken with Bob, but I told them I had nothing to say about her, that I had met her only a couple of times, that there was no story with me. I wasn't giving them anything. It's in my blood that I hate rats; I can't stand people who sell out others for money. So I told the *Enquirer* straight up that I didn't want to see anything negative printed about Bianca because, as far as I was concerned, she was a very nice girl. The only things I did say were very positive.

The *Enquirer* would come back and say, "Well, your friend Bob says she's a little crazy and loves to party. What do you think about that?"

Every time I would reply, "I didn't say that. Bianca is a nice girl." And that was that.

When the story finally came out, it became apparent that the magazine writers had decided to twist things around for their own benefit. Because I'm in the media, and I have the retarded-looking arms, it apparently made sense to the *Enquirer* writers to quote me as the one who trashed Bianca a little. They slapped my name onto everything Bob had said that wasn't exactly nice or uplifting. They quoted me as talking about Bianca flashing her tits in the clubs, making out with other girls, and all kinds of things that I absolutely had not said. I wasn't even there when these things supposedly happened, yet I was the one credited with mentioning them. To this day, I haven't talked to Bianca about any of it.

Now, I'm not saying that anyone lied, but these were words spoken by other people, and it was very unfair of that magazine to claim I had said them. This was the *National Enquirer* putting its famous spin on some bullshit scandal. And, to make matters worse, Bob got paid to tell these stories, and I became the asshole who had no idea any of it had happened. Honestly, the only reason I'm comfortable even alluding to the fact that these stories might be true is because I know Bob so well and know he wouldn't lie. If he says she did these things, that's fine, then I believe she did, but I repeat that I never saw them and never told anyone anything about her.

The *Enquirer* also printed pictures of me looking completely jacked up. Think about what the better story is: quoting a gym owner and the friend of a girl filing a $100 million lawsuit, or the guy Ripley's labeled "The Man with the World's Biggest Arms" who looks like a freak. The *Enquirer* made its choice clear.

That was in the spring of 2006. In late August of that year, after I appeared on the Tyra Banks show, I got a call from the Maury Povich show. They offered me some money to be a guest for just fifteen minutes. They wanted to do what everyone loves to do: talk about my arms. Since the show is in Manhattan, it was a short trip for me and, with the fee, sounded like a perfect afternoon. I signed the contract and set it up.

When the day came to shoot, I brought my daughter Gina to the set with me because I wanted her to see how a television show is put together. I wanted her to see her dad in action, learn about the side of an industry she hadn't seen before, that sort of thing.

When we got to the set of the show for taping, it was a very quick process to get the filming rolling. They started an interview with me, and I noticed only a few minutes into it that one producer was talking to another, and they kept looking over and pointing at me. When the show took a break to change the set lighting, I was called over to them. I just had a feeling that there was some sort of drama brewing.

One of Maury Povich's crew members had recognized me as the guy whom the *National Enquirer* called an "ex-lover" of Bianca. To them, I was the guy who had bashed her. If that was actually the case, then it would have been good for Povich because it degraded the character of the girl suing him. But it would become a conflict of interest because it would appear to the unknowing public that I was getting a pat on the back, so to speak, for coming out against this girl. It would look as if he was trading publicity for me for some negative press on Bianca.

Right in the middle of the interview, after it was discovered who I was — or who they thought I was — the lawyers for the show were called and quickly decided I couldn't be a guest. Just as I figured, they thought that Bianca's lawyers would try to play it up and say that I was partnering with Maury and that I had bashed Bianca only to get myself on the show.

In the end, I was given half of the original agreed-upon fee, a pat on the back, an apology, and a proverbial kick in the ass on the way out the door. Honestly, it was embarrassing having my daughter there for that, but I feel lucky that she was a little too young then to realize exactly what went on there. Along with being embarrassed, I was angry, because the whole problem had come about from no actions of my own. If anything, I had been an advocate for Bianca as a nice girl, not a hater of her like I had been made out to be.

I've found over time that people's opinions of me can have a drastic effect on my life even though I couldn't care less what they think. People hate out of anger, fear, and greed. That's their problem. But as soon as you get a little notoriety, it's very unfair that people's bias against you can cause problems. Whether that's trying to build your name as a brand or just trying to get paid for an appearance, it's wrong that others can prevent someone from achieving things just by their hatred. That said, there was another situation before this drama that was a prime example of the costs that can arise from people spewing their hate. And in this case, it wasn't money, it was a life. The ultimate price to pay.

Chapter 33
A CRAZY LITTLE THING I CALLED RAVEN

In case I sound righteous or reformed, it should be noted that I do still find trouble or make the odd mistake. In fact, the craziness of my life never ceases. Whether it's bodybuilding, drugs, or women, if I'm involved, it's safe to say things aren't going to be normal.

Bob Bonham had met a girl who was very much into the "dark side," if you know what I mean. She was a goth in every sense of the word: white makeup, dark lipstick, dark nails, the whole bit. After Bob hooked up with her, he called me the next day to tell me his girl had a friend who had seen me on television a few times and wanted to meet me. I figured I'd done a lot worse in the past than any gothic girl could have done, so I agreed to meet her. Looking back, I should have known right then that the girl would be fucked up in the head.

A couple of days later I met Bob and these two goth girls in the city. At first I saw Bob's girl, who was very petite and cute and didn't scare me. Then I met her friend Doreen, the girl who wanted to meet me. I was on edge right from the start. Right away she told me that she didn't want to be called Doreen, that she went by the name Raven. And she was no-nonsense about that. I hadn't known her long at all when I slipped and used her real name, and she flipped out on me. She

200

grabbed my hand and dug her nails into it and said from then on she'd only answer to Raven. I looked down, and my hand was bleeding.

"If you ever do that shit again," I told her, "I'll crack you in the fucking jaw. There's no need to get all crazy like that."

She smiled. I think she liked me telling her straight up what would happen if she acted like a bitch again. She said something in response, but I missed it because I suddenly realized this girl was even more fucked up than I had originally thought. She lived a totally goth lifestyle, all the way down to the permanent fangs I now noticed were implanted in her mouth.

At this point, I figured this girl might actually, somehow, be for me. She was attractive, with jet black eyes, big red lips, and long, silky, wavy black hair, and now she had a vampire mystique about her. It might be the thing of dreams — or nightmares — but I'm sure many guys would love to hook up with a real-life vampire if they existed. Well, at least for me, one did now. And she was into me.

That night we all went out and had a really great time. To close the night, we went and grabbed a bite at the Market Diner. As we were leaving, Raven asked me to come back to her apartment. She had been looking me up and down all night, very much into putting her hands on me, so I knew what she was after. And I was much obliged to help her out. She had been kissing me and biting my ear, and I was due for a turn.

Raven lived in a loft that was very well furnished and had a very cool vibe to it. It was a few blocks past Canal Street right off the Westside Highway, and it just screamed "unique." Just like this girl. The inside of the place was all dark, like I imagined a castle being, and it was littered with gothic-looking statues, pictures, and paintings.

"This chick has money," I said to myself under my breath.

When I walked around to look for the bathroom, I glanced

up and noticed a hangman's noose hanging from a beam in the ceiling. "What the fuck is that?" I asked, pointing upward.

Raven gave me a very unconvincing smile as she said, "Oh, that's for Chicky, my pet bird," and she went about lighting some candles while swaying back and forth to some eerie gothic music she had put on. The song inspired thoughts of Satan to me, but I didn't know why.

When I came back from the bathroom, Raven showed me a skull on her lamp table. "It's real," she said.

I asked her why she would want something like that as well as how the hell she would get something like that — hoping she wouldn't give me an answer that would scare the shit out of me. She laughed and said she had bought it from a flea market in Chelsea. When I pressed on to find out why, she merely said it was because she liked it.

At this point, I was a little freaked out. My feeling of unease was compounded when I saw a shadow moving around on the other side of the room. I screamed like a fucking teenage girl in a horror movie and thought I was going to have a heart attack.

"What's the matter?" Raven yelled. "What are you screaming about?"

I told her straight up that she had a ghost in her apartment and that it was in the room at that very moment.

"Oh," she said nonchalantly. "I know. But it hasn't been around for a few months."

Raven went about playing with her two jet black cats, which had mysteriously appeared to me for the first time, and I finally told her to turn some lights on. I also told her I was allergic to cats and asked her to keep the little bastards away from me.

She stood up from the couch and directed the cats away. She started off toward the bathroom and looked over her shoulder and showed me her fangs. "Go into the bedroom," she said. "And take your clothes off."

I hit the off button to her stereo to silence the creepy, serial-killer-inspiring music and made my way to the bedroom. As soon as I walked in, I screamed again like a dog getting its tail stepped on.

Raven rushed out of the bathroom. "What now?"

"You have a fucking casket next to your bed!" I yelled, pointing toward the wooden casket on the floor. "What the hell is with that shit?"

She rolled her eyes. "I keep my personal stuff in there."

A moment later she had it open and showed me all kinds of "goods" in there, from dildos to butt plugs to strap-on cocks. She also had hoods, latex masks, studded bracelets, whips, all kinds of restraints and harnesses, as well as one thing I hadn't seen before: a giant arm with a fist at the end.

"What the fuck is that for?"

Raven didn't answer, instead just closing the casket lid and standing back up.

"Get naked," she ordered me.

I shook my head. I felt caught in a predicament. One part of me wanted to look past all of the weird shit and fuck the girl, and the other had me wondering why Bob couldn't have chosen this one and passed along his polite and petite goth to me instead.

Against my better judgment, I took my clothes off and got onto the bed as she walked back into the bathroom. A few minutes later she walked back into the room looking sexy as hell and climbed onto the bed next to me and started kissing me.

After we made out for a while and allowed our hands to wander, I put her on her back and got on top of her. Just as I was ready to move to the next step, I saw something move to my right and realized it was the bedsheet, slowly moving on its own.

Once again I screamed and jumped up. "Your bedsheet is fucking moving!"

"Oh, relax," she said. "It's just Ozzy."

"Is Ozzy the ghost?" I asked her.

"No, don't be silly. Say hi to my baby Ozzy." Raven pulled back the sheet and showed me a big, hairy, scary-as-fuck-looking tarantula.

I screamed again and crawled backward on the bed as fast as I could.

Raven started talking baby talk to this spider, which was now sitting in her palm. She started petting it and twice kissed it on its back before she got off the bed and placed the spider into a dresser drawer.

"You don't have a cage for that fucking thing?"

She looked back at me, pissed off. "Don't call Ozzy a 'fucking thing,' he is my baby. And, no, I don't believe in cages."

"Well, at least close the drawer all the way."

"No way. I let him roam free. Don't worry, he won't come back to the bed anyway. He's sleepy."

I looked at her awkwardly, my pulse racing, my breathing heavy. It had been clear from the moment I met Raven that she was crazy, but now it was obvious that she was unlike any woman I had ever met. And, for a lifelong New Yorker, that's saying something.

"Do you have any other surprises for me?"

Instead of answering, she slowly walked back toward the bed, crawled toward me, and straddled her legs around me. As she started kissing me again, I recalled that her lips had just been on a fat, hairy spider, but she was very good at what she was doing, and it got me back into the mood. I even told her to bite my neck a little, fantasizing about those teeth while she did. It hurt, but I liked it.

I turned her over and pinned her to the bed and started in on her. She pulled my head down and began kissing and biting my neck. As she was doing this, I felt her finger on my ass and told her to be gentle. She was scratching me.

Raven stopped kissing me and raised an eyebrow. "I'm not touching your ass." Then she showed me both of her hands.

I screamed, yet again, and jumped up quickly. I turned around and saw that it was one of her fucking black cats that had been licking my ass pipe. In retrospect, I should have blasted that damn cat with muddy creatine right in its fucking feline face. "Now my ass is going to itch for the rest of the night!" I yelled to Raven. "I'm allergic to those little fuckers!"

I told her I had endured enough of the bizarre bullshit and was going to leave. I put my clothes on as fast as I could and headed toward the door.

"I found out some things tonight," I yelled to Raven as I walked. "I like gothic babes, but when you live in a haunted house you've got issues."

I was thinking that at least with ghetto girls it's only roaches and rats, things I'm used to and can deal with. But hangman's nooses, coffins, human skulls, giant spiders, ghosts, and black cats licking my ass were not my idea of fun.

As I stormed into the living room, it felt as if someone was walking with me. In the darkness, as my eyes tried to adjust, I saw two eyes staring at me, and I heard a voice.

"Hello. Goodbye."

I thought I was going to die of a heart attack. I felt a stabbing in my chest and ran back into the bedroom.

"You have a fucking ghost in your living room, and it just yelled at me!" I told Raven.

"It's just Chicky," she said. She called for her bird, and like a ghost this white bird cut through the blackness and landed on her forearm.

"Keep it away from me, or I'll feed your pet spider to it."

She smacked me and laughed. "Come on, Gregg, just stay, and I promise no ghost will get you. I'll even close the door so the bird and the cats can't bother us."

I wanted to say no. I was prepared to say no. But she flashed those fangs at me, and I gave in. We ended up back on the bed, back in action, and it was well worth it.

The next morning I woke up and kissed Raven goodbye and told her I'd let myself out. As I was heading out, I peeked into the dresser drawer, and sure enough the spider was gone. I wiped my face because suddenly I felt very disgusting. Throughout the night, I had woken up now and then because I thought Raven was tickling my face. But when I had turned around, she was asleep with her back toward me. My mind went straight back to the image of her holding a very big, very hairy spider.

Raven and I dated for a while, and things seemed to be coming along well enough. One year, a couple of days before the New York Night of Champions professional bodybuilding show, I took her out to the movies, and we saw *Van Helsing*. We had a nice time at the movie, we ate dinner, and then we stopped by a club called the Old Flamingo Club. It was goth night, so sure enough Raven wanted to go out until the early morning. It was after 5:30 a.m. when we left and headed back to her place.

By this point, I had been to her place hundreds of times, but each time I walked through the door the noose hanging from the ceiling freaked me out. I was always afraid I'd walk in and see someone hanging there. And, even worse, I'd had night-mares about Raven drugging me and somehow hanging me from it. To add to my displeasure over going to her place, I still didn't care for any of her possessed pets from hell. For a while, the bird would take a swan dive at my head every time I entered, and one of the cats would wait until I was lying on the bed, nice and relaxed, before it terrorized my allergies by rub-bing itself all over me.

On this early morning, we walked into her apartment, and she put on her slow, deep, grinding gothic music as I went to the refrigerator and got a bottle of water. She told me she wanted me to take a shower with her, and initially I declined, but once I turned around and took a drink of water I noticed she was completely naked. Sure enough, I changed my mind and followed her like a crackhead follows a crack pipe.

When we were done in the shower, we hit the bed, still naked, and she climbed on top of me. I noticed right away that one of the cats was on the bed to my right. I wanted to prevent the little shit from causing me any grief, so I reached toward the night stand on the other side of the bed, grabbed a bottle of lotion, and tossed it at the cat. I hit it squarely on its head, causing it to scramble out of the room after it fell loudly to the floor.

After Raven and I finished our business, we fell asleep. Later in the morning, she cooked breakfast for me. She prepared a nice, juicy steak and six eggs over-easy. Once I had cleared my plate I sat down and relaxed on the couch, hanging out like a bloated Buddha. In a matter of minutes, I started to doze off.

I woke up suddenly when I felt a tiny tickle on the inside of my upper arm that went all the way to the back side of my arm. I had a strange feeling overtake me, like a drop of boiling water was traveling down my arm. I looked back and saw a spider on me. I jumped up and hollered like in a horror movie, swung my hand around, and squashed it to death. But I still felt that burning sensation. I scratched at the point of the pain and tried to wipe away this odd feeling, but there was nothing there, and my arm was totally dry.

At this point, Raven came into the room and asked what I was yelling at.

I pointed toward the spider and told her the fucking thing had bitten me, so I had killed it. I watched as the little color that had been there drained from her face.

"Oh, no," she said. "Shit. . . ."

"What?"

"You fucking idiot. You just killed Little Nicky. Now I'm completely screwed."

"Who the fuck is Little Nicky? Don't tell me you have a second pet spider."

She shook her head. "Hell, no, the one you killed was Little Nicky. He's a pet of my best friend, Mel."

"So what? The damn thing bit me. Why is Mel's fucking spider in your house?"

"I was pet-sitting, asshole!"

I laughed. "You're baby-sitting a spider? A spider named Little fucking Nicky? You two chicks are nuts."

Raven didn't answer me and instead just started freaking out.

I apologized but explained that the spider had bitten me and that it was a natural reaction to squish it. I also added that it wouldn't have happened if she and her friends had normal pets instead of bugs that bit people.

As I was talking, Raven started running around the apartment in a frenzy. I asked her why she was acting all crazy, and she stopped, turned on her heel, and pointed her finger at my face.

"That, my dear, was not only a poisonous spider that bit you, but there were three other brown spiders in the box with Little Nicky."

"Okay. And what does that mean? What are you trying to tell me?"

Raven pointed toward an end table just outside her bedroom. I looked and saw a spider box upside down on the floor.

"Oh, shit," I said. "Don't tell me that means there are three other poisonous spiders fucking floating around this house."

"Yeah, asshole, that's exactly what it means."

Right then I started running around the apartment too, trying to find the remaining spiders. Then it occurred to me that Raven called the spider I had killed by a specific name.

"Raven," I started. "You called the spider that bit me Little Nicky. How do you know that was the one that bit me?"

"Gregg, come here, please."

I went into the bedroom, where she was looking under the

bed frame, and gazed down to her view. I saw the biggest spider I had ever seen in my life. I freaked.

"What the fuck is that!" I yelled, more as a statement than as a question. "Is that real?"

"That's how I knew it was Little Nicky that bit you." Raven then went into a closet and pulled out a small butterfly net she sometimes used for her own pet spider and scooped up the big brown spider and put it back into its box. We then started looking for the other two.

Two minutes later I hear Raven scream, "I gotcha, you little fucker!" She had found another spider by the casket next to her bed.

After an hour and a half of looking for the last one, at times with flashlights, I gave up and sat down on the couch. When I looked up toward that creepy noose, I saw the spider crawling on it. Then I brainstormed an idea.

Raven's bird was at the end of the couch, sitting there, staring eerily at me like it always did. I took my flashlight and got its attention with the beam; then I shone the beam right on the spider and wiggled it. Like a bolt of lightning, Chicky screeched across the room and snatched the spider up like a frog snatches a fly.

"Yes!" I screamed.

Raven heard me yell and ran into the room. "Did you find it?"

I didn't say a word. I just looked into her eyes and grinned from ear to ear. She asked me again if I had found it, and I merely flashed the light beam up toward the ceiling and onto my new favorite pet, Chicky.

Raven gasped. "Do something, you idiot!"

"I did," I said, noticing the bird was still chewing.

"This is just great. You killed Little Nicky, and then with your help Chicky killed one of the others. How am I going to explain this to Mel?"

"Like I give a fuck," I said. "That Little Nicky bit me. I don't feel bad for it, and neither should you. It got what it deserved. The fucked-up part is that you care more about that bird than you care about me."

Raven rolled her eyes. "Fuck you!" she yelled before walking into the bathroom and locking herself in.

I was so pissed off that I walked over to her bedroom door and opened it, allowing her cats to come into the room. Then I took the flashlight to get Chicky's attention again. Finally, I knocked the box that housed the other spiders off the table, and I watched in amusement as both the cats and the bird went after them. Once the spiders were taken care of, I left Raven's apartment and slammed the door as hard as possible on the way out.

Hours after I left, I got a fever. I thought I was just catching a cold. But after two days, I realized it was an infection at the bite location, and I was in bad shape. I wound up going to the hospital because my body felt like it was shutting down. I was feeling weak and flushed, and my fever wouldn't go away without a combination of Tylenol and Advil. Once those medicines wore off, though, the fever came right back.

My motivation to do anything had long since passed. At one point, I even tried taking some tablets of Ephedra for some energy, and I still couldn't get going. Despite feeling so run down, though, I couldn't sleep at night because of the fever. And, to top it off, my shoulder and arm were swelling up to massive proportions. I wasn't on any juice, so I knew it wasn't a bad injection, but something was having its way with me. Then, like a guy trying to catch a Monday flight on Wednesday, I remembered the spider bite. Being the self-medicating guy that I am, the first thing I tried to do at this point was remove the fluid that had built up.

I took an 18-g needle and attached it to a syringe, and I pierced the center of the swelling and tried to withdraw whatever pus or blood was in there. That didn't work. Later I'd learn it was edema, which can't be drained, so I was using myself as a pin cushion for no good reason.

After my failed attempt to self-serve, I ended up at the emergency room in the Hudson Valley Hospital. The doctor there immediately started lecturing me about using steroids before I even told her why I was there.

"Listen, lady," I told her. "I haven't used a steroid since April 17, 2001. If you don't believe me, test my blood."

She looked at me, confused and frustrated. "Well, why are your arms so big, then?"

"Are you fucking serious?" I asked her. "Can you please worry more about the fever and the edema in my arm instead of why I'm muscular?"

After a few words back and forth, and her noticing I was getting very pissed off, she wrote me a prescription for Cephlexen and then went to get me a release form. When she handed it to me, she included a pamphlet on the "dangers of steroid use."

"You don't listen," I told her as I looked her straight in the eye. "I don't use steroids right now. I swear to God."

She then stuck her face just inches in front of mine and said, "Yeah, right."

"You need some Scope, lady. Your breath stinks from talking so much shit."

She walked away, and I made my way toward the pharmacy to get my prescription filled. A couple of days after I started taking it, I felt as if I was getting sicker and sicker. On top of feeling worse, I now had huge pockets of fluid popping up from my shoulder all the way down to my wrist. My hand was even huge with fluid, and each finger looked like a fat penis. My fevers too were rampant.

I wound up going back to the ER, and fortunately the bitch of a doctor I had talked to the first time wasn't there. It was an

Indian doctor now who took a few blood samples and then left me sitting in the waiting room for an hour. When he finally returned with a clipboard in his hand, he told me that I had a collapsed lung and that I was bleeding from one of my kidneys.

I completely freaked out. "You can tell all that from a fucking blood test?" I asked him.

"Oh, wrong chart, sorry." The doctor paused and looked confused for a moment before adding, "Oh, you're Valentino. Right. You have a very bad infection, and we need to admit you."

Now I was in shock. I was still getting over my initial freakout over hearing I had a failing lung and kidney, and then he admitted he was an idiot, and now I was going to be admitted under his care.

I wound up in the Critical Care Ward in a room with an Italian gentleman in his eighties. At night, the guy would pass gas so loudly that it would wake me up. Then I would have trouble falling back asleep because he would grunt nonstop. He also made frequent trips to the bathroom that caused him to walk past my bed, in front of which he'd continue to fart loudly. To make matters worse, he'd walk past me completely naked to get to the bathroom.

Adding to my inability to sleep, my disgusting roommate, and my worsening infection, I really felt like I was dying. The skin on my arm looked like that of an alligator, and I was getting very bad cellulitis. My fevers were in the high 103° range. I was on intravenous antibiotics — Levaquin — but they weren't working. The doctors wanted to put me on morphine for the pain, but I refused it and instead only took Advil and Tylenol, which I'd take every three hours. They didn't help the pain at all, but at least they kept my fevers in check.

After I had been in the hospital for quite some time, Steve Blechman called me. Steve is the owner of *Muscular Development* and a great friend to me. "Have you talked to Dr. Colker?" he asked me.

"No, I haven't. I don't want to bother him because he's busy with a big project he has going on right now."

Like a firecracker, Steve blew up on me. He told me that I was crazy and that he would call Carlon Colker himself and explain what was going on.

Fast-forward a day, and Carlon himself called me. "What the fuck is wrong with you?" he asked me. "Why didn't you call me first? I thought we were friends!"

I've known Carlon for more than twenty years, and because we were such good friends I didn't want to bother him. He's the type of guy who always has some sort of iron in the fire, and to me all I had was an infection. Nothing more. I'd had them before, so I figured that some reject doctor at a hospital could fix me up.

"I thought you were busy," I told him lamely.

"Well, what the fuck are friends for?"

With that call, things finally started turning around for me, and I owe it all to my friends Steve and Carlon.

Carlon asked me what the doctors were using to treat me, and I explained their methods to him.

Right away I could hear his disapproval. "Get the fuck out of there right now," he said. "That's completely wrong. The medicine they're giving you is totally wrong. Demand to get released and go to my facility right away."

I proceeded to argue with the doctors at Hudson Valley until they finally gave in and allowed me to sign myself out. I made my way directly to Greenwich General in Connecticut to see Dr. Sabetta, a friend of Carlon's. Carlon was away in Chicago. As I was heading toward Greenwich General, I felt my chest tighten, and it was becoming very difficult to breathe. Carlon had told me that I was pre-septic and that once sepsis gets a full grip on a person vital organs begin to shut down, leading to death.

As soon as I entered the hospital, I was taken to a room.

Carlon had set it up, and the staff was expecting me. As I was being wheeled in, Dr. Sabetta was called, and I learned that he was an infectious diseases doctor.

In brief, he told me that the drugs the Hudson Valley Hospital had me on were absolutely horrible when it comes to the treatment I needed. Immediately, he put me on intravenous Rocefen, and within a matter of hours I felt a major difference. My fevers went down to just once a day — they would onset, last only temporarily, and then subside — and my breathing eased up significantly.

Just as Carlon had predicted, Dr. Sabetta confirmed that I was probably just hours away from sepsis. Staying at Hudson Valley might well have killed me. Lucky for me, I've got good friends.

Dr. Sabetta even tried to help out with an additional step by calling another surgeon, a Dr. Crowe, telling him I needed drains put in to get the fluid out of my body. So I was sent over and sat down in Dr. Crowe's office. As soon as this asshole found out I didn't have medical benefits and wasn't carrying cash, he suddenly refused to see me. He even told his reception-ist to have me call a friend to bring me some cash. I also watched a couple who came in shortly after me who were turned away for lack of cash or benefits. I couldn't believe this guy.

"Listen," I told Dr. Crowe's receptionist. "I pay all of my bills. Ask Sabetta."

I was quickly, and rudely, told to get lost.

"This shit is poisonous," I added. "Sabetta wants this drained."

"No can do."

I told the entire office staff standing there that I felt Crowe should lose his license to practice medicine. He was supposed to help people, and instead, if you don't have cash, he wouldn't give a fuck if you were lying there in his office dying. He'd call an ambulance, if you were lucky, and ask the attendants to take you somewhere else. Then, I imagine, he'd bill you for his time to make the call.

Other doctors I ended up talking to after my visit to the scum that is Dr. Crowe gave me a myriad of responses. Some were shocked that a doctor would be so inconsiderate to a patient in need; others just shrugged and said, "Yeah, that's Crowe."

At least I have great friends — Steve, Carlon, and even Raven are three of whom I still talk with today — and because of a couple of them, I'm still above ground and breathing.

Chapter 34
MY LIFE TODAY

Life for me these days is much different from my drug-dealing, two-timing past. Things have fallen into place for me, and I'm successful and happy, enjoying a job as a columnist for *Muscular Development* magazine and pursuing other interests. That said, though, as my days involved in steroids have come to an end, the political interest in the drugs has only increased. And there are times when everything I've done comes back and hits me like a freight train.

These days cops are looking for a reason to search muscular guys in the hope they're behind the next big bust. Having muscles today makes you a target. Our knowledge of nutrition and our training techniques are more advanced than ever, yet having fifteen-inch arms these days makes you a target. It's political bullshit. And in my case, it's even worse because many cops around New York know me, and some of them would just love to see me locked up again. But, every once in a while, I do run into a cop who also happens to love bodybuilding.

During the promotion for the movie *Bigger Stronger Faster*, I was out at the AMC Theater in Times Square doing interviews and autographs. I didn't end up leaving until 4 a.m. and was so tired I was practically driving on autopilot to get home.

I wasn't thinking much of anything when I saw the red and blue flash in my rearview mirror, and, sure enough, there wasn't just one but two New York state troopers behind me. I quickly pulled over and rolled down my window.

One of the officers came to my driver's window, while the other stood on the passenger's side, shining his flashlight directly at my face.

"License and registration," the officer said flatly.

I asked him if I had been speeding, because I was sure I had been going exactly the speed limit. He then told me we'd talk about that once I showed him my license and registration.

I handed over my paperwork, and the officer looked over at his partner and smiled. "No shit, you're Gregg Valentino, the Ramblin' Freak!" he said excitedly.

"That's me," I said.

"You've got to get out and show my buddy your arms!"

I quickly unbuckled my seatbelt and stepped out, the other officer now having made his way around to the driver's side. I hit a few shots on the side of the highway, laughing at how ridiculous I must have looked to the people in the cars driving by and honking their horns. But the cops didn't care; they were giddy. They told me I represented "us short guys," because they were short just like me. The officers were impressed enough that they admitted they had pulled me over only because they thought it was me. I had the new issue of *Muscular Development* in my trunk, of which I gave each a fresh copy. They had me sign them, asked me a couple of training questions, took pictures with me. And then I was on my way again.

Much like the officers, many people recognize me today. They love my humor and my column, or they just want to talk training or old gym stories. It hasn't, of course, always been like that.

I once did an interview with a guy who worked for a useless waste of the Internet called *Testosterone Magazine*. When the piece hit cyberspace, it was titled "Gregg Valentino: The Most Hated Man in Bodybuilding." And naturally the guy who wrote it up was, is, and always will be nobody in the sport of bodybuilding.

I've seen the real side of bodybuilding that most people never will. And it isn't all glitz and glamour. I've seen a past Mr. Olympia, a winner of the crown jewel of the sport, off his rocker from Ecstasy. I've known dozens of professional, top-level bodybuilders who use hard drugs like coke, Ecstasy, Nubain, Special-K. And let's not forget Vicodin, Percoset, and good old Valium, all in addition to their steroids. I've known professional bodybuilders who have beaten their wives and girlfriends, sold drugs, prostituted themselves, sold fake gym memberships and fake steroids. Yet this interviewer had the balls to call me the worst of it all.

The interview came out entirely one-sided, with the interviewer spinning his own bullshit. He called me hated, and I couldn't understand it. What made me hated in bodybuilding? People hate crack and heroin dealers because they sell poison to kids. I never did that. I crack jokes and tell people what's real on the streets and in the gym. I looked retarded, and people laughed at me. I never fought back. I've never been rude to anyone who hasn't disrespected me first. So again I wanted to know what made me hated.

I feel I'm misunderstood, not hated. Morons who don't know me and judge me are suffering from their own inadequacies, with which I can't help them. If they have nowhere else to place their hatred, then that's their problem. This interviewer was one of those guys.

Later, after I became a columnist for *Muscular Development* magazine, started doing appearances, talk shows, movies, and the like, I gave the same interviewer a chance to do an updated interview. He never got back to me. It seems that giving him the chance to talk to me after the world saw who I really am would make him look like the fool he is. All I wanted to say was "Look at how far I've come. Look at me for the man I really am. Not bad for a man you call hated, is it?"

He and his hater squad can't handle the fact that I now write the most popular column in the sport of bodybuilding. They were all betting against me, and they all went broke on that bet. I live by a quotation from the bodybuilding god himself, Arnold Schwarzenegger: "The worst thing I can be is the same as everybody else. I hate that."

The hatred against me ran for a long time. I'm like a chick with big tits: some people love it, and others think it's gross, but I had just as many fans back then as I did haters. It's just that the negativity in articles fueled the haters, and it wasn't until Steve Blechman came into the picture that everyone — fans and haters alike — got to see the other side of me. Steve, the brain behind *Muscular Development*, came to me years ago and said he wanted me to write for his publication. But people inside his team, the very people who now read my column, the very people who have their material printed alongside mine, told Steve not to hire me. They told him that I was a stain on bodybuilding and that I would bring down the value of his magazine.

"Don't hire Valentino, he's going to embarrass you," another *MD* columnist told Blechman. And I'm not going to lie: that hurt.

A good friend of mine whom I've known for more than thirty years, Dr. Carlon Colker, told Boss Blechman not to listen to the egos and the voices telling him I was bad for his magazine. Colker told Blechman instead that I would rock the house at *MD* and that I was what the magazine needed. I truly love the people who stand by me even when there's a chorus of others against me, even when they've never met me.

I have never pretended that I didn't look retarded with my massive arms, and I don't pretend that many of the things I've done in my life were the right things to do. But one thing I will never do is judge a man I've never met, and I expect the same from other people. If a person can look me in the eye, have a conversation with me, and then say that he hates me or that I'm an asshole, fine. But until that day comes, it is absolutely wrong to judge me. My children and their friends read the bullshit written about me, and it hurts them to read these things. And it hurts me when they come to me and say, "Daddy, is this true?" A man shouldn't have to defend himself from lies to his own children. Misconceptions have lived on about me for too long.

People claim that I don't take care of my children, and that couldn't be further from the truth. I have joint custody of my children and take care of them four days a week. When my ex-wife and I got divorced, I gave her over $210,000 in cash. When I got out of jail, despite having no job, I still paid her $1,000 a month for our kids. Whether that meant I had to clean up puke from the gym floor or recycle soda bottles, I did it to make sure my kids had whatever they needed, because that's what a man does. The cops came and went shopping in my house, took all of my money, and thought they had finished me off, but I wouldn't let that happen, and my children are the reason why.

I've passed up countless opportunities to make big money by appearing on shows or in movies or to endorse products. I say no because they require me to travel and be away from my children, and I won't do it. I will never miss a day that I'm responsible for my kids. Period.

Another fun fact about me that the haters don't like to admit is that I go all over now, at my own expense, to speak at high schools and other community events. I also participate in as many benefit events as I can that raise money for charitable causes. I don't do it for my image, I do it because I believe in it, and I believe that we as people have a responsibility to help others. I bring posters, pictures, and T-shirts for the kids I visit, sign and personalize every one of them, and stay as long as it takes to meet everyone who wants to meet me. I don't think that's too bad for a "scumbag" like me.

I've helped to coach boys' and girls' baseball teams, assisted with lacrosse, basketball, and wrestling, and helped out with all of my kids' school functions. I used to volunteer with children who have Down syndrome. I used to help with the homeless people who live on the streets of New York City. And still I sit down time after time and pick up a magazine or read on the Internet that I'm a "disgrace." But you know what, if I do all of these things with a clean conscience and a pure heart, then I wish everyone was as "bad" as I am. The world wouldn't be such a bad place.

I'm not saying it's wrong to do it, but I've never tasted coffee or tea. I've never drunk alcohol or smoked a cigarette. I've never taken a party drug or even thought about doing so. My love affair with drugs was limited to steroids, and I strongly believe that in many ways steroids made my life better. I'm a man of convictions, but when I believe in something I believe in it 100 percent. I believe in myself, my ethics, and I think that all people are inherently good and deserve to be treated well. And I've never hurt anyone worse than I've hurt myself. Not bad values, I think, for a man who is so "hated."

These days I'm completely drug-free. I loved steroids, I had an affair of sorts with them, but now I'm as clean as the driven snow. The extent of my supplements is the occasional Halodrol gel cap from Gaspari Nutrition, and that's about it. But it isn't often that a week goes by without me thinking about the good old days of juicing and training.

When I was a natural bodybuilder, I used to get sick all the time. I had allergies, and I had to take antibiotics and cold medicines so often that my wife called me "Mr. Healthy" as a sarcastic remark about being such a figure of health yet needing so much medicine. I lived a supposedly very healthy lifestyle, yet I was the poster boy for antibiotics and the flu shot.

After I started taking steroids, though, I rarely ever got sick. I don't know why, and I'm not saying anyone should take steroids for any reason, I'm merely saying what happened in my own experience.

Before I started taking steroids, I'd heard they wear you down by messing with your immune system. The muscle magazines I read called the drugs dangerous: they would turn off your liver, cause your kidneys to fail, and put a huge strain on your heart. Decades ago I heard the same hysteria that the media push to this day. But none of that stopped me from my love affair with steroids. I decided to find out the truth for myself, and after more than twenty years as a natural I felt I deserved to give it a try.

At my peak, I was hitting 3,000 mg of testosterone Propionate or Enanthate each week. I had a motto of "up the reps and increase the dosage." And once I started that, I never had tonsillitis again, even though growing up and through all my natural years I'd have a bout of it almost monthly. Even today, when I go to the doctor, with the exception of my natural testosterone and estrogen levels, I'm healthier now than when I was a natural, drug-free, amateur bodybuilder. That's no lie.

After six years, my probation ended May 1, 2007. I had been to jail for a short period of time, had put up with a drug program designed for alcoholics and crack addicts, and had reported my every move. The day I could do what I wanted again, when I wanted to do it, was a glorious day. I had been owned by the State of New York for six years, and it wasn't a second too soon that I became a free man again.

While the state looks at me as reformed, and I feel comfortable where I am in life and proud of the work I'm doing now, there are times when I feel the weight of the world crashing down on me. Sometimes in life you just don't see that an army of emotion is preparing to attack until all of its guns start firing.

I picked my daughter Gina up from school one afternoon, and she told me that her friends, other seventh-grade students, had talked to her about a film in class on teenage drug addiction and its consequences. She added that all of her friends suddenly started cheering while watching because they saw me. I was included in this video as a poster boy for steroid abuse. Not Alex Rodriguez, not Marion Jones, just me. Gina told me that all of her friends ran up to her and told her they had seen me in this video. "But it's okay. Alex Rodriguez took steroids, and look how cool and famous he is. Your dad is cool and famous too!"

One of my daughter's friends actually started making up stories and bragging to other kids that Gina is her cousin and that I'm her famous uncle. When I saw the look on my little girl's face — Gina looked so proud — an alarm went off in my head. My ears started ringing, I felt anxiety rush over me, and I almost drove my car off the road. My chest started tightening, I felt as if I couldn't breathe, and I was literally gasping for air and feeling as if I were going to pass out.

I quickly drove over to my sister's house, dropped off my daughter, then returned home and vomited. I shivered in a cold sweat for some time, completely overwhelmed with anxiety and depression. I had been punished for what I had done, and now almost a decade later it seems I'm still paying for it. And, to make matters worse, my daughter has to pay for it now too.

People can't let go of what I've done. Athletes and politicians can use drugs, and for most of them it's forgotten within the same season. For me, no one will let it go no matter how much time passes.

After it came out that Alex Rodriguez used drugs, I was interviewed for New York television. I gave them great material, and we interviewed for quite a while, yet when it came time to view the finished product I watched in horror. They played only a few seconds of what I had said about A-Rod — the supposed point of the interview — and several minutes about my arrest eight years prior. I've lived a very clean life since my arrest, but I'm treated like a repeat offender.

I had always considered people who experienced fear or anxiety or depression as weak-minded and pathetic. I learned that I was very wrong. These emotions attacked me, and they had me down to tears, causing me to do nothing but stay in bed curled up in a ball as if I was back in a jail cell or back to dealing with the wrong people and having guns to my head. Completely and utterly helpless. I never saw it coming.

It was the perfect storm that brought all of my inner demons to life. I had done hours and hours of taping with ESPN for the segment they did on me for their *E:60* program. I talked about the old days, my life on the streets, dealing drugs, taking drugs, the dangers and results of what I had done. Coupled with my daughter's revelation that I had now become classroom curriculum, it simply cracked the dam of emotions I had sitting inside me. It definitely caused me to re-evaluate some things, and it showed me who my friends really are. The ones who check up on me, the ones who are always there even when you don't ask them to be. But as I've come to find, it takes a lot for your friends to stand by you when you're in the public eye, because they catch heat just for associating with you.

In 2009, the online site Dealbreaker flipped some shit to my good friend Charlie Gasparino, an on-air financial editor for CNBC, because he and I had gone to school together. It absolutely doesn't affect his job, but simply because they found out he's friends with a guy who has fucked-up arms they try to make it news. Charlie doesn't care, and I appreciate that, but he and I have known each other for decades. How do people in the media have the balls to even bring up our association? It's pathetic. But Charlie and I grew up together, fought together, and trained together, and he's as strong mentally as he is physically. I truly believe that bodybuilding helps people to develop strong minds as well as bodies. Ultimately, the sport of body-

building might have many assholes in it, but it also has some of
the most genuine people you could ever meet. I know this first-
hand.

And when it comes to the sport, I know I'm not the poster
boy for bodybuilding, and that's fine. I don't want to be. These
days I don't want to be known as the guy with the fucking
retarded arms, and I surely don't want to be known as the guy
who ran his own drug empire. I want to be known for entertainment, for making people laugh, and for giving them things
to think about.

I'll always be attached to bodybuilding no matter how bad
it gets. Many people bring out their Nostradamus-like predic-
tions and say that the sport is on its way out and that, in the
near future, there will be no bodybuilding shows, professionals,
or magazines. I don't think that's true. There's a lot of work that
needs to be done to make bodybuilding viable again, to make it
respected like it was in Arnold's prime, but I believe it's possible. I've seen the potential in the sport — how it can actually
enrich someone's life — and I know the people who can change
the general public's perception of the sport.

On a Saturday one year at the Arnold Classic Expo in
Columbus, Ohio, the *Muscular Development* crew maintained a
booth, and it was an absolute madhouse. We had huge names
there, including Paul "Triple H" Levesque and José Canseco. I
went up on stage with Dr. Colker, and we got the crowd going.
I brought a kid up to get his shirt signed by Triple H, a couple
of our guys were giving out shirts and other items, we were all
signing weight belts, gym bags, shirts, whatever else people had
for us. It was a lot of fun, and I was doing my best to get stuff
to all the kids in the crowd. For me, seeing a kid's face light up
is what it's all about.

What gives me faith in the future of bodybuilding is that we
have some genuine stars in the sport. We also have some of the
best fans in the world, who range from your average Joe to

international superstars. Paul, one of the greatest wrestlers in the world, is one of the latter.

I'm not into celebrity worship, and wrestling itself isn't my thing. I hang out with celebrities all the time, and who they are or what they do has never impressed me. It's about character. If they're assholes, that doesn't change no matter how many movies they've made or how much money is in their bank accounts. But if they're genuinely good people, then I want to call them my friends.

Paul was signing autographs and taking pictures with fans for hours at the Arnold. His line was nonstop because everyone knows his name, and he is a guy everyone wants to shake hands with. When the day started winding down, he was starving like everyone else. He kept saying how he really needed to eat and was ready to go out with some people to grab a bite. Being the great guy he is, just before he left, he shook everyone's hand, signed even more autographs, and posed for even more photos. From there, a group of bodybuilders escorted him out toward the door.

I saw a girl in a wheelchair in the back corner of the big crowd we had at the booth. I saw she was crying. I walked up to her, where she sat with her parents, and asked her what was wrong. Without missing a beat, she said through her tears, "Triple H ignored me. He didn't even see me." There were honest tears streaming down her cheeks. This kid was a big fan of Paul's, and even her parents looked distraught that their child didn't get a chance to meet her hero.

"Don't move," I told them as I ran toward the doorway.

I grabbed Paul's arm just as he was walking out and explained to him the girl's story. Without hesitation, Paul turned right around. "Where is she?" he asked. "Take me to her."

Paul and I walked over, and the little girl's eyes just lit up. Paul shook her hand, talked with her, and even gave her a kiss on the cheek. Her parents caught a picture, and I swear to God I had tears in my eyes over this.

After that, Paul slapped me on the shoulder and walked out to finally go eat. The mother pointed at me and mouthed the words "Thank you."

"Don't thank me," I told her. "Thank him. You won't find another celebrity like that anywhere. That guy is the real deal."

Paul is the type of guy who could get backstage access to any concert, front-row seats to any sporting event in the world, or a meeting with any name in any sport. Yet he's a sincere fan of bodybuilding. And we are all the better for it.

Ultimately, the important thing for our sport, and for life in general, is that people learn to use their own thoughts to drive their opinions. Bodybuilding, just like me, has been affected for years by undue hate and negativity. I'm not the guy whom people make me out to be or the crook whom people want me to be. And bodybuilding, as ugly as it can be, has done a lot of good for a lot of people. Just like me.

Hate is ugly. Life is beautiful. Judge people — all people — by how they treat you. Don't judge anyone based on a preconceived notion of what he or she is supposed to be. Find out for yourself, or do the world a favor and don't say anything at all. And most of all, learn from the mistakes of others so that you can avoid them yourself. God knows I've made enough for all of us.

The Ramblin' Freak Speaks

Many of my supporters also love the sport of bodybuilding. They love the stories of guys like Arnold Schwarzenegger, Vic Richards, the Barbarian Brothers, and so many others. Much of my life and many memories, both good and bad, have come because of my association with bodybuilding. But I've never felt that my life was dictated either by the sport or by my passion for lifting weights or living a healthy lifestyle. I have loved and lost, been trusted and betrayed, lived through my own hell and found redemption. None of that happened because of bodybuilding.

The bodybuilding I know isn't glitz and glamour. Many years ago it lost that appeal for me and became a very different scene in my eyes. People hear about the "Golden Years" of bodybuilding and the "Mecca of Bodybuilding" that was Gold's Gym. Those are gone now. I've met all of the greatest body-builders in the world, and I've trained at the most historic gyms. Those too are all more or less "retired" now.

Bodybuilding isn't as pure as it used to be. At least not to me. The best athletes are long gone, and the sport has become something that I don't even recognize anymore. If bodybuild-ing had been in my youth what it is today, I would never have picked up the magazines, let alone a weight. Not with the pas-sion that I had back then.

Today everything is vanity. There isn't the camaraderie that Arnold and Franco and Lou and Frank and many others shared in their day. People are looking out for themselves only, and frankly, in the age of growth hormones and diuretics and experimental drugs, bodybuilding today is a dangerous endeavor. For being a sport that supposedly represents "health and fitness," bodybuilding wreaks havoc on the insides of many otherwise intelligent would-be athletes.

For all its inadequacies and indifferences, loving bodybuild-ing is a curse. And it's a curse that I know very well. It's like a flu of its own, a sickness. I think that what ails bodybuilding today can be cured, but I don't know if it ever will. That said, when people are sick, the best thing to do is think of what it feels like to be better, do what it takes to make progress toward feeling better, and remember times that make you laugh and make you happy.

Although I don't consider my life a bodybuilding story, I do have many stories to share that do include it. And, to ensure that I don't disappoint the countless people who will read about my life in the hope of gaining some great information about what bodybuilding used to be like, I'm including some of my favorite memories from my days as a kid in love with the sport of bodybuilding. I'm also adding some of my more entertaining experiences that many have come to expect of the Ramblin' Freak.

Victor Richards

Back in late 1982 and into 1983, I was training at Gold's Gym in Venice Beach, California. At that time and for many years thereafter, it was known as the "Mecca of Bodybuilding" because of its relation to so many great bodybuilders who called the place home.

On one occasion, I was bullshitting with my friends David Paul and Peter Paul, more affectionately known as the Barbarian Brothers, when Big Vic Richards came over to us and asked me to spot him on a set of incline flyes. There was a great sense of camaraderie at Gold's, so I said sure, of course.

I had been spotting Big Vic for quite some time. We were both at the gym every day, and he had come to treat me more like his little slave spot boy. He knew I was in awe of how massive he was, so he would always take advantage of me and demand I give him a spot, even if I was in the middle of a set of my own. Naturally, he expected me to drop everything I was doing to help him out. At first, I was honored that a professional bodybuilder wanted me to spot him, because he was known at the time as the "biggest and strongest bodybuilder on the planet." But then he'd start barking at me to bring him the 265 lb dumbbells, and he'd expect them post haste. Sometimes it would take me five minutes just to bring him the fucking dumbbells. But, like a star-struck pinhead, I did it.

In any case, on this particular day, I was getting a little tired of him telling me to stop what I was doing and help him. He'd been wearing on my nerves for a few months by that point.

"Get the 265s," he said, as usual.

The funniest part was that at this time I was a lean 160 lbs, so those dumbbells were closing in on doubling my own weight.

"Hurry the fuck up," he said after he thought I was taking too long.

I remember thinking to myself, "He's just being a fucking bully now." And I was no longer awed by his size, his professional status, or his strength. I now thought of him as a selfish asshole who was about to see little Valentino from the Bronx go off on him New York style.

After Big Vic screamed at me for taking so long yet again, I helped him get the dumbbells in place and watched him pump out a few reps. After the sixth rep, he screamed at me to help him out by cupping his elbows with my hands and pushing them up to help force out a few more reps. But his arms had oil on them, and I just couldn't keep my hands in place; they just kept slipping off. He started freaking out about this and yelled at me because my hands were slipping off his greasy elbows. "What a pair of brass balls this guy must have," I thought to myself. "Fuck you!" was all I could think.

"My hands are slipping because you decided to oil up before you worked out today," I told him.

From that point on, with his thick Caribbean accent, Big Vic started calling me "Little Man." When he was ready to do his next set, he told me to watch him closely and that I'd "better not" let my hands slip. Of course, in hindsight, I should have told him off and just not spotted him, but at the time I didn't think to do that and kept on helping him out.

As expected, my hands slipped off his arms again, and this time, along with screaming at me, he dropped the dumbbells to the floor. He yelled so loudly that the entire gym looked over at us. Despite how pissed off I was, I still didn't say anything.

Instead I went over to my gym bag and pulled out two sponges that I used instead of gloves on things like pulldowns and rows to keep from tearing my hands up. I decided to use these sponges for his next set to keep my hands on his elbows.

Once again, after six reps, he screamed for my help, and the sponges ended up working great.

One of the Barbarian Brothers came over after that last set to ask me why Big Vic kept screaming at me and why I was using sponges. I told him about the oil and that my hands had been slipping, explaining the whole thing. He then yelled the whole story to his brother, and both of them started breaking Big Vic's balls about oiling up for a workout. Just as I expected, this hazing caused Big Vic to completely freak out. Instead of getting mad at the Barbarian Brothers for heckling him, though, he got mad at me for telling them his arms were oiled up.

"Little Man, I'm going to kick your ass," he told me. He kept saying it over and over so the whole gym could hear Mr. Big Mouth spouting off.

A couple of the other guys there, including Rick Valente and Mr. Olympia Samir Bannout, were laughing their asses off at this. I was getting extremely agitated with the name calling, but I was afraid that if I went off on Big Vic these other pro body-builders would practice their kick-offs with my head. Samir especially was giving me a weird vibe.

Eventually, I decided things were going to go badly either way. I'd be looked at like a total pussy if I did nothing, or I'd get my ass kicked by standing up for myself. Being born and raised a proud New Yorker, the choice was clear.

"Fuck you, motherfucker," I said right in Vic Richards' face. "You ain't kicking nobody's ass, motherfucker. I ain't afraid of you or your big, oiled-up ass." And I just kept on popping bull-shit out of my mouth. "Yo, my man," I said. "As big as you are, you ain't shit compared to what I've had to deal with. I'm from New York, and if you want to press me I'll kick your fucking ass." Even in my own head I realized how corny that sounded. But it worked.

Big Vic stopped dead in his tracks, and for some reason he was startled. He hesitated. I became very bold at that moment and started spewing more punk bullshit out of my mouth and exuding total confidence, but inside I was nervous as hell and ready to shit my pants. I was mimicking his accent and mouthing off like I'd never mouthed off before. I knew that if he took one more step toward me I'd absolutely have to blast him as hard as I could in the mouth, kick him in the balls, and run like a motherfucker before the rest of the gym jumped on me.

Finally, one of the Barbarian Brothers and Rick Valente came over and stepped between us. Big Vic said nothing, just turned his back to me, and walked away while he talked shit about me to Samir Bannout, with whom I'd later become friends.

The next time I saw Big Vic he was completely cool with me and even complimented me on the size of my arms, "for a Little Man."

The moral of the story is that you've got to stand up for yourself. Sometimes it might backfire, and you might get hurt, but it won't hurt as much as letting people constantly take away your self-worth with their words. And in some cases, you might even gain the respect of a 300-plus-pound bodybuilder who, at one time, was dead set on kicking your ass.

Arnold and Lou

The first time I met Arnold Schwarzenegger I was sixteen years old. He was at a Macy's store in White Plains, New York, promoting his book that had yet to come out titled *Education of a Bodybuilder*. At the time, he wasn't even close to being famous. Gyms weren't big then; the entire "fitness generation" was still more than twenty years away. To most people, he was no more famous than Chesty Morgan, the freaky stripper with sixty-inch tits who would run around on a baseball field and kiss players.

To most people, Arnold was a muscle freak who every once in a while would get a bit part in a TV show or a little movie. The documentary titled *Pumping Iron*, now famous in the bodybuilding world, had just come out, and Arnold was slowly starting his rise to stardom. But to us rare fellow bodybuilders, he was practically our Moses. He was leading the way for other bodybuilders and inspiring the world to train and to show everyone that our underground world existed. And, perhaps most importantly, he was giving the rest of us a belief that maybe we too could form a career out of this passion called bodybuilding.

Of course, Arnold wasn't the first bodybuilder to hit it big. Steve Reeves was. But unlike Reeves, Arnold brought bodybuilding to the public instead of leaving bodybuilding for the public. Arnold has charisma and a dominating demeanor. When I first met him, that's what I remembered. He looked big in pictures and on my tiny TV screen, but he was larger than life in person. The biggest man I'd ever seen. I remember thinking that all of the pictures I had in my room of him didn't do him justice.

My father used to get upset about that too. He'd tell my mother, "Most young boys have pictures of girls or baseball players on their walls. My son has pictures of greased-up muscle men in their underwear on his walls."

What hit me most is that Arnold talked to me as if I was actually somebody important. Here was a guy whom I practically worshipped, someone I read about and looked up to every day of my life, and he was two feet away from me, speaking to me, looking me straight in the eye. I thought to myself, "Oh, my God, Arnold actually notices me, he's talking to me, and he knows I exist." For a teenage kid, it doesn't get much better than that. I remember talking to him and not shutting up, I remember shaking his hand and not wanting to let go, as if by holding on to his hand I'd somehow get some of his strength and ability.

"Don't get so emotional," Arnold said, grinning and laughing. He then patted me on the shoulder, and I thought I had just met a prophet in the flesh.

Since that day at Macy's, I've met Arnold close to twenty more times. Once was actually at a restaurant in California, with my ex-wife, who started speaking to the "Austrian Oak" in German. Arnold grinned that wide, friendly smile of his and rambled off shit back and forth with my then-wife. I thought it was all rather amusing, because he looked like he was actually blushing a bit. I couldn't help but think he was getting smitten with my wife, which I actually took as a compliment. Before we left, he grabbed her, gave her a tight hug, kissed her on the cheek, and told her how cute she was. I even caught him staring at her ass as she walked away. Like I said, I just didn't care.

Arnold has been a very upstanding guy each time I've met him and spoken to him. Unfortunately, I can't say that for many other bodybuilders, and that includes two people whom Arnold was close to in his competitive days and beyond: Franco Columbu and Lou Ferrigno.

Without getting into too much detail about Franco, I will say that he too tried to pick up my then-wife. Very uncool of him because of his persistence and general lack of understanding that, when a woman says no, she means it.

As for Ferrigno, "The Incredible Hulk" himself, he's an asshole in the truest sense of the word. He sued his own family, his brother Andy, for using their last name on a gym. Andy and their father, Matt, started Ferrigno Fitness in 1980 with no help from Lou. Then, almost thirty years later, Lou got the balls to sue his own brother and family because he somehow got the idea that they were profiting from his name. I talked to Andy, and he told me how distraught he and their mother are that Lou would do such a ridiculous thing.

"My dad died brokenhearted over my brother Lou's selfish ways," Andy told me. "He verbally back-stabbed my father in the remake of the *Pumping Iron* movie. Myself, my mother, and my sister are all very hurt that Lou could bad-mouth our father the way he did and then hit the family with a lawsuit just because my dad and I used our own last name for our business." Andy added, "Gregg, what really kills me is that two years ago my niece, Lou's oldest daughter, graduated. My wife was in the hospital with breast cancer and got out the very same day. We drove four hours in a snowstorm to attend the graduation, and Lou talked to me the whole time like nothing was wrong. Then a few days later I get a letter in the mail from his lawyer with the lawsuit. He knew my wife was fighting for her life at that time, and my brother stabs her and myself in the heart with a threatening lawsuit. The man has no balls himself."

And, to call a spade a spade, if it wasn't for Matt Ferrigno's drive and genius in the movie *Pumping Iron*, it would have lost a lot of its punch, and Lou might never have gone on to be a television star. And, if anything, in my opinion Matt and Andy helped to build the Ferrigno name as one of quality.

Over the years, I've bought a lot of weight equipment from the Ferrignos, as far back as 1982, and I know how nice the Ferrigno family really are. I still use their equipment in my basement, where I train today, all of my weights branded with their name. They made quality equipment and had amazing service. In the industry, their name was more respected than Lou himself. All I can say is I hope Lou changes his ways, because what goes around most definitely comes around. It's bad karma to screw someone, but to screw your own family is a cardinal sin.

Ray Mentzer and Onions
By 1982, I was spending time in Venice Beach and hanging out

at the gym every day. If I wasn't at Gold's Gym, then I was at World's Gym. Since this was before the popularity of low-volume workouts, I enjoyed as much as four hours a day of training in the gym throughout the morning. Then in the evenings I'd go back just to hang out and watch the pro body-builders train.

In the 1980s, Gold's and World's dominated the bodybuild-ing landscape. Gold's was like a circus atmosphere, and World's was the more serious training environment, at least to me. Gold's seemed like a real-life animal house with crazy body-builders and nuts all packed into one big gym. World's, on the other hand, still had the original machines made by Joe Gold himself. They weren't as fancy as the new stuff at Gold's, but they had history.

In the winter of 1983, during spring break, my friend Carlon Colker came out to hang with me for a couple of weeks. My pattern was regular, and by this time I was spending at least three days a week at World's Gym. I really enjoyed the smaller feel of it, the more focused crowd there, and the fact that they didn't play any music. I hate listening to music when I train, so it was wonderful for me.

On one of my days at Gold's, I was at the front desk talking to Kent Kuehn, the 1964 Mr. America, one of the few people who can out-talk me. In walked Carlon with my good friend and his training partner, Dave "Onions" Goodman. We all hugged and shot the shit for about fifteen minutes and then headed upstairs for the locker room.

When we walked in, Robby Robinson — Mr. America, Mr. World, and Mr. Universe winner — was sitting on a bench look-ing like he was in a trance. He was wearing only his underwear. Carlon walked over to Robby to shake his hand, and though Robby did so he didn't even look up. He never took his eyes off the locker. We all looked at each other, wondering what the hell was going on, when out of nowhere Andreas Cahling, a Mr.

International winner, came storming in and bitching about all the bikes being in use and how he couldn't do his cardio. After a few seconds of realizing we were all watching Robby, Andreas turned around to leave, and as he left he said, "This is bullshit, no one cares!" We all laughed and finally left Robby alone.

Back down on the gym floor, the Barbarian Brothers were carrying on with Lyle Alzado and future lightweight national champion Dean Tornabene, and Carlon, Dave, and I trained while we took in the action around us.

Toward the end of the day, Carlon and I were talking again with Kent up front. We noticed Dave walking toward us with Ray Mentzer, a fellow bodybuilder. Dave told us that we needed to give Ray a ride because he and his girlfriend had gotten into an argument, and she had left him there with no ride. So, as friends, we all went outside and got into Dave's old, unreliable white van, which he drove both for pleasure and for work. To help pay his way through medical school, Dave delivered newspapers.

At the time, I lived only about ten blocks from the gym, so usually I just walked to and from it. But since Ray was getting a ride, Carlon and Dave insisted they give me a ride too. Once we were all situated in the van, with Ray in the passenger's seat, Dave reached into his gym bag just as we were pulling out onto Hampton Drive and pulled out a giant onion. He began to eat it, peel and all, right there in the van, and the onion was no less than the size of a softball. That was Dave; he did this twice a day, every day, and it's what not only earned him his nickname of Onions but also what made him stink like a New York City homeless bum's asshole. He reeked horribly from his pores, his sweat, his breath.

Ray, not used to this kind of thing from Dave, gagged. "What the fuck are you eating?" Ray asked him. "Are you really eating an onion?"

Carlon and I looked at each other and grinned because we

knew the drill. Dave, not missing a beat, pulled another onion from his bag and put it right in Ray's face and asked him if he wanted one too. Ray, of course, covered his nose and told Dave to get the onion away from him.

At the same time, we reached my place, and I got out and told them to call me the next day because I was going to be hanging out with my girlfriend that night.

Early in the morning — it was almost 3 a.m. — I heard a knock on my door. It was Carlon and Dave, who reeked of alcohol. Both of them were giddy like schoolkids who had just gotten away with something bad. They told me I had to go out to the van and see what they had in there.

I threw on some sandals and went outside and watched as they popped open the back door of the van. And there I saw Ray Mentzer lying in the back totally out like a light and drunk as a skunk.

Apparently, when they got back to Ray's house earlier, they realized his girl wasn't there, so they went to look for her at, ironically enough, a bar called The Red Onion, where all the bodybuilders used to hang out. Mentzer ended up finding his girl and getting into a fight again because she was with a guy named Tim Belknap; after the two men had words, his girl left. So my three amigos sat at the bar and started drinking. When Ray had had too much, Carlon and Dave literally carried him outside and laid him in the back of the van, where he remained all the way to my place.

Fast-forward to the next day, and I was supposed to meet the guys at Gold's for a workout. I was running late because I had to walk, and when I got to the driveway I noticed the three of them sitting outside talking and laughing, all eating giant onions. Ray later told me that it was the best secret anyone had ever taught him, that onions "totally got rid" of his hangover and actually made him feel rejuvenated. I just stood there in awe as these guys were sitting there munching on onions as if they were big, juicy, delicious apples.

Later that day, his breath stinking like I couldn't believe, I said to Ray, "Your breath is so stinky I don't know whether I should give you a breath mint or toilet paper."

A Date at Gold's Gym

I met a number of celebrities during my time training in Gold's Gym. And I was never really star-struck; professional bodybuilders to me were, for the most part, just people. With the exception of Arnold Schwarzenegger, I never did a double-take when I saw someone whom an amateur bodybuilder would consider a star. It was an everyday thing for me at Gold's. Then something happened that, for any born and bred New Yorker, was life-changing.

One day Reggie Jackson, Mr. October himself, came into Gold's to train. Being the huge New York Yankees fan that I am, a feeling of damn near arousal came over me. I was in the gym doing my thing, and next I knew Reggie was training biceps right next to me.

I started up a conversation with him and verbally caressed him, as I'm sure every other Yankee fan who has ever met him has done. Once I had said my bit, though, he started talking my ear off right back. He loved to talk. Except, of course, when a gorgeous girl walked by. He'd immediately stop talking and turn to stare in whatever direction necessary to keep the girl in his view. He'd make loud comments about her ass or whatever and just smile like it was no big deal. Then, when the girl was gone, he'd turn back and pick up right where he had left off with his story.

Because of the mix of personalities who strolled in and out of the gym, and because it was like a second home to me, nothing could shock me. My comfort, I later realized, didn't transfer to people around me who weren't as versed in the gym lifestyle.

In 1982, I made the mistake of taking a young Mexican girl I was dating to Gold's Gym to watch me train. She was eighteen years old and very into the fact that I was built. Put those two things together, and she was the perfect girl for twenty-one-year-old me. She wanted to know more about the bodybuilding lifestyle that I led and the life I sacrificed so much for, so I said I'd take her to the gym.

When we arrived, I immediately started hitting the weights hard to impress her. She sat next to me during every exercise I did and watched my every move. The way her eyes lit up when my muscles would contract or when I'd grunt during the last couple of reps during each set made me feel very powerful.

When I moved on to do some heavy shoulder presses, the Barbarian Brothers walked in to start their daily show. It was like clockwork that these guys would come in and completely turn the place upside down. There was always something crazy when they came in, you could count on it.

As they walked past where my girl and I were sitting, one of them said to me, "Hey, buffed Peter Seigel, what's up?"

My girl looked at me and asked why he had said that, if my name was really Peter, and why I'd tell her it was Gregg. I had to explain that he was joking and that, yes, I was really named Gregg.

Later I moved over to work on a power rack while my girl sat on a flat bench right next to me. At about the same time, the two brothers came over to the next power rack, about ten feet away, and geared up to do some heavy squats. They immediately started screaming at each other to psych one another up, but while they did this they scared the hell out of my girl.

She looked over at me with giant, scared eyes. Her mouth was slightly open, and I could tell she was terrified. The two massive monsters right next to her were literally putting the fear of God into her. She was afraid that these two giant men were going to hurt someone badly.

"It's normal," I told her.

Then, just as one of the brothers was about to start his set, shaking and screaming to get himself excited, he quieted down and stepped back from the bar. Then he lifted his leg and farted loudly. The whole gym started laughing at this blast of epic proportions.

His brother looked at him, shook his head disapprovingly, and said, "That's disgusting." He then promptly lifted his leg and farted as well.

The two brothers went back to screaming and yelling, and each time they did it caused my girl to jump. She stood close to me and at times grabbed my arm tightly because she was so frightened. I kept telling her not to worry, that everything was cool, that it was normal for them, but she just looked at them in both amazement and fear. Both of them were close to 300 lbs and were extremely intimidating to people who didn't know, or understand, them.

Just as my girl sat back down, one of the brothers slapped the other one in the face and called him a pussy.

My girl gasped and jumped back off the flat bench. "Oh, my God, he's hitting his brother!" she said, terrified. "That's not normal. I don't like that. They scare me, Gregg."

"Relax. It's normal for them. Trust me. Very, very normal," I said as flatly as possible.

She naturally didn't understand the game they were playing, doing what they needed to do to get the job at hand done well. To her, they were just monsters, big and mean and terrifying.

As their sets started, they began swearing at each other on every other rep. At one point, my girl clawed her nails so tightly into my arms that they left indentations. With her attached to me like that, I couldn't do my own workout properly.

One of the brothers looked at me and noticed my girl problem. He yelled out, "Yo Seigel, are you training, or are you going to take your little girlfriend to a motel room?"

The other added, "Don't make me come over there and slap you to get you going, you little limp dick, pussy motherfucker."

My girl gasped, and her eyes started bugging out of her head. "Maybe we should leave," she said. "He might hit you."

I told her they were only playing, it was okay, and yet again not to worry. Then, as fate would have it, more taunting came.

"Come on, Seigel, get your ass over here and do some squats. I'll kick your ass if you don't, you pussy, get over here right fucking now!"

My girl was literally shaking in her sneakers now. Her eyes just kept growing wider and wider, to the point that her appearance started to freak me out. She just couldn't grasp that he was only joking about hitting me, and now she feared for my safety. In her mind, these guys were real-life monsters, violent and angry and set on destruction. No matter how many times I told her they were good guys and just very serious about their training, she wouldn't listen.

"I want to leave," my girl told me.

I sighed. "Just a few more sets and, fine, we'll go."

As luck would have it, when the Barbarian Brothers started doing their sets again, they began to spit in each other's face, causing my girl to panic. It was clear she was ready to bolt out of the gym, and she had real, honest-to-God tears in her eyes. I stopped my set to put my hand on her shoulder, asking her if she was okay, and she screamed at me not to touch her and to take her home right that second. No matter what I said or did, there was no calming her down by that point.

Part asshole, part serious bodybuilder, I told her we weren't leaving until I was done with my workout. She got upset and said she was going to sit on the bench she saw outside the locker rooms and wait for me there. That was perfect, I thought.

A few minutes later the brothers did another set, with one brother squatting his ass off, screaming, pushing, punishing himself under hundreds of pounds of weight. The other brother was slapping him, degrading him, yelling at him to continue pushing the heavy weights until his legs reached their failing point. When the set was finally done, the brother who was working out fell to the floor and starting choking up some thick brown vomit. He got up as quickly as he could and ran for the bathroom.

The other brother came over to me and asked what had happened to my cute little girlfriend. I explained she was a little freaked out by the whole scene but that she'd be okay. And then, like in a horror movie, we heard a high-pitched shriek.

I ran toward it, and sure as the sun shines it was my girl. She was standing by the locker room doors, shaking her hands by her head, and looking down at the floor. On the floor was the squatting Barbarian Brother, throwing up all over the floor by her feet. He had tried to make it into the bathroom, but he couldn't make it, and his puke was splashing all over, including onto my girls' shoes. He kept heaving and heaving while his brother stood there, laughing, doing play-by-play.

"There's the chocolate milk," he said, followed by "those twenty egg whites from this morning, the whole wheat toast, there's the chicken breast from last night . . ."

The puking brother was hacking it up, grunting and growling as brown, smelly milk and solid materials pumped out of him and onto the floor.

"Hey," the other brother added, "do you want to order a pizza with peppers and onions?"

More heaving.

"Anchovies?"

More grunting.

"Oh, fuck, I could definitely go for some sushi right now."

"Fuck . . . ," his brother said, pausing to heave again, ". . . you."

My girl had had enough and bolted for the door. I ran out after her, and when I passed through the door I saw her ripping off her sneakers and throwing them into the street. She was bawling, screaming at me, and demanding I take her home.

I had borrowed a friend's car that day for my little date, so even though she lived more than half an hour away I took her home before coming all the way back to finish my workout. After that, she never returned any of my calls or messages, and I've never seen her again.

The Jacket Story

I was out with my partner Paul one evening, and it was a typical cold night in New York City. It was fall, and the night started coming earlier, daylight was becoming less and less common, and it was wise to bundle up before heading out.

My favorite jacket at the time was a thick, quilted, varsity-type jacket with leather sleeves that came from Gold's Gym. One sleeve read "Gold," the other said "Gym," in stitched yellow letters. The sleeves themselves were red, and the body of the jacket was a black flannel material. Before this night, I had worn the jacket for nearly seven years running, causing Paul to joke that I lived in it. He hated the sight of the thing, but I absolutely loved it.

On this particular evening, I got into Paul's car, and with a straight face he immediately turned to me and said, "Bro', that jacket stinks." He waved his hand in front of his nose and then said to me, "Bro', we own a Powerhouse Gym, why are you wearing a beat-up, stinking old Gold's jacket? You realize you're promoting a different gym, right?"

I told him that I well knew what it said but that I had got the jacket at the original and famous Gold's in Venice Beach, California. Of course, Paul didn't care where I had bought it from and really started grilling me for wearing it. He reached over me and popped open his glove box, took out a bottle of cologne, and started spraying me with this musty-smelling spray. I hate cologne anyway, so it really bothered me that he was dousing me with this stuff.

Naturally, I got pissed off, and Paul started being a drama queen and told me I smelled so bad he couldn't breathe. With that, he opened the window while driving and stuck his head outside while screaming, "You smell like shit!" and "Get that fucking jacket out of my car. It reeks!"

We were heading to a nightclub, and throughout the ride there he was bitching about my jacket, how it stunk, how it was time to get a new one. Every five minutes when it was quiet he'd glance over at me, make a face like someone had just let one rip, and shake his head.

When we finally parked the car and started walking, Paul pushed me and told me to walk on the other side of the street because of how bad my jacket stank. "I don't want people to think it's me that stinks like that," he said.

When we got into the club and went to hang our jackets up, he told the girl at the coat closet to throw my coat on the floor and not to hang it anywhere near his. He told her my jacket had boogers on it and all kinds of childish bullshit, adding that I slept in the jacket. The girl laughed right in my face and held my jacket out away from her.

While we were in the club, Paul and I met a couple of girls. I was talking with a Latina, and he was with a blonde who was a stripper in Midtown. When we all decided to leave together, we picked up our jackets — Paul trying to get me to leave mine — and hit the street.

As soon as we stepped out into the night air, we saw a large crowd at the end of the block watching as a guy was catching one hell of a beating. Paul and I ran over and saw a young bodybuilder-type Latino kid kicking the hell out of an old man with a toupee. The old man wasn't even fighting back. As he got back to his feet, the kid knocked him down again, ripped his wig off, and threw it out into the middle of 11th Avenue. The old guy was full of blood, and the crowd somehow thought this was funny and started laughing.

I quickly had enough and yelled at the kid and told him to cool it.

The kid turned around and looked at me, took in a deep breath to expand his chest to try to make himself look like a bad-ass, and said, "Hey, fuck you. Shut your mouth, or you'll be next." Then he pointed straight at me before turning back to the old man.

Paul grabbed me and held me back because I tried to lunge at the kid.

In the short amount of time the punk had been distracted, the old man had stepped out into the street to grab his hairpiece and started walking off to the street corner. The guy looked groggy and spaced out, and I figured he was drunk. While I was still being held back, the kid ran after the old man and clocked him up against the back of his head, knocking him out cold.

I ripped Paul's arms away from me and ran at the kid, ripping off my jacket on the way. As soon as I jumped on the kid, I put him in a headlock and started punching him straight in the nose. I slammed him down onto the street hard just as people were grabbing at me to pull me away. Some guys were punching me in the head, including a big black drag queen who looked a hell of a lot like the professional bodybuilder Ronnie Coleman.

Paul jumped into the crowd and started pulling people off me so I could keep blasting this punk kid in his head. I looked up at one point and saw Paul seemingly fly across the sidewalk and smash a black guy across his cheek, sending one of the guy's teeth flying out of his mouth.

Eventually, the police came and first tended to the old man, then started breaking up the brawl I was in. The Latino kid made a run for it as soon as the cops pulled me away, and none of the cops went after him.

When all was said and done, after telling the police what

had happened, I went over to the parking lot, where Paul was now standing, and I saw an old, homeless black man walking down the street wearing my jacket. I started yelling that he had stolen my coat as I ran after him, but Paul grabbed my arm and told me, with a shit-eating grin on his face, that the guy hadn't stolen it. Paul had given it to him.

I told Paul, "Fuck that," and started to try to run after the guy, but I couldn't break free.

"Look, bro," he said. "That jacket has ripped pockets, it's old, it has boogers on it, it stinks, and it's cold outside. The guy is homeless, let him have the fucking jacket."

Paul and I started such a heated argument that he finally took off his own $500 leather jacket and handed it to me. But I didn't want his jacket, I wanted my Gold's Gym varsity jacket, which I never saw again.

Two days later, though, I inadvertently got Paul back. We went out to the movies with the same two girls we had been with at the club and stopped off at a McDonald's. When we got to the theater, Paul and his girl sat two rows behind me and my girl so they could do whatever intimate things they wanted to do in a theater.

My girl had brought in some McDonald's cherry pies. Halfway through the movie she took one out and bit into it, and suddenly a big, gooey piece of cherry flew out and hit my lap. I picked it up and shook my hand to get it off, and as soon as I sent it away I heard a guy scream and yell, "Oh, my God, something is in my fucking eye! It burns!" I couldn't help it. I started laughing so hard I couldn't breathe.

Paul started such a commotion, yelling, "Who threw a fucking cherry at me?" He started interrogating people who were sitting around him, even those behind him. "Hey!" he yelled to the usher, who had come running in. "I'm going to cave someone's fucking head in if I don't find out who threw a fucking cherry into my eye!"

Paul ended up leaving because he was so pissed off, and I just sat there, laughing, thinking to myself, "That's for my jacket, asshole!"

New York Rat Trap

One weekend my friends Bob Bonham and Steve Zaccaro came out with me to the Exit nightclub. All three of us were in shape at the time, and there were a bunch of Dominican women from Washington Heights there at the club. That's exactly my flavor, and I was having a great night. I always joke that it helps to build my testosterone levels back up now that I'm off steroids.

Steve was cracking one-liners, and Bob was talking shit, as we walked past some hood rat "tough guys" with their ghetto bitches. It was just another crazy night for the three of us, and each of us ended up with a lady on his arm. One of them invited us all back to her place for an "after party," so to speak, so of course we all obliged.

As soon as we left the club, we realized that all three of these girls looked better in the dark atmosphere of the club. But their bodies were hot, and it was late at night, so we kept following them back to this girl's place.

When we reached her place, the three of us sat on the couch in the living room while the girls went into a bedroom. We started looking around and noticed that there were roaches crawling over every wall and surface in the apartment. It was an infestation of epic proportions, but it didn't really freak me out; I was relatively used to seeing that, given the girls I tended to hang out with.

Bob nudged me and said, "Bro', let's get the fuck out of here, this place is disgusting."

"Just wait a few minutes," I said. "I know how these girls operate."

Bob whispered to me that we needed to leave anyway

because he thought the girl Steve was with was really a guy. Steve heard this and started in on Bob, and soon enough they were bitching back and forth, calling each other's girl names and all sorts of other things.

What finally broke them apart was a loud noise coming from the kitchen. It was a pounding noise, as if someone was banging on some pipes. Steve got up to look and came back to say there was no one there except for some big roaches. Then there was a big crash in the kitchen, and Steve checked once more. Still nothing. Whatever it was, it sounded very violent, and all of us were surprised that no one was actually there.

Steve sat back down and asked what was taking the girls so long.

Bob looked at him and said, "Steve, your girl is probably washing her dick off for you."

As soon as Bob finished, the door to the bedroom opened, and the girls came walking out. We could immediately smell marijuana and knew the girls had been in there smoking joints. None of us guys was cool with that, so it totally killed the mood, but before leaving I asked what the sound coming from the kitchen was. Bob even asked if the place was haunted.

My girl looked at me as if I was crazy but walked into the kitchen anyway. A few seconds later she came back with a metal bucket in her hand and said, "Oh, this is what you guys heard." She tilted the pail for us, and we looked inside to see the two biggest, most well-fed rats I have ever seen in my life. It was disgusting. They looked diseased with bloodied scabs over their bodies, their eyes red, their teeth showing.

Bob shivered. "What the hell do you do with them? You can't just reach in there."

The girl laughed. "Hell, no, I ain't putting my hand in there. I just get rid of them like this." She walked over to the window, opened it up, and dumped the rats out of the pail onto the street eight floors below us.

"What the fuck!" Bob yelled. "Are you crazy? Suppose some-one's walking right below down there when you drop those bastards out."

The girl grinned and said, "Shit, I guess that's their bad luck."

The girl Steve had brought back laughed. "She's crazy, right? She does that shit all of the time."

Bob turned to me and gave me the look that said it was time to go. Steve was still laughing from the rats being dropped out of the window, and he slammed his first down hard onto the arm of the couch. Suddenly, half a dozen rats came running out from under the couch, across the living room floor. One ran over Bob's foot, causing him to scream. Without a word, the three of us just ran out the door.

We hopped into Bob's Jaguar and sped off. As we drove down a street with a slower speed limit, we saw a rat running in the road, a not-so-uncommon occurrence at night in New York City. Instead of avoiding it, Bob floored it as he yelled, "You ruined my night, you little motherfucker. Take this shit!" And with that, he swerved right over that nasty little New York rat.

Fat Boy

One of the most popular columns I've ever written centered on my run-in with a famous rapper who dissed me but ended up suffering the ultimate ghetto girl revenge — you know the type, the raised-tough street girls who don't complain but take mat-ters into their own hands.

At the time, I was dating a girl named Mercedes. She had just been to her best friend Rita's house party in the Bronx in honor of her sister Lizette's upcoming wedding. At the party, there was the whole gamut of thugs and wannabe thugs and gang-bangers, the whole nine. There was bling-bling, do-rags, FUBU, and all that hood flare everywhere. At the same time, there were a bunch of rappers there, including a big, fat fuck whose name I can't mention for legal reasons. I'll call him "Fat Boy" and leave it at that. In any case, I found out that this now-famous fat rapper had grown up with Mercedes, and they had been childhood friends. I wasn't impressed, didn't care in the least, and the party went on.

The next day Mercedes called me, and I drove over to her apartment to find her waiting out on the steps. Now, the only time a ghetto girl is outside her apartment is if she's waiting to beat another girl's ass or drinking on her steps with a few of the other hoodies. Or, of course, she might be kicking it to some thug from the block. Regardless, I knew something wasn't right when she ran and hopped into my car, kissed me hard on the lips, and threw on a big smile.

"Hey," I said. "I left my cash at home, so we can't go to Fordham road today."

She looked at me and said, "No, stupid, we're going to my friend Fat Boy's house. He wants me to be in his next music video."

Still I wasn't impressed and told her so and asked her why I needed to go with her.

"I told him about your muscles, and he said he might want you in the video too."

I knew it was bullshit, and no one lies better than a ghetto girl. "I'm not stupid," I said. "You needed a ride, and I'm the only idiot with a car who would take you all the way over there."

Instantly, Mercedes reached over and grabbed my dick and told me if I gave her a ride, and could wake my dead dick up when we got back, her ass would be all mine.

"Fat Boy, fire up the grill, 'cause here we come," I yelled.

As soon as I started driving, though, Mercedes started throwing out rules to me. Don't say anything — let her do the talking — and don't embarrass her in any way, lest I pay dearly for it in the end. I told her to relax, I was just there for support, and everything would be cool.

When we got to Fat Boy's place, I gagged. The house was ridiculous in every way. It was opulent and seemed to go on forever.

"I've got to learn how to rap," I said.

Right away a big, bald bodyguard greeted us and asked us what we were doing there, and then he noticed Mercedes. He walked to her side of the car, leaned in, gave her a kiss hello, and told her to get out and walk with him. At the same time, a skinny, seven-foot-tall guy who looked like he should be playing basketball introduced himself to me as Kamal and pointed out where I was to park.

I then walked with him through this castle of a house to the swimming pool area, where Mercedes was already sitting with Fat Boy. I walked over, introduced myself to this famous fat-ass, and the first thing this arrogant prick said to me was "Yo, are those arms real or implants?"

I told him they were as real as his big, fat gut, and he looked at me as if he wasn't sure how to take that. He then put his hand on Mercedes' lap, laughed, and said, "Son, this gut gets a lot more fine ass and makes a lot more money than those big arms."

"I bet it does," I said, "but I tell you this, bro', I would rather have these arms than that fat gut."

Mercedes kicked her leg out and stomped my foot incredibly hard, causing me to let out an embarrassing scream like a girl in a horror movie.

"Yo, why you screaming like that?" Fat Boy said, apparently oblivious to me getting stomped. "Chill, bro', chill out."

I noticed Mercedes' nostrils were flaring a little, and she gave me a mean stare. I also noticed Fat Boy rubbing her leg as he told me to go get something to eat. Now, I didn't like this diss — his hand on my girl's leg — but I was hungry, and my foot hurt, so I let it go and went to fill up a plate with sliced roast beef and salad.

As I was eating, I saw a mini pit bull roaming around with a bad limp. I called him over to me and found he was especially friendly.

All of a sudden, Fat Boy showed up and said, "I'm gonna snap that useless mutt's neck."

I grabbed the dog and said, "Hey, he's not bothering anyone."

"Yo, I hate that mangy mutt. I'm going to shoot it and put it out of its fucking misery."

"Relax, bro', keep talking to Mercedes, I'll play with the dog, myself." So out of impulse I started feeding him some of the roast beef, and Fat Boy went off to kick it to Mercedes in the worst way.

I tossed a couple of pieces of roast beef out into the yard, and even with a limp the dog was pretty spry and went right after them. Finally, though, I tossed a piece a little too far, and the dog grabbed it but went sliding like a baseball player right into the pool.

Fat Boy jumped up and ran to the pool and yelled out to Kamal to get him a gun to shoot the dog. Right then I saw that the dog must have taken in too much water, because he puked some of the roast beef back up into the pool. Fat Boy freaked out over it, but I just looked at him and apologized, telling him not to blame the dog.

"Fine," Fat Boy said. "Then I'll just shoot you and the fucking dog."

Mercedes then stepped in and asked to talk to me privately. She looked me right in the eyes and said, "You're a dead man!" Then she pinched me on my gut so hard I screamed again.

"What is it now?" Fat Boy asked.

"I think I got stung by a bee," I said.

Fat Boy ignored me, then said to Mercedes, "Come here, baby."

By this point, I was getting tired of him kicking it to her like that, so I decided it was payback time. I said I needed to go to the bathroom, and Fat Boy had Kamal show me where it was.

As I was walking away, I heard Fat Boy scream and looked back in time to see him kick the little dog in the head. Mercedes started pulling him away, and she looked back at me, nostrils flaring, to make sure I knew I was in deep shit with her.

Speaking of which, when I reached the bathroom, I stopped to do what I do best and dropped a bomb. As my dumb luck would have it, there was no toilet paper in the bathroom. Fortunately, there were paper towels on the sink, so I used them instead.

I walked back out to where Fat Boy and Mercedes were sitting, and, as I expected, he had his hand in her lap. I asked him where the dog was; he said he didn't know and didn't care and hoped the dog was dead. Mercedes slapped him on the arm, and he brushed it off and told us all to head in and watch his new music video with a famous Latina actress-turned-singer.

As we stepped inside, there was a woman with a mop. Fat Boy asked what she was doing, and she said that the toilet had flooded out the whole bathroom. "Someone flushed paper towels down the toilet," she said, causing both Fat Boy and Mercedes to look directly at me.

I 'fessed up. "I'm sorry, I didn't see any toilet paper."

The woman then pointed to a little flat drawer in the cabinet base and said, "It's in there."

I felt like an idiot, but at the same time I figured there was no way for me to know that. I'm not a rich guy, and my toilet paper hangs off a roll holder on the wall like everyone else's.

I knew Mercedes was even more angry with me than she had been, and now of course so was Fat Boy. But he just shrugged and said, "Pay it. If you ruin my floors, I'll just send you the bill." Then he turned, asked everyone to follow him, and went on deeper into the house. After Fat Boy turned his back, Mercedes made a fist, smacked me squarely in the balls, and told me off. I screamed, yet again.

The fat-ass stopped walking and turned back toward us. "Yo man, why you always screaming? What's wrong with you now?" Then he turned to Mercedes and said, "Where did you find this guy?"

I didn't say anything because I felt my balls floating up into my gut.

Finally, we reached a room that looked like a mini movie theater. It had an eighty-inch projection screen on the wall. Before he put in the film, Fat Boy asked Mercedes if she wanted a drink. I chimed in and said, "I'll have a diet Coke," and Mercedes said she'd have a regular Coke.

"That's not what I had in mind," Fat Boy answered, "but okay."

After he brought our drinks, he sat down and put his arm all around Mercedes, completely out of disrespect for me. She shrugged his arm off and looked at me with some evil eyes. Fat Boy then turned on his screen, which showed the uncut video he had shot with this Latina singer. Afterward, he said to Mercedes there was something he wanted to show her, and they got up.

She looked at me strangely and said, "Come on, baby."

I knew something was up. She had called me baby. Then it finally hit me: she kept getting mad at me not because I was acting up or doing something she didn't want me to do but because I kept leaving her alone with him, which allowed Fat Ass to grope her and kick it to her. I had figured that was what she wanted and that she'd get upset if I said anything, but I was wrong. She wanted me to get him away from her. Clearly, I was an idiot, but I followed them to the side of the house, where he had a giant garage and a whole bunch of expensive cars, which he began to show off.

He was showing Mercedes his white Lincoln Navigator as I was walking around looking at his other rides. I still had my soda in my hand, and I noticed that Fat Boy had pulled Mercedes into the SUV with him. I caught her eye, and it told me she wanted help.

I did some quick thinking in my little brain and saw the dog running around. I called him over to me and made it look like I wasn't even thinking and just wanted to play with the dog. I set my soda glass down on the hood of one of Fat Boy's expensive cars and started wrestling with the dog on purpose to get some attention so Fat Ass would see the soda. Right away I heard him scream.

"Yo, motherfucker, that car cost more than your mother-fucking life is worth. Get that drink off that car right now!"

That was it for me. I reached up with the dog in my arms and "accidentally" knocked over and spilled the soda on the hood of what I found out later was a $100,000 car. Fat Boy jumped right out of the SUV screaming like a crazed fat man at a barbecue and was totally ready to fight me.

"Bring it on, Fat Man," I said.

At the same time, his boys came running around to see what he was screaming at.

Mercedes jumped in between us, and Fat Boy grabbed her arm and said, "You stupid, fucking, dumb-ass cunt. This is your fault. Why did you bring a man with you? This was supposed to be about just me and you."

I grinned from ear to ear and held the dog tightly. I know that you never, ever, dare call any girl a cunt, especially a ghetto, thug girl. The word *cunt* is the keyword to enter Satan's Lair.

As expected, Mercedes flipped out. "Who the fuck are you calling a cunt, you fat pig?"

Then the Spanish shit started flying out of her mouth, and I had no idea what she was saying, but Fat Boy was yelling back, and even Kamal tried to shut Mercedes up and put his hand on her shoulder, which then pissed me off.

"Back off, man — I may be half your height, but I'm the toy

cannon. You pull my string, and I'll take you to the ground in a split second. I said, get your fucking hands off of her."

Kamal then told me to get Mercedes off the property, and watching the two spit Spanish back and forth was like watching *Telemundo*. Big famous rap star talking shit just like a low-life street punk also showed me that you can take the boy out of the hood, but you can't take the hood out of the boy.

I grabbed Mercedes and pulled her away, and her mouth just kept going and going. We got outside, to the car, and as I was driving away I saw the dog limping toward the car, stopping once he reached the end of the property. He had such sad eyes that it hurt me. Thirty seconds later Mercedes grabbed me and told me to stop the car and get out because she wanted to drive. She was pissed, so I didn't argue.

As Mercedes was slipping into the driver's seat, she took out her cell phone and called her girl Rita. "Rita, get Emily on the phone, and both of you stay on the phone and don't say a word. Just listen, it's very important. Hurry up . . . now, bitch!" All of a sudden she pulled the shifter to drive and pulled a u-turn and drove straight back to Fat Boy's house, where he and his boys came running down the driveway.

Mercedes jumped out of the car, and I immediately followed to grab her, but she called me off. "Hey, Gregg, I got it, I got it. Watch this, just back off . . . watch how a Latin bitch works a man."

With the phone still in her hand, Mercedes ran up to Fat Boy and his crew. "Yo pa, how long we know each other?" she asked. "I'm sorry I didn't know you wanted me in that way, or I wouldn't have brought that asshole with me," she said, pointing to me. "Please give me another chance. I want to stay here with you. Tell me what you want from me, and I'll give you whatever it is, no questions asked. I'll make him leave right now."

Fat Boy smiled. "Yo girl, you know I always wanted you. I invited you here to bring our friendship to the next level, you know what I'm sayin'? I always had this crazy love for you and wanted to make love to you, but then you bring this fucking asshole," he said, also pointing at me, "with you. I wanted it to be just you and me, you know. Make it special between us, no one has to know our business. We can keep it on the down-low. So why don't you go tell your muscle boy to go lift weights and take some steroids? As in, get the fuck lost. Then, Mercedes, you can stay here with me all weekend. I promise by Sunday night you'll fall in love with me."

Mercedes turned her head. "Well, what about your girl, what if she finds out or comes home and sees us together?"

"Damn, Mercedes, why you gotta bring my girl into this? Yo fuck that, all right? She ain't coming here. She's away until Monday morning. So now whatcha gonna do? You stayin' here with me, or you goin' home with steroid boy? I'm tired of this game, so what's up, baby? It's your game now. Make the right call, mami."

Fat Boy extended his arms out as if to call Mercedes in to him for a hug. His boys were next to him, and he had a smug look on his face.

Mercedes let out a big sigh and put a big, beautiful grin on her face. "Ay, papi, I can't do that. You know why? 'Cause I really care about Gregg, plus I gotta' tell ya that you are wrong about something. See, you called me a cunt, and well, pa, you're dead wrong about that. I'm a bitch, not a cunt. Watch, I'll show you!" She brought the cell phone up to her ear and said, "Oh, I made the right call, trust me, pa. Hey, Rita, did you and Emily hear all that drama and bullshit? Yo Emily, I'm sorry, mama, but you really needed to hear that bullshit for yourself, 'cause this piece of shit ain't worth it, girl."

Fat Boy looked like a deer caught in a pair of Ford F-150 headlights. "Oh, shit!" he yelled. "I'll fucking kill you, you motherfuckin' bitch!"

Mercedes laughed and said into the phone, "I'll call ya'll

later." Then she looked at me. "Baby, run!"

We both ran as Fat Boy and his boys came after us. I scooped up the dog on the way down the driveway and took him with us, tossing him in between the two front seats as I started the car and drove off.

Emily, the girl Mercedes had called, turned out to be Fat Boy's "official" other half. And that's why I love a ghetto bitch!

And, just for reference, Mercedes loved her new puppy, which she named Jeter, after Yankee god Derek Jeter.

The New Freak

[As printed in *Muscular Development Magazine*]

IM STEPPING OUT OF MY RAMBLIN FREAK PERSONA THIS MONTH AND IM COME TO YOU AS GREGG VALENTINO THE HUMAN BEING.. I TAKE A BIG RISK EXPOSING MYSELF TO YOU , BUT I HOPE BY THE END OF THIS COLUMN YOU WILL ALL UNDERSTAND... TRUST ME, THIS IS BY FAR THE HARDEST COLUMN I HAVE EVER HAD TO WRITE... SO IF YOUR LOOKING FOR LAUGHS AND CRAZY SHIT , THAN MAYBE THIS MONTHS COLUMN IS NOT FOR YOU... JUST TO REMIND YOU, I AM GOING INTO MY 7TH YEAR WITH MD AND ITS BEEN A GREAT RIDE FOR ME AND IT HAS ACTUALLY SAVED MY LIFE ...YA SEE, WORKING FOR MD HAS ALLOWED ME TO BE AN ACTIVE FATHER FOR MY CHILDREN, ESPECIALLY MY DAUGHTER GINA WHO IS MY LIFE' ....NOT WORKING A NORMAL 9 to 5 JOB HAS GIVEN ME THE FLEXIBLE HOURS TO BE THE FATHER I NEED TO BE...FOR THIS I THANK STEVE BLECHMAN WITH ALL MY HEART, I LOVE STEVE FOR WHAT HE HAS DONE FOR ME... SINCE DAY ONE HERE AT MD I BEEN IN THE LIMELIGHT AND I HAVE HAD MANY GREAT EXPE-

RIENCES, MEETING LOTS OF MAIN STREAM CELEBER-
TIES , BEING ON A TON OF TV SHOWS, FEW MOVIES ,
TONS OF MAGAZINES ect ....I AM HONORED AND
BLESSED...I HAVE HAD TO OVERCOME A LOT OF BAD
THINGS IN MY LIFE AND I HAVE ALWAYS CARRIED
MYSELF IN A WAY THAT I FELT WAS CORRECT...NOT
POLITICALLY CORRECT.
FIRST, A LITTLE HISTORY ABOUT ME ..... MOST OF YOU
LONG TIME READERS HAVE READ ABOUT ME & MY
DAUGHTER GINA IN PAST COLUMNS, BUT I HAVE A SON
PAUL TOO BY THE SAME MOTHER (MY EX-WIFE) ....HE
IS NOW 18 GOING ON 19 YEARSOLD AND HE WANTS
NOTHING TO DO WITH ME....HE IS PART OF MY
BROKEN HEART BECAUSE WE WERE INSEPERTABLE...
MY SON AND I DID EVERYTHING TOGETHER AND FOR
THE LONGEST TIME I WAS HIS HERO...THAT ALL
CHANGED NOT LONG AFTER MY ARREST , HE IS AN
ADULT NOW, BUT IN MY HEART HE IS STILL MY BABY
AND MY PAST LIFESTYLE RUINED ALL THAT...I
EMBARASSED HIM & LET HIM DOWN] NO WONDER MY
SON HATES BODYBUILDING.... NOW I ONLY SEE HIM IN
MY HEART!! ..TO THIS DAY I LOVE HIM TO DEATH BUT I
LOST HIM LONG AGO....MY ONLY HOPE NOW IS THAT
ONE DAY WE WILL BE A FATHER & SON AGAIN....I MISS
MY LITTLE BOY, ITS LIKE A DEATH IN MY FAMILY....HE
HAS NOTHING TO DO WITH ANYONE IN MY FAMILY ,
YET WE (MY FAMILY & I) ALL LOVE & MISS MY BOY
VERY MUCH, I WOULD DIE FOR HIM ...I DON'T EVEN
GET ANY RECENT PICTURES OF HIM..I LOVE HIM & I
SEE HIM NOW, ONLY IN MY HEART ...GOD I MISS HIM!!!
..BUT IT WASN'T ALWAYS LIKE THIS.
   "Any man can father a child, but only a real man can be a
dad"....IN THE SUMMER OF 1999 I PROVED TO BE MY
SONS HERO.....THERE IS A LOCAL KID JOEY AND HIS

FATHER, JOE sr. WHO USED TO PRACTICE BASEBALL EVERYDAY .....EVEN IN WINTER TIME, THE FATHER (JOE sr) IS A "WHACKO" , HE'S HOPING TO TURN HIS SON JOEY INTO A PROFESSIONAL BASEBALL PLAYER SOMEDAY AND HE IS SO OBSEESED TO THE POINT THAT HE CLEARED OUT HIS LIVING ROOM & TURNED IT INTO A PLACE WHERE HE COULD HAVE HIS SON JOEY DO BASEBALL DRILLS.....THIS NUT-JOB (JOE sr) MADE A KILLING IN THE 80's FROM INTEL STOCKS SO HE HAD A LOT OF MONEY AND HE DIDN'T NEED TO WORK.....ANYWAY MY SON PAUL AND HIS SCHOOL FRIEND CHRIS WERE HITTING BASEBALLS ON A LOCAL BASEBALL FIELD.....I PITCHED TO EACH KID AS THEY HIT AND THEN THEY PLAYED THE FIELD FOR THE OTHER KID TO HIT.... JOE sr. AND HIS KID JOEY CAME TO THE FEILD AND ASK IF THEY (JOEY & JOE sr.) COULD PLAY AGAINST MY SON AND HIS FRIEND......I DIDN'T FEEL LIKE PLAYIN SO I JUST WATCHED...AT FIRST , MY SON & HIS FRIEND HELD THEIR OWN BUT THE FATHER JOE sr. STARTED THROWING FAST BALLS LIKE NOLAN RYAN AND TAKING THINGS WAY TOO SERIOUS...YES , JOEY & JOE sr. WERE NOW BEATING MY SON & HIS PAL REALLY BAD.... JOE sr WAS PITCHING AND ACTING LIKE A JERK, MOCKING MY SON & HIS FRIEND IF THEY STUCK OUT ....I DIDN'T WANT TO START A FIGHT BUT I DIDN'T LIKE HIM MOCKING MY KIDS , I JUST KEPT MY MOUTH CLOSED BUT I WAS FUMING INSIDE...FINALLY MY SON BEGGED ME TO GET UP AT BAT,....HE KNEW HOW GOOD A BASEBALL PLAYER I WAS AND HE WANTED ME TO "SHOW UP" JOEY & HIS PINHEAD FATHER JOE sr. ....FINALLY I GAVE IN AND I USED A KIDS T-BALL BAT...IT WAS A SMALL BAT, THESE KIDS WERE 9 YEARSOLD FOR GOD SAKE.....ANYWAY JOE sr. THOUGHT HE WAS GOING TO

STRIKE ME OUT AND HE THREW A FASTBALL RIGHT DOWN THE PIPE...YO, I DRILLED IT OVER THE FENCE INTO THE TENNIS COURTS NEXT DOOR ....MY SON & HIS FRIEND WHERE ECSTATIC , THEY WERE CHEERING AND HOOTING AS I RAN THE BASES LIKE REGGIE JACKSON......MY SON LOOKED AT ME WITH PRIDE & TEARS IN HIS EYES, AND HE GAVE ME A HUGE HUG....HE THEN TURNED TO HIS FRIEND CHRIS AND SAID, "YA SEE, I TOLD YA, MY DAD IS AWESOME!!!!!".... THAT WAS ONE OF THE GREATEST FATHER & SON MOMENTS I EVER HAD.... JOE sr. WAS STUTTERING TO HIMSELF, IT KILLED HIM THAT I MADE A FOOL OF HIM AFTER HE HAD BEEN BULLYING MY 9 YEAROLD SON & HIS FRIEND.....BUT DON'T BE FOOLED THESE WERE JUST HAPPY MOMENTS FROM THAT TIME.....WHEN NIGHT TIME CAME, MY OTHER LIFE TOOK OVER!!!!

"It takes a long time and many steps to climb to the top of a mountain, but in only an instant, it takes just one wrong step to fall all the way down and crash at the bottom" . BACK IN 2001 AFTER I WAS ARRESTED , WHEN I GOT INTO THE COURT ROOM , I REMEMBER AS I WAS STANDING BEFORE THE JUDGE & I QUICKLY LOOKED OVER MY SHOULDER....I COULD SEE MY FATHER SITTING THERE WITH A PAIR OF SUN GLASSES ON , HE HAD TEARS DRIPPING DOWN HIS CHEEKS....HE WAS CRYING SILENTLY TO HIMSELF, HE DIDN'T WANT TO LOOK WEAK FOR ME...MY ARREST BROKE HIS HEART...I ALWAYS PRIDED MYSELF BY NEVER DRINKING ALCOHOL OR DOING DRUGS...NEVER SMOKING POT OR CIGARETTES....ALL THIS WAS BECAUSE OF THAT MAN SITTING THERE]] MY DAD!!!!...I IDOLISED MY FATHER GROWING UP....HE WAS BIG & STRONG AND HE NEVER DRANK OR SMOKED OR DONE ANY DRUGS...NOW HE IS SITTING IN A COURT ROOM WATCHING HIS LOSER

SON BEING CHARGED WITH DRUG DEALING ....I REALLY HURT MY FATHER BUT HE STOOD BY ME REGUARDLESS OF HIS HUMILIATION.. "We never know the love our parents have for us till we have become parents ourselves."

WHY ALL THE DRAMA NOW... I BEEN VERY SICK AS OF LATE...IT ALL STARTED WHEN I FILMED MY FIRST SEGMENT FOR AN ESPN PIECE ON STEROIDS IN SPORTS...OF COURSE WHO ELSE BETTER TO USE THEN "BIG MOUTH" GREGG VALENTINO...WE (ESPN & I) SPENT ABOUT 10 HOURS FILIMNG AT BOB BONHAM's STRONG & SHAPELY GYM AS I TOLD THE STORY OF MY DRUG DEALING DAYS BACK IN THE MID 90s BEFORE I WAS ARRESTED...I TALKED ABOUT MY ARREST , MY PAST STEROIDS USAGE AND MY FAMILY DRAMA AFTER MY ARREST etc ..AT THE END OF THAT NIGHT OF FIL-IMNG WITH ESPN, I HAD LITTLE PANGS OF PANIC ANXIETY, NOTHING TOO MAJOR YET, BUT ENOUGH THAT MY GIRLFRIEND NOTICED IT RIGHT AWAY...A FEW DAYS LATER THE WHOLE A-ROD SCANDAL BROKE AND I WAS GETTING A BUNCH OF PHONE CALLS FROM A FEW TV NEWS STATIONS WANTING MY OPINION ON A-ROD.....I WENT ON NEWS 12 WESTCHESTER WHO ONLY SHOWED FILM CLIPS FROM MY ARREST 8 YEARS AGO, MEANWHILE THE PIECE WAS SUPPOSED TO BE ON MY OPINION OF A-ROD TAKING STEROIDS... THAT NIGHT WHEN I WATCHED NEWS 12 I GAGGED] I WAS VERY UPSET AND FELT TOTALLY BETRAYED THAT THEY USED OLD NEWS FOOTAGE ABOUT ME AND MY ARREST 8 YEARS AGO INSTEAD OF WHAT I HAD TO SAY ABOUT A-ROD.....THIS REALLY BOTHERED ME A LOT AND THAT PANIC ANXIETY PANG CAME BACK A LOT STRONGER...VERY STORNG!!!...AS A MATTER OF FACT, I BEEN WEARING A BASEBALL HAT EVERYDAY SINCE

THAT SHOW AIRED, TO HIDE MY BALD HEAD AND CHANGE MY LOOK, I JUST WANNA BE INVISIBLE / UNRECOGNIZABLE …I KEPT SAYING TO MY FAMILY & FRIENDS]] "THAT SHIT IS 8 YEARSOLD WHY CAN'T THEY JUST LET IT BE AND PUT ON WHAT I SAID ABOUT A-ROD, WHY CALL ME AND ASK MY OPINION IF YOU DON'T WANT TO USE WHAT I SAID"…..I WAS REALLY FEELING THE OLD WOUNDS OF MY ARREST AND MY PAST MISTAKES …….THEN A FEW DAYS LATER I LOGGED ONTO MD.COM WERE I SAW A VIDEO ABOUT SOME BODYBUILDER BEING ARRESTED AND ALTHOUGH HE IS A TOTAL STRANGER TO ME , I DON'T EVEN KNOW HIM, JUST SEEING THE PAIN ON HIS FACE IN THE ARREST VIDEO PUSHED ME EVEN DEEPER INTO MY OWN PERSONAL POST TRAUMATIC ANXIETY ….BY NOW EVERYTHING WAS SETTING ME OFF…..FINALLY, THE STRAW THAT BROKE THE CAMELS BACK CAME JUST ONE DAY LATER WHEN I PICKED UP MY DAUGH-TER FROM SCHOOL AND SHE TOLD ME THAT HER 7TH GRADE FRIENDS WATCHED A FILM ON TEENAGE DRUG ADDICTION AND IT'S CONSEQUENCES ..SHE TOLD ME THAT ALL HER FRIENDS WHERE CHEERING BECAUSE IN THIS FILM THEY HAD A FEW CLIPS OF ME TO SHOW STEROID ABUSE!!! …NOT BARRY BONDS….NOT A-ROD]] ME!!!….SHE SAID ALL HER GIRLFRIENDS RAN UP TO HER AND TOLD HER THEY SAW HER DAD (ME) IN THIS SCHOOL DRUG VIDEO "BUT ITS OK BECAUSE A-ROD TOOK STEROIDS AND LOOK HOW COOL & FAMOUS HE IS, YOUR DAD IS SO COOL & FAMOUS TOO!!!!"….OH YES THEY SAID THAT!!!!….ONE GIRL (MY DAUGHTERS FRIEND) ACTUALLY BRAGGED TO THE OTHER KIDS THAT GINA IS HER COUSIN AND I AM HER FAMOUS UNCLE (TOTALLY NOT TRUE!!!!) …YO', WHEN THIS CAME OUT OF MY DAUGHTERS MOUTH AND I SAW

THE PROUD LOOK ON HER (GINA'S) FACE AN ALARM WENT OFF IN MY EARS…..I ALMOST DROVE OFF THE ROAD!!!! …...I COULDN'T BREATH, I WAS TOTALLY GASPING FOR AIR, I FELT LIKE I WAS GOING TO PASS OUT…MY HEAD GOT REAL HOT AND I STARTED TO SWEAT, ALL WHILE I COULD NOT BREATH…..I HAD TO TRY REAL HARD TO HIDE MY TREMBLING AND MY SHEER FEAR / ANXIETY ATTACK FROM MY DAUGHTER WHO WAS SITTING IN THE BACK SEAT OF MY CAR!!!!… ALL THESE EVENTS HAPPENED WITHIN JUST A FEW DAYS OF EACH OTHER AND NOW A HUGE DAM OF " EMOTION" EXPLODED DEEP INSIDE ME, I WAS A TOTAL MESS!!!!…I HAD EXTREME FEAR AND ANXIETY LIKE NOTHING I HAVE EVER EXPERIENCED IN MY LIFE……AT THIS POINT, EVERYTHING SET ME OFF…AT A RED LIGHT I SAW A BUMPER STICKER THAT SAID "SAY NO TO DRUGS", WHICH HAD ME TREMBLING IN MY SEAT (NOT AN EXAGERATION IT REALLY HAPPENED) & BROUGHT "BOILING HOT" TEARS BURING DOWN MY CHEEKS ….I QUICKLY DROVE OVER TO MY SISTERS HOUSE DROPPED OFF MY DAUGHTER, THEN RAN TO MY HOUSE , PUKED A FEW TIMES THEN SHIVERED IN A COLD SWEAT AND IN UTTER FEAR / ANXIETY / DEPRESSION ON MY BED….I WAS HAVING POST TRAUMATIC STRESS FROM MY OWN –LONG TIME - BOTTLED UP FEELINGS FROM 8 YEARS AGO…LISTEN, I HAVE DONE NOTHING WRONG AND I LIVE A VERY CLEAN LIFE (NO STEROIDS) SINCE MY ARREST 8 YEARS AGO AND EVEN THOUGH SOME OF THESE EVENTS HAD NOTHING TO DO WITH ME PERSONALLY , I COULDN'T BREATH, EAT OR FUNCTION NORMALLY..HELL, I LOST ABOUT 15 to 20 POUNDS IN JUST A FEW DAYS JUST FROM FASTING…..MY MUSCLES DISAPEARED & MY BODY TURNED TO A PILE OF MUSH…...I WENT DAYS WITH-

OUT ANY FOOD AT ALL AND WENT 2 WEEKS WITHOUT EVEN SHOWERING , NOT TO MENTION NO MORE THAN AN HOUR SLEEP EACH NIGHT......ITS LIKE THIS OPENED UP -A CLOSED DOOR DEEP INSIDE ME....IT'S A NIGHTMARE...THE CRAZY THING IS, I ALWAYS FELT THAT PEOPLE WHO EXPERIENCE FEAR / ANXIETY / DEPRESSION WERE WEAK MINDED & PATHETIC ...I WAS WRONG!!!!!!!...AT THIS POINT, I WAS GOOD FOR NOTHING , I COULD ONLY LAY ON MY BED CURLED UP IN A BALL , SOMETIMES CRYING, SOMETIMES IN FULL FLEDGED FEAR LIKE WAS BACK IN A JAIL CELL OR A WAR ZONE WITH GUNS TO MY HEAD AGAIN...I WAS GETTING PARANOID DILLUISIONS TOO...I FELT EVERY-ONE WAS WATCHING ME AND OUT TO GET ME!!!....MY GIRLFRIEND CALLED ME MEL, SHE SAID I REMINDED HER OF MEL GIBSON IN THE MOVIE "CONSPIRACY THEORY"...MY PARANOIA WAS GETTING OUT OF CON-TROL & PUSHING ME DEEPER INTO FEAR & DEPRESSION.....ASIDE FROM NON-STOP DIZZY-NOSE BLEEDS, I WAS CONSTANTLTY FREEZING YET IT WAS 75 DEGREES IN MY HOUSE...I HAD MASSIVE DIARRHEA & OCCASIONAL VOMITING YET I HAD NOT EATEN FOOD IN DAYS...I WAS AFFRIAD TO LEAVE MY BED, I WAS HAVING A TOTAL PARANOID NERVOUS BREAK-DOWN...MY PARANOID MIND SAW EX-DRUG DEALERS IN MY ROOM WAITING FOR ME AGAIN....KEEP IN MIND, I HAVE NO MEDICAL BENEFITS SO I CAN'T SEE A DOCTOR.....AT ONE POINT , I ACTUALLY WANTED TO DIE, TO JUST GO TO SLEEP AND NOT WAKE UP... MY PAST DEMONS WERE RIPPING ME APART FROM THE INSIDE–OUT.....IM NOT ON MEDICATION , IM RUFFING IT OUT MYSELF, I DID THIS TO ME, NOW I GOTTA FIX IT... IT WAS ALL SOMETHING LOCKED DEEP INSIDE ME AND THE ESPN TAPING WHERE I WAS RE-LIVING MY

PAST STARTED CRACKING MY INNER "DAM OF EMO-
TIONS" (BAD STUFF MY MIND BURIED) TILL FINALLY
MY DAUGHTERS SCHOOL FILM BOUGHT IT OUT INTO
TOTAL A "POST TRAUMATIC STRESS" NEVERVOUS
BREAKDOWN... INCASE YOUR WONDERING, NO] I DO
NOT TAKE ANY HEAD MEDICATIONS OR PARTY DRUGS,
THIS IS NOT BROUGHT ON BY A BAD NIGHT OF PARTY-
ING, I DO NOT DRINK, I DO NOT SMOKE & I'M
CERTAINLY NOT ON STEROIDS....THIS WAS SIMPLY
BROUGHT ON BY NATURAL DEEP INNER HIDDEN EMO-
TION AND A VERY BAD PAST... THIS IS NOW A NEW
CHAPTER IN MY LIFE...

MY NEW MISSION STATEMENT....I AM NO LONGER
GOING TO VERBALLY GIVE STEROIDS THEIR GLORY,
BUT IM NOT GOING TO BASH THEM EITHER...I JUST
WANT NO PART OF DISCUSSING THE WHOLE STEROID
SUBJECT...NO, I HAVENT SOLD OUT AND I AM NOT A
HYPOCRYTE...IM ONLY SPEAKING MY MIND AS I
ALWAYS DO , WHAT HAPPENED TO ME IS NOT THE
STEROIDS FAULT] IT'S THE WHOLE "JUICE HEAD"
LIFESTYLE I LIVED A LONG TIME AGO THAT I AM EMO-
TIONALLY PAYING FOR NOW ....FIRST OFF "STEROIDS
ARE ILLEGAL" SO FUCKING AROUND WITH STEROIDS IS
BREAKING THE LAW...IT DOESN'T MATTER WETHER I
THINK THEY SHOULD OR SHOULDN'T BE ILLEGAL,
WHAT MATTERS IS "THEY ARE ILLEGAL" [BOTTOM
LINE!!!...ME OPENING MY BIG MOUTH,IN THE MEDIA
HAS DISGRACED MYSELF AND MY FAMILY
ENOUGH!!!....NO MORE!!!!....TO HAVE MY DAUGHTERS
SCHOOL WATCH ME AS A FEATURED DRUG ABUSER ON
THEIR SCHOOL FILM NOT BECAUSE OF MY ACCOM-
PLISHMENTS BUT INSTEAD BECAUSE I'M AN
EX-STEROID USER, IS THE STRAW THAT BROKE THE
CAMELS BACK...AND THEN TO HAVE THE KIDS AT MY

DAUGHTERS SCHOOL THINK THAT JUST BECAUSE IM ON TV , "ITS COOL" , NOT REALIZING ITS NOT FOR A GOOD THING, IT'S BECOME A REAL EYE OPENER FOR ME & VERY HURTFUL FOR MY FAMILY…..MY DAUGH-TERS FRIENDS WERE TOO YOUNG TO REALIZE THERE IS NO GLORY IN ME BEING IN A SCHOOL FILM ABOUT DRUG ABUSE, IT WAS A TOTAL EMBARRASSMENT FOR ME & MY FAMILY… .KEEP IN MIND, I HEARD ABOUT THIS FILM FROM A FEW OF MY FRIENDS WHO'S KIDS SEEN IT IN THEIR SCHOOL TOO, BUT NOW MY DAUGH-TER HAS TO SEE IT NEXT YEAR WHEN SHE IS A 7TH GRADER…… ITS HUMILIATING TO KNOW THAT THE KIDS THOUGHT IT WAS COOL TO SEE GINA'S DAD IN A SCHOOL DRUG ABUSE VIDEO..THEIR QUOTE:] "IF A-ROD IS A MILLIONARE SUPER STAR & HE DID STEROIDS, THEN I GUESS WHAT YOUR DAD DID AINT SO BAD"..BULLSHIT!!!.... 8 YEARS AGO, I BROKE THE LAW AND I PAID THE PRICE FOR IT…..AND NOW 8 YEARS LATER IM SUFFERING "POST TRAUMATIC STRESS" IN A WAY I WOULDN'T WISH ON MY WORST ENEMY …. IN THE 90's , WHAT I WENT THROUGH ON THE STREETS OF NEW YORK CITY , WAS HORRIBLE] I WAS ALMOST KILLED WITH GUNS TO MY HEAD A BUNCH OF TIMES, MY MOM DIED, MY WIFE LEFT ME, MY GIRLFRIEND KILLED HERSELF WITH A DRUG OVERDOSE AND THEN GETTING ARRESTED & LOSING EVERYTHING FROM MY MONEY , MY CAR, MY GYM , MY DIGNITY , I WAS LEFT WITH NOTHING!!!!… AND TO TOP IT ALL OFF , MY SON TURNED AWAY FROM ME TOO… YES THIS WAS ALL LONG AGO BUT I BURIED ALL THOSE FEELINGS .. NOW I AM LIKE A VIETNAM VET WHO ALMOST 10 YEARS LATER HAS A SERIOUS CASE OF "BOMBS BURSTING IN HIS EARS" aka "POST TRAUMATIC STRESS"… I ACTUALLY CONSIDERED LEAVING THIS SPORT, BUT NOW IM

THINKING] MAYBE I CAN HELP OTHERS FROM FALLING INTO THE BLACK HOLE THAT I FELL INTO YEARS AGO....IN BODYBUILDING THE DRUG USE IS OUT OF CONTROL AND ITS NOT WORTH IT, WITHOUT A SUPPLEMENT CONTRACT THERE'S NO MONEY IN PRO-BODYBUILDING!!!!...IT COSTS A LOT OF MONEY TO PREPARE FOR A SHOW, THATS WHY THE DRUG DEALING IS SO WIDE SPREAD AMONG PRO & AMATURE COMPETITORS... I MAKE MORE MONEY WITH MY MD CONTRACT THAN MOST PROS MAKE FROM BODY-BUILDING ALONE... YES STEROIDS HAVE A PLACE IN MEDICINE FOR MEN WHO NEED THEM WITH A DOC-TORS CARE , BUT SELLING THAT SHIT OR BUYING IT ON THE STREET / IN THE GYM OR OFF THE INTERNET]"IS AGAINST THE LAW AND WILL PUT YOU IN JAIL" ...WARNING] DON'T CRY OR RAT OUT YOUR FRIEND WHEN YOUR SITTING IN JAIL.."IF YOU CANT DO THE TIME THEN DON'T DO THE CRIME!!!".. BE A MAN!!!.. I TOOK MY LUMPS MYSELF!!!...."YO', ITS JUST A MATTER OF TIME TILL PRO-BODYBUILDING GETS SHUT DOWN BY LAW ENFORCEMENT WITH A BIG SHOW LIKE THE OLYMPIA GETTING RAIDED & THE COMPETITORS ALL SUBPOENAED..BODYBUILDING MUST CLEAN UP ITS ACT NOW!!!!" ... THE REALLY SAD THING IS] MOST JUICE HEADS DON'T EVEN COMPETE , THEY JUST TAKE STEROIDS TO LOOK BIG AND IMPRESS ALL THE LITTLE GIRLIES AT THE MALL , TO BE MR. MALL , MR.BEACH OR MR.NIGHTCLUB , BUT NOT FOR COMPETITION... "IF I SIT HERE AND GLORIFY STEROIDS AND THEN SOME KID HEARS MY BULLSHIT AND HE BREAKS THE LAW , GETS ARRESTED DESTORYING HIMSELF, HIS FAMILY LIKE I DID , THEN I FAILED HIM!!!] AND AS A PARENT WITH A VOICE IN THE MEDIA, I AM OBLIGATED TO HELP HIM... IT AINT WORTH THE CONSEQUENCES (

JAIL)...NOW I KNOW WHAT YOUR THINKING]
VALENTINO ARN'T YOU THE GUY WHO SAID
"STEROIDS ARE AS AMERICAN AS APPLE PIE" IN THE
MOVIE "BIGGER, STRONGER , FASTER"....YES I AM , BUT
I AM ALSO THE FATHER WHO HAS TO HAVE HIS 11
YEAROLD DAUGHTER & HER FRIENDS WATCH A
SCHOOL VIDEO WITH HER DAD (ME) STARRING AS A
FEATURED "DRUG ADDICT"... NOT GOOD!!!!... I NOW
SAY "I'M SORRY" TO ALL THE PARENTS WHO HAVE
YOUNG KIDS WHO LOOK UP TO ME AS A "BODYBUILD-
ING MEDIA VOICE".. THEY SEE ME ON A MOVIE SCREEN
GLORIFYING STEROID USE IN SPORTS , I AM NOW
ASHAMED & A DISGRACE TO PARENTHOOD , I BEG
YOUR PARENTAL FORGIVENESS!!!... YES, NOW IT IS MY
CHILD WHO WILL SUFFER HUMILIATION FOR MY PAST
STUPIDITY ..... THE SAD THING IS, I WAS ONCE A AWE-
SOME NATURAL BODYBUILDER, FOR 23 YEARS I WAS
100% DRUG FREE , I HAD PRIDE ....I NEVER EVEN TOOK
A TYLANOL BACK IN MY DAYS AND NO-ONE IN MY
CLASS COULD BEAT ME!!!! ... NOW IM STARRING IN A
MIDDLE SCHOOL DRUG ADDICTION VIDEO!!! ...I
RUINED A GREAT PYSIQUE TO LOOK LIKE A SIDE SHOW
FREAK... ITS MY FAULT FOR MAKING POOR CHOICES &
FOR OPENING MY BIG MOUTH ON TV SHOWS , MOVIES
AND SHOOTING A SHIT LOAD OF OIL BASED STEROIDS
INTO MY ARMS (NOT SYNTHOL DON'T START WITH
THAT BULLSHIT- FUCK YOU!!!) ... I GAINED FAME, BUT
NOT IN A GOOD WAY, AFTER ALL CHARLES MANSON IS
FAMOUS TOO ..IT TAKES A LOT OF GUTS TO SIT HERE
AND OPEN UP TO YOU ALL LIKE THIS....I KNOW, I WILL
EAT MY OWN SHIT FOR THIS BUT CAN TELL YA THIS
MUCH] I WANT MY LIFE BACK, I WANNA FEEL NORMAL
AGAIN AND I WANT MY SON TO BE WITH ME AGAIN
...YOU CAN ALL KEEP YOUR "NEED TO BE HUGE" BULL-

SHIT] I DON'T WANT IT ANYMORE!!!... YO', I DIDN'T
NEED EVEN STEROIDS, I WAS SUPER BUILT WITHOUT
THEM AT 36 YEARS OLD WHEN I STARTED ... AND THE
SAD THING IS A-ROD DIDN'T NEED STEROIDS EITHER,
HE WAS ONLY 20-SOMETHING (TOO YOUNG) AND THE
BEST HITTER IN BASEBALL WITHOUT THEM!! .... NOW
A-ROD LOST EVERYONES RESPECT AND WILL BE
"LABLED FOR LIFE" WHEN THERE WAS NO NEED FOR
THAT SHIT... SO NOW WHEN I SEE MY DAUGHTER
LATER TODAY I GOTTA TELL HER TO TELL HER FRIENDS
THAT DADDY & A-ROD WERE WRONG AND WHAT WE
DID WAS ILLEGAL AND COULD DESTORY LIVES & PUT
YOU IN JAIL!!!!.... WHAT HURTS ME THE MOST IS NEXT
YEAR MY DAUGHTER HAS TO WATCH THAT "ANTI-
DRUG USE VIDEO" AND SEE HER DAD (ME) AS AN
EXAMPLE OF STEROID ABUSE... I AM SO ASHAMED!!!!...
BUT I KNOW SHE WILL UNDERSTAND BECAUSE SHE
LOVES HER DAD AND HER DAD LOVES HER WITH ALL
MY HEART ... I KNOW I MAY LOSE A FEW "FANS" AFTER
READING THIS, BUT I DON'T CARE, I LOST MYSELF A
LONG TIME AGO & NOW I WANT ME BACK!!!!.. NEXT
MONTH] BACK TO NORMAL.. GV